IMAGES
of America

WEST LAS VEGAS

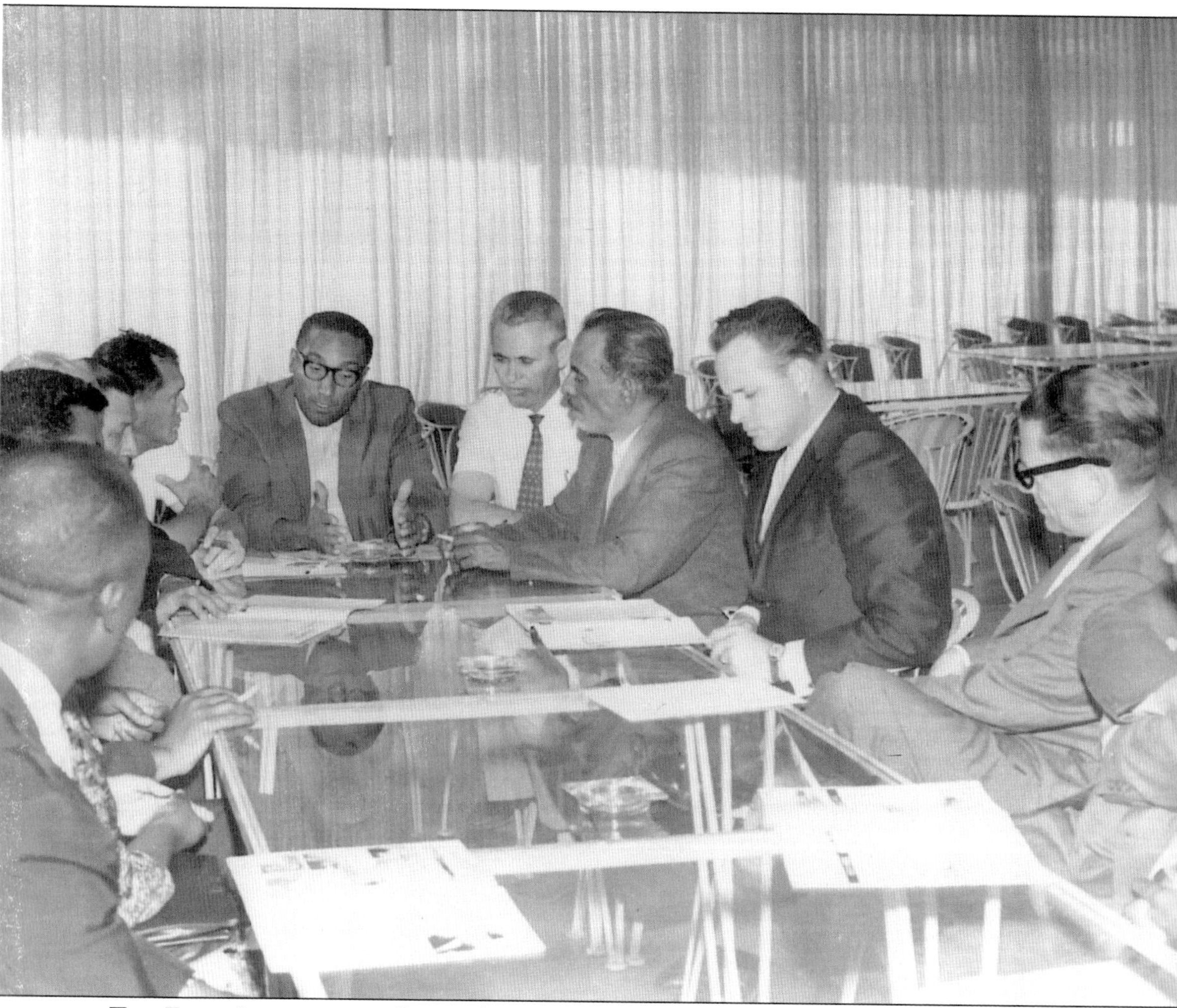

THE FIRST INTERRACIAL CASINO/HOTEL. The Moulin Rouge was the site for the historic announcement to end segregation on the Strip in March 1960. Seated from left to right are Woodrow Wilson; Lubertha Warden-Johnson; Bob Bailey; County Commissioner Clesse Turner; Sheriff Bruce Leypoldt; Hank Greenspun, *Las Vegas Sun* publisher; Dr. James McMillan, then NAACP president; Mayor Oran Gragson; Dr. Charles I. West; Ray K. Shaeffer, police chief; Art Olsen; unidentified; and Donald Clark. (Courtesy Marie McMillan.)

ON THE COVER: MOULIN ROUGE BEAUTIES. Dancing beauties grace the flowered bed of the iconic float in the spring 1955 Helldorado Parade. Handsome gendarmes stand guard below the platform carrying the unidentified Miss Moulin Rouge. (Courtesy Nevada State Museum, Las Vegas.)

IMAGES
of America

West Las Vegas

Patricia Hershwitzky

ARCADIA
PUBLISHING

ISBN 978-0-7385-8196-5

Published by Arcadia Publishing
Charleston, South Carolina

Printed in the United States of America

Library of Congress Control Number: 2010934399

For all general information, please contact Arcadia Publishing:
Telephone 843-853-2070
Fax 843-853-0044
E-mail sales@arcadiapublishing.com
For customer service and orders:
Toll-Free 1-888-313-2665

Visit us on the Internet at www.arcadiapublishing.com

To all the pioneer families of West Las Vegas who dared to dream and still refuse to let their vision die.

Contents

ACKNOWLEDGMENTS

When I accepted a teaching position in West Las Vegas, little prepared me for that area's incredible history. While the dry climate was prescriptive for my husband's health, I dreaded leaving the 250-year-old landmarks of Frederick, Maryland. Las Vegas represented only the "cha-chink" of slot machines, blaring neon lights, mammoth casinos on the Strip, and boisterous, bawdy entertainment.

Fortunately, I was blessed to land near the original Las Vegas, and over the decade, I became acquainted with its fascinating stories that occurred over a span of nearly 100 years. My gratitude extends to those who brought me to the shocking realization that my education was short shrifted on racism. Many introduced me to that inspirational area in Las Vegas. Thanks to Claytee White and Kelli Luchs at the University of Nevada, Las Vegas Department of Special Collections. They responded to my questions and needs, often steering me to great resources. The insights and images provided by Dennis McBride and Paul Carson of the Nevada State Museum, Las Vegas, were unparalleled. Viewing original newspapers and learning historical tidbits about Las Vegas in general kept me on target. Katie Duncan provided the springboard. Photographer Don Walker boosted this project, along with guidance and editorial oversight from Mahlon Chute. Local legends and leaders who provided irreplaceable context include Trish Geran, Sam Wright, Marie McMillan, Sarann Knight Preddy, Elijah Green, Saul Willis, Jarmilla McMillan Arnold, Erma Jai Walker, Katherine Joseph, Dr. Linda Young, Brenda Williams, Nancy Forman, Dee Dee Jasmin, Richard Taylor, Barbara Coleman, Dr. S.S. Rogers, Arby Hambric, Agnes Marshall, Sam Smith, Hannah Brown, Anthony Snowden, Louie Overstreet, Edna Mae Williams, and Mimi Williams. Others like Jim Campiglia of the Official US Casino Chip Price Guide provided rare gaming images. The advice of Brian Sobel and other historians gave me perspective. My apologies to anyone I missed, as there were dozens of Westside residents who provided their memories. To those pursuing their personal stories in a different way, know that I respect your dreams. Hopefully, this photo essay will spark widespread interest so that the deepest richness of West Las Vegas history can experience full bloom. Much appreciation is due Debbie Seracini at Arcadia Publishing for her wonderful guidance as editor and knack for picture-perfect pages. Finally, a huge thanks to my husband, Lloyd, without whom this could not have been completed.

All images used in this book come from UNLV Special Collections, unless otherwise noted.

Introduction

What is today known as the Westside, later expanding to a disputable boundary area known as West Las Vegas, was destined to be a truly incredible and unique setting of American diversity and indomitable spirit, sometimes triumphing and at other times flailing against big power and mega-money. In 1905, J.T. McWilliams had barely begun his 80-acre townsite for diverse immigrants between today's A and H Streets to the east and west and Washington Avenue and Bonanza Road to the north and south when Sen. William Clark, well connected with railroad magnates and owner of nearly all the water sources, brazenly auctioned his land, resulting in the McWilliams landowners literally pulling their structures on skids to Clark's more desirable townsite. Ever since, West Las Vegas and Downtown have been in a tug-of-war over development, entertainment, leadership, and economic prosperity.

By late 1905, and for several decades, the land would be dotted with rickety shacks, tents, and cardboard housing lacking services and resources on the west side of the tracks. Yet the pioneer tenacity of those who relocated to what became the Westside would trump the rest of Las Vegas in sheer community, jubilant entertainment, joyful spirituality, and perseverance to build up their area literally and figuratively.

The meager opportunities in Las Vegas for those of color, immigrants, and Native Americans were better than those from where they relocated. First-generation blacks were greatly encouraged by significant increases in wages. Many migrated from small Southern plantations and had grown up picking cotton for a few daily dollars.

Yet as the Depression impressed its hardships on the rest of the country, Las Vegas, too, began to experience an emergence of social and economic ranking by ethnicity. Mayor Ernie W. Cragin, elected in 1931, was confronted by both prejudiced working-class whites who flocked west to the Boulder (Hoover) Dam project and wealthier racist Southern whites who spent money in Las Vegas and balked at associating with blacks. Then the city allegedly demanded that black business owners who wanted to renew business licenses had to reestablish the businesses on the Westside. For nearly 30 years, African Americans in Las Vegas would chafe against many injustices.

Even so, the Westside grew in population as the need for unskilled labor also rose with the newly built Basic Magnesium plant, the gunnery school, the atomic test site, and the burgeoning Strip. The black population exploded despite severe conditions, including virtual confinement to the Westside after work shifts ended.

What occurred in the 1940s and 1950s was nothing short of astonishing, given the significant barriers to economic success. The work of dozens of minority leaders would sprout success. From the seeds of segregation would grow numerous integrated nightclubs and hotels that would be located on the Jackson Street Strip, including the Town Tavern, the Cotton Club, the El Moracco, the Brown Derby, and many other hot spots. Service businesses grew, from grocery shops to liquor stores and from barbershops and hair salons to restaurants and retail shops.

The Moulin Rouge opened with great fanfare in May 1955. *Life* magazine featured the first interracial casino and hotel with a front-cover story that June. Though the casino closed under suspicious circumstances after just five months, it was miraculously revived time and again. The casino and hotel was later reopened in the 1980s and 1990s by Sarann Knight Preddy, the first black woman in the world to obtain a nonrestricted gaming license, and her husband, Joe. Two fires would later extinguish the main facility, so that by 2009, it was a mere hull of its original grandeur. But the name Moulin Rouge alone, even in controversy, continues to outlive many establishments that were imploded on the Strip. Additionally, it was the site of the famous desegregation announcement in 1960 and later hosted numerous civil rights events through the 1990s.

Concurrently and ironically, the area was being impaired by civil rights concessions. By the early 1960s, following a formal handshake for integration, blacks on the Westside took increasing advantage of their elevated status in Las Vegas and began to patronize Downtown and the Strip and move away from the Westside. Eventually this, coupled with a city opposed to permitting property upgrades, would lead to the demise of the Jackson Street Strip and demolition of private property. Some, like the Carver Hotel, the Brown Derby, and other places, would be destroyed in quick succession.

The area became increasingly blighted, though churches and storefront prayer sites grew in number proportionately. In the late 1960s, the area erupted in racial fury, and the late desegregation of schools in 1972 did little to neutralize injustice. In the 1980s, the depressed black population was reeling from economic downturns, despite the tireless efforts of activists like Ruby Duncan, who strove to ensure economic independence and a rightful share of the American dream. The distress, coupled with the invisibility of the black people, attracted such groups as the Black Panthers, followed by major gangs migrating from other areas, including Southern California.

Fortunately, this was not the last chapter. As in previous decades, the challenges to the Westside were met by dozens of prominent citizens who refused to permit the ill effects of racism to destroy the area. On the heels of early successful black pioneer families from the 1920 through the 1940s came fresh young faces now ready to turn over the baton to others.

Among those combating the downward spiraling of the community were the veteran middle-class African Americans like Dr. Charles I. West, Dr. James McMillan, Sarann Knight Preddy, and Anna and Bob Bailey, who remained loyal to the Westside community. They, along with strong church and educational leaders like the Reverend Jesse Scott, Marion Bennett, Dr. S.S. Rogers, Mabel Hoggard, Shirley Barber, and Dr. Linda Young, kept the original Las Vegas alive. Bold legislators like Woodrow Wilson, Gene Collins, and Joe Neal would be followed by Assemblyman Harvey Mumford, County Commissioner Larry Weekly, City Councilman Ricki Barlow, and Sen. Steven Horsford.

Efforts by Pioneer Trail historians like Sam Wright have enshrined and preserved valuable sites. Gwen Walker's African American Museum houses numerous artifacts. A police station named for Officer Larry Bolden, the first black deputy chief of a Nevada police department, symbolizes the pride of his family and community.

West Las Vegas has expanded over time to include the once-segregated Bonanza Village. Gersan Park, formerly a housing project riddled with gangs and violence, was torn down in the late 1990s and now boasts a gated community with over 200 one- and two-story homes built by Frank Hawkins, a former football Raider and the 2010 president of the NAACP Las Vegas Branch.

Faces have changed but not the dynamics as a new generation arises. To name a few: Dina Neal follows in the footsteps of her famous father, Sen. Joe Neal by being elected to the state assembly; Trish Geran upholds her family's pioneer spirit, coleading a group to reopen F Street, site of a wall that obstructed a popular residential way to Downtown; Jarmilla McMillan Arnold multitasks in community work like her father, Dr. James McMillan. Most importantly, there still resounds the "we can; we will" cry that keeps the Westside alive.

One

Original Las Vegas
Recalling an Often Forgotten History

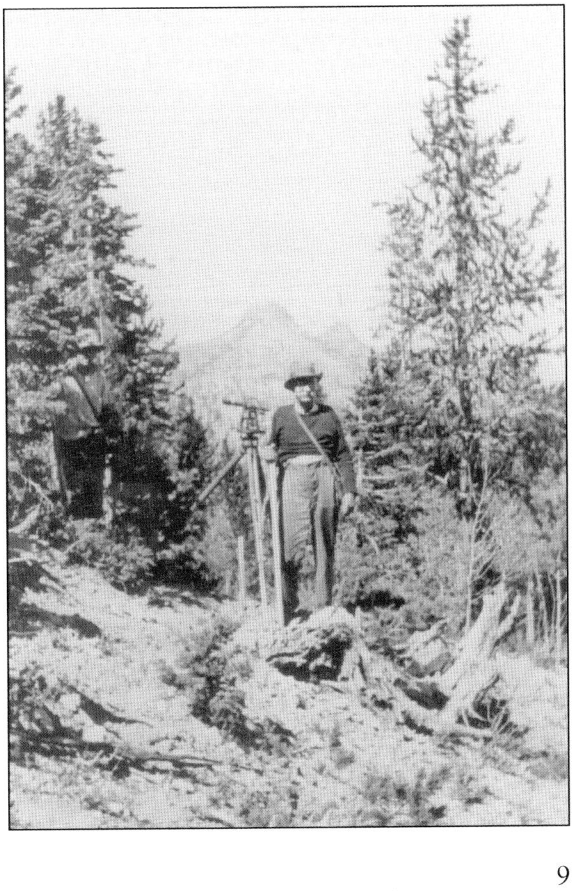

Founder of the Original Las Vegas. John Thomas "J.T." McWilliams's fiery red hair matched his fervid vision and determination to build an 80-acre community townsite in Las Vegas. He saw the advantage of the Las Vegas Creek and accessibility to roads leading to mining towns. Unfortunately, William A. Clark, J.T.'s old nemesis from a previous land right fracas, would confound his plans again. The earlier battle over 1,300 acres of lumber land claimed by J.T. McWilliams, a railroad surveyor with a penchant for the common man, went all the way to Teddy Roosevelt's White House to secure McWilliams's property rights. However, no allies came through when Clark lorded over Las Vegas and the creek and wells would not suffice for McWilliams townsite. After reaching a population from 2,000 to 3,000, the experimental town faltered and fell into ruin. McWilliams never admitted defeat, however. Today, this pioneer is celebrated for his grit and generosity in building up southern Nevada.

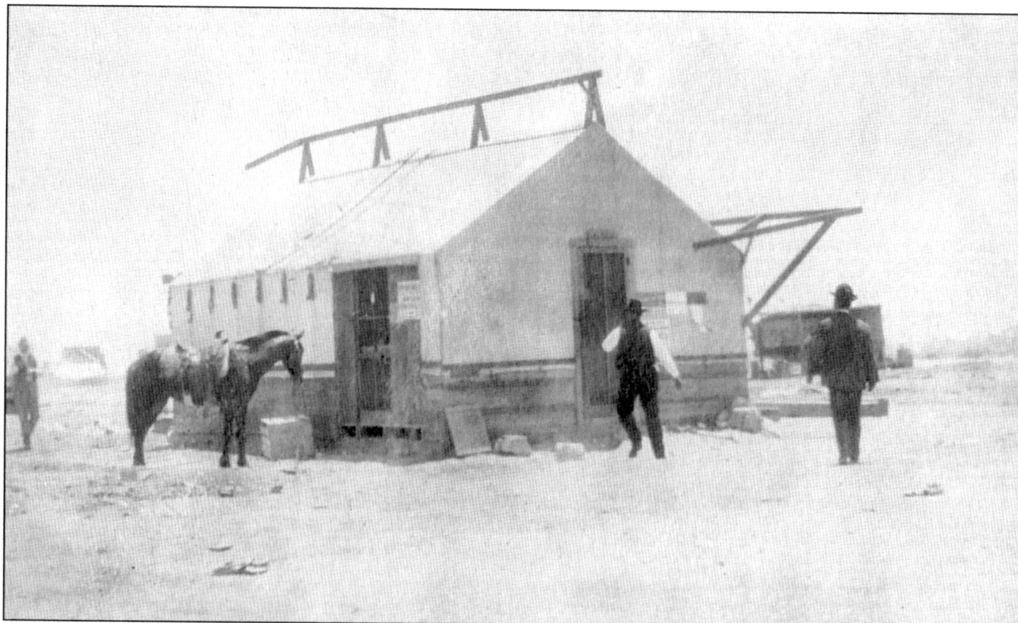

A Different Painting on Canvas. Like many sturdy pioneers across the country, early settlers in Las Vegas used whatever resources at hand for shelter. Canvas and wood created the business atmosphere of early Las Vegas, as can be seen in this photograph of a post office most likely in the McWilliams townsite. For over a year, this area bloomed, and people were optimistic with the railroad being built through Las Vegas, Spanish for "the meadows."

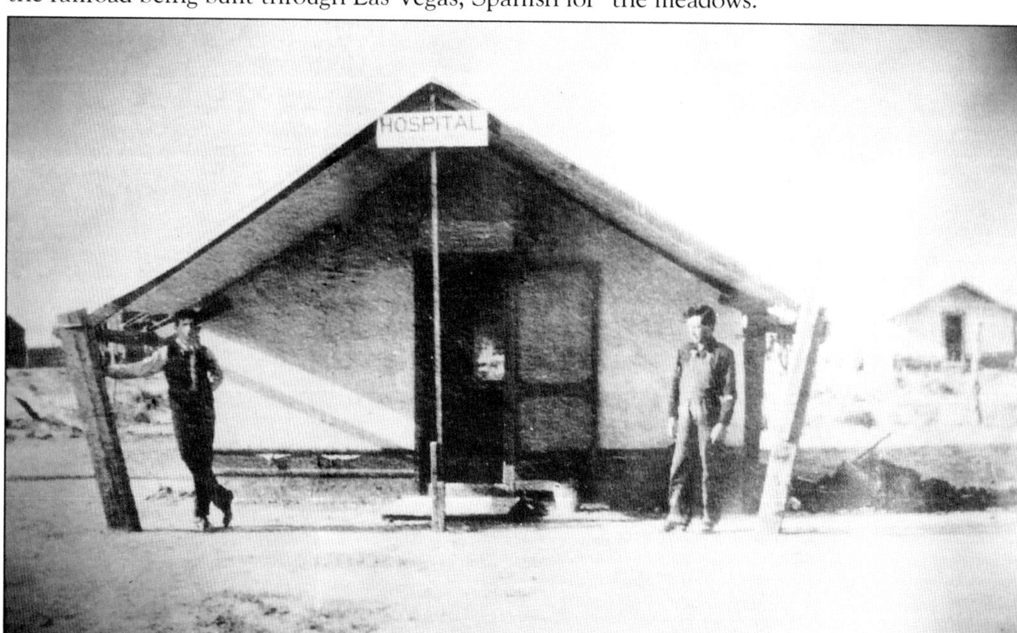

First Tent Hospital. This crude set-up served the first people to settle Las Vegas, though it hardly looks like an inviting emergency center. It served injured or ill miners, railroad personnel, and their loved ones. The Westside would have to wait 50 years for a real doctor's local care when Dr. Charles I. West opened offices on Bonanza.

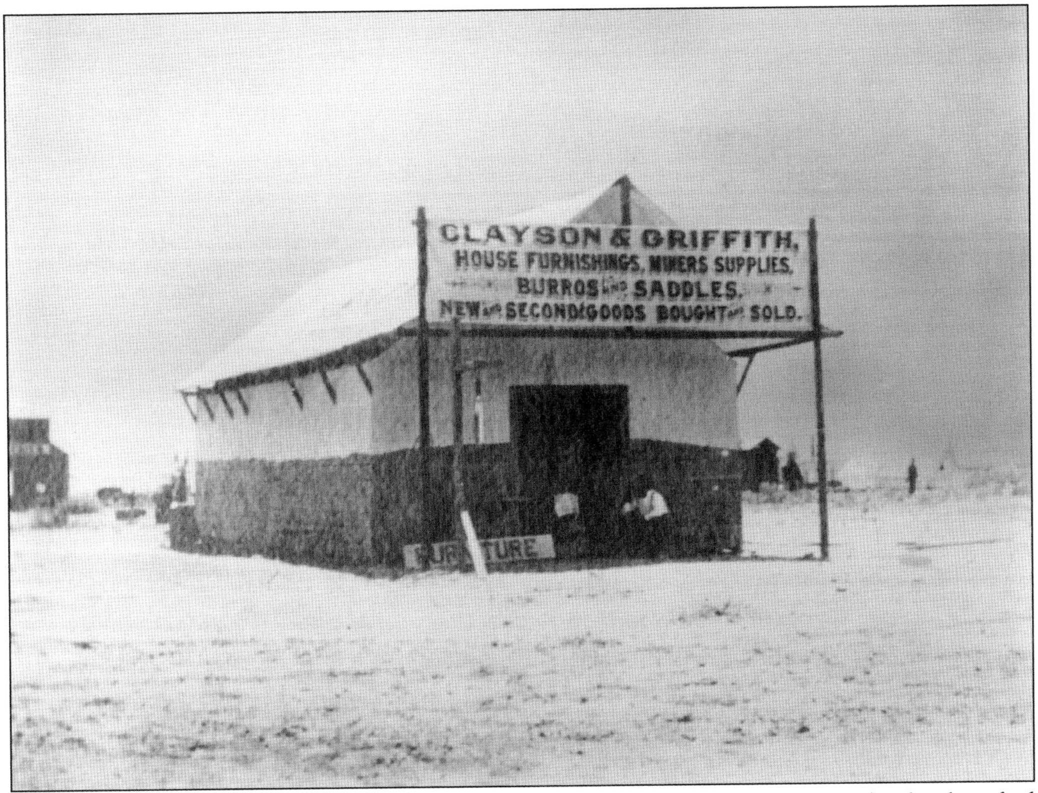

ATTRACTION THROUGH SIGNAGE. Early businesses provided bold signage that clearly identified their goods. Canvas often kept out dust better than loosely joined wood plats, which was as scarce as forestation. Early retail stores were often one step above a camp tent and needed to be securely pegged against strong winds that swirled viciously on the desert terrain.

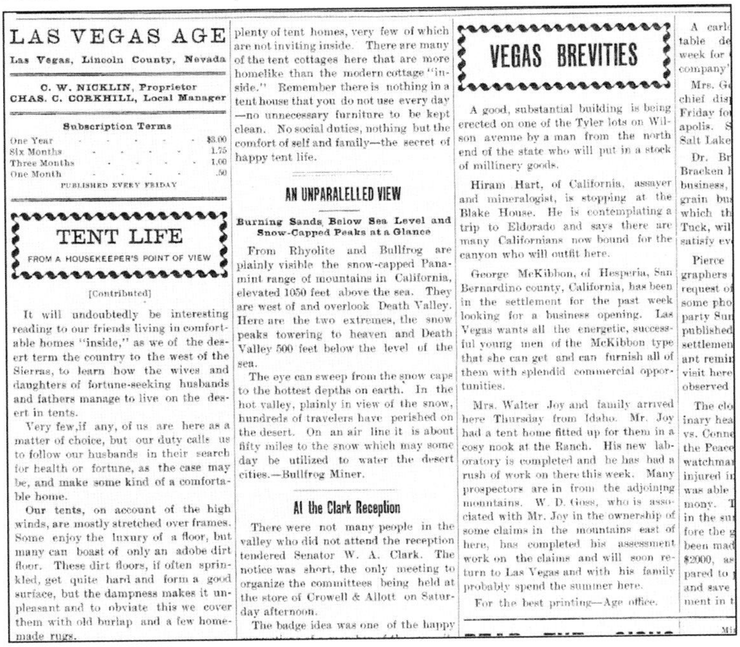

LAS VEGAS AGE

Las Vegas, Lincoln County, Nevada

C. W. NICKLIN, Proprietor
CHAS. C. CORKHILL, Local Manager

Subscription Terms

One Year	$3.00
Six Months	1.75
Three Months	1.00
One Month	.50

PUBLISHED EVERY FRIDAY

TENT LIFE

FROM A HOUSEKEEPER'S POINT OF VIEW

[Contributed]

It will undoubtedly be interesting reading to our friends living in comfortable homes "inside," as we of the desert term the country to the west of the Sierras, to learn how the wives and daughters of fortune-seeking husbands and fathers manage to live on the desert in tents.

Very few, if any, of us are here as a matter of choice, but our duty calls us to follow our husbands in their search for health or fortune, as the case may be, and make some kind of a comfortable home.

Our tents, on account of the high winds, are mostly stretched over frames. Some enjoy the luxury of a floor, but many can boast of only an adobe dirt floor. These dirt floors, if often sprinkled, get quite hard and form a good surface, but the dampness makes it unpleasant and to obviate this we cover them with old burlap and a few home-made rugs.

plenty of tent homes, very few of which are not inviting inside. There are many of the tent cottages here that are more homelike than the modern cottage "inside." Remember there is nothing in a tent house that you do not use every day—no unnecessary furniture to be kept clean. No social duties, nothing but the comfort of self and family—the secret of happy tent life.

AN UNPARALELLED VIEW

Burning Sands, Below Sea Level and Snow-Capped Peaks at a Glance

From Rhyolite and Bullfrog are plainly visible the snow-capped Panamint range of mountains in California, elevated 1050 feet above the sea. They are west of and overlook Death Valley. Here are the two extremes, the snow peaks towering to heaven and Death Valley 500 feet below the level of the sea.

The eye can sweep from the snow caps to the hottest depths on earth. In the hot valley, plainly in view of the snow, hundreds of travelers have perished on the desert. On an air line it is about fifty miles to the snow which may some day be utilized to water the desert cities.—Bullfrog Miner.

At the Clark Reception

There were not many people in the valley who did not attend the reception tendered Senator W. A. Clark. The notice was short, the only meeting to organize the committees being held at the store of Crowell & Allott on Saturday afternoon.

The badge idea was one of the happy

VEGAS BREVITIES

A good, substantial building is being erected on one of the Tyler lots on Wilson avenue by a man from the north end of the state who will put in a stock of millinery goods.

Hiram Hart, of California, assayer and mineralogist, is stopping at the Blake House. He is contemplating a trip to Eldorado and says there are many Californians now bound for the canyon who will outfit here.

George McKibbon, of Hesperia, San Bernardino county, California, has been in the settlement for the past week looking for a business opening. Las Vegas wants all the energetic, successful young men of the McKibbon type that she can get and can furnish all of them with splendid commercial opportunities.

Mrs. Walter Joy and family arrived here Thursday from Idaho. Mr. Joy had a tent home fitted up for them in a cosy nook at the Ranch. His new laboratory is completed and he has had a rush of work on there this week. Many prospectors are in from the adjoining mountains. W. D. Goss, who is associated with Mr. Joy in the ownership of some claims in the mountains east of here, has completed his assessment work on the claims and will soon return to Las Vegas and with his family probably spend the summer here.

For the best printing—Age office.

TENT LIVING LOOKING INVITING. A hearty group made tent living look and sound like a preferred alternative lifestyle. One spirited housekeeper wrote in *Las Vegas Age* in 1905 about the secret of happy tent life, noting, "These tents may appear comfortless to many, but it is always a pleasant surprise to step inside and see how happy and contented you will find the occupants." (Courtesy Nevada State Museum, Las Vegas)

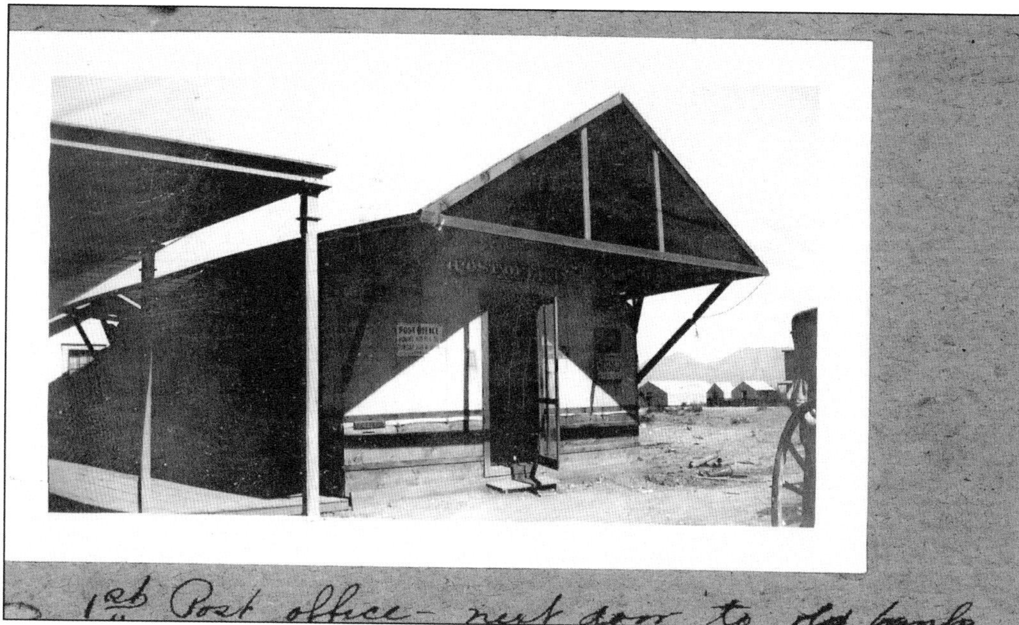

BUILDING SMARTER, NOT HARDER. Although tents remained the staple for many stores and residents, natives learned to overlay tent tops with a wood fly to deflect the scorching heat, especially as lumber became a more available import.

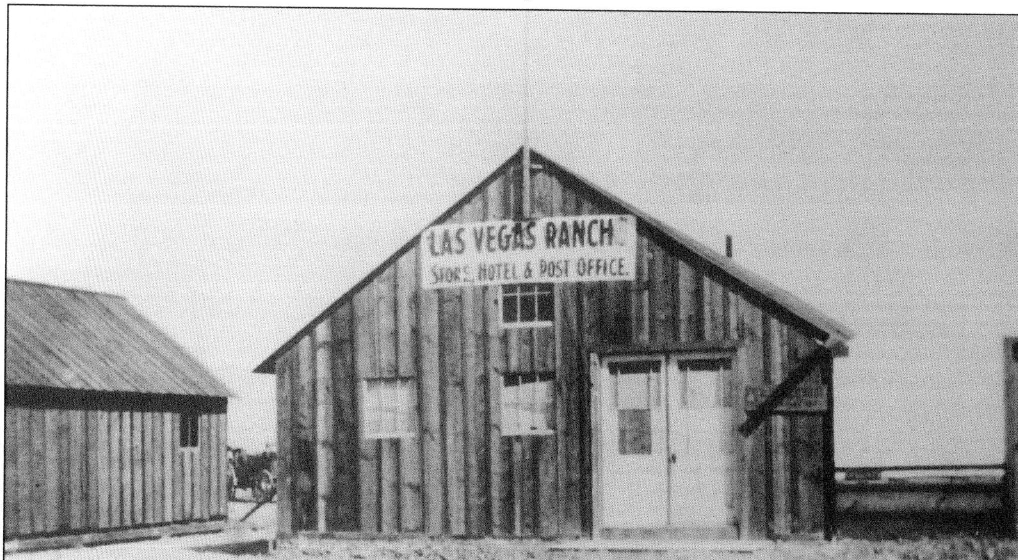

EARLY WOOD STRUCTURES. Simple one-story wood structures emerged as the small townsite grew. Yet the building lines were initially quite simple and likely uneven, with a sense that a strong gale could quickly topple them. Still, tents would dominate Las Vegas, especially the Westside, for several more decades.

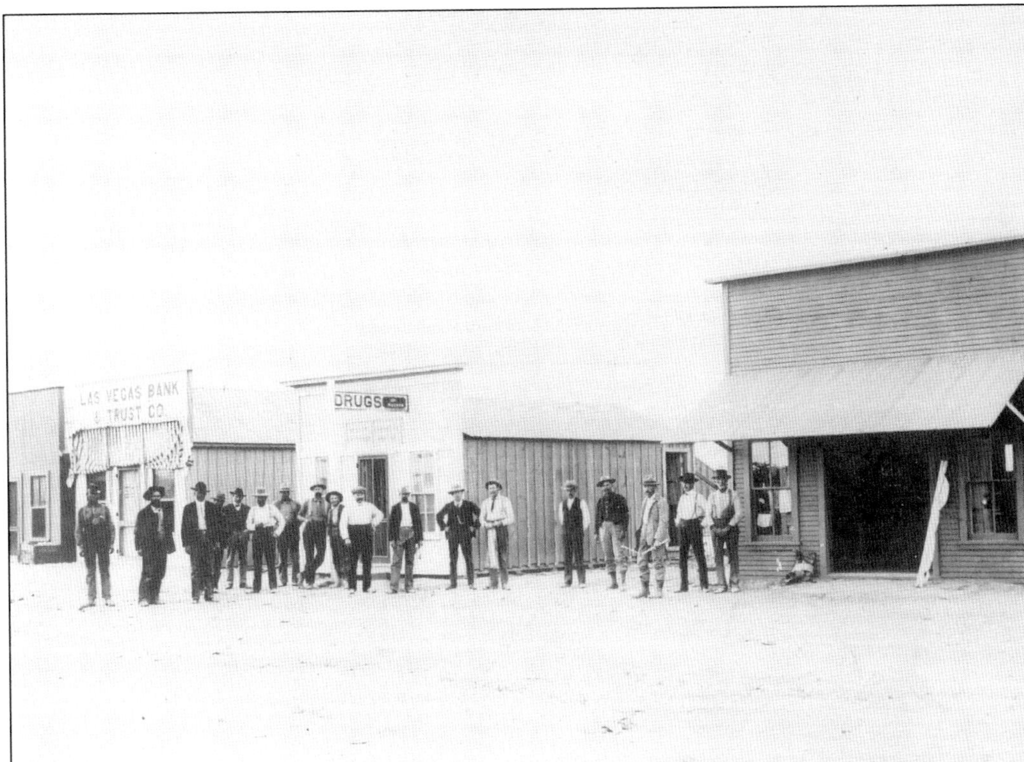

TOWNSITE FROM ANOTHER VIEWPOINT. As buildings rose, so did the offerings, as can be clearly seen here. The town boasted a strange sophistication in goods and services even though the environment was rather bleak. Ironically, the town for all of its expanse would look as barren even in the 1950s in many parts of town.

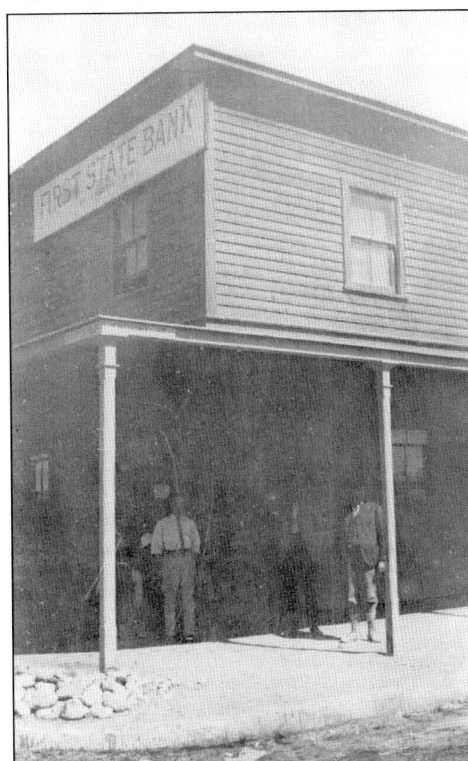

ADDING A PORCHED ENTRY OR ANOTHER STORY. Through the end of 1904 and into 1905, architectural individuality increased, as can be seen with the addition of covered entries. Any shield against the sun was a bonus, and early settlers learned how to adapt to the environment.

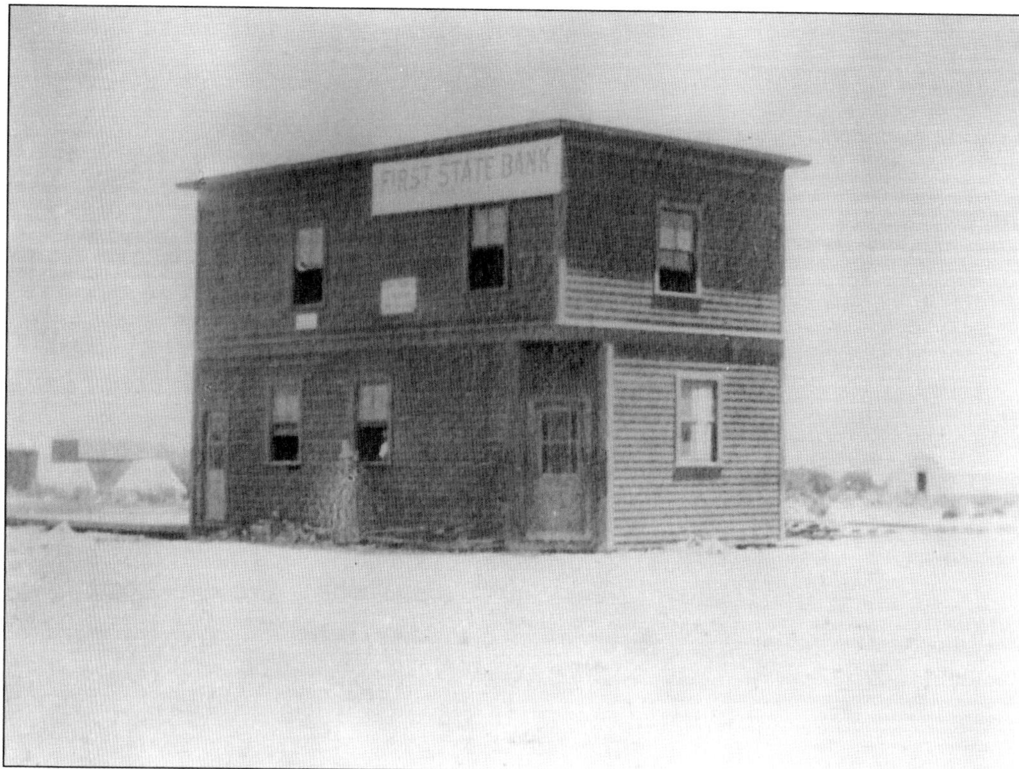

FIRST BANK, FIRST STATE. While it is difficult to imagine a thriving business at this bank, it served the local population, business, and miners quite well. Much business transpired simply through serving the miners. Numerous tent outlines can be seen in the background.

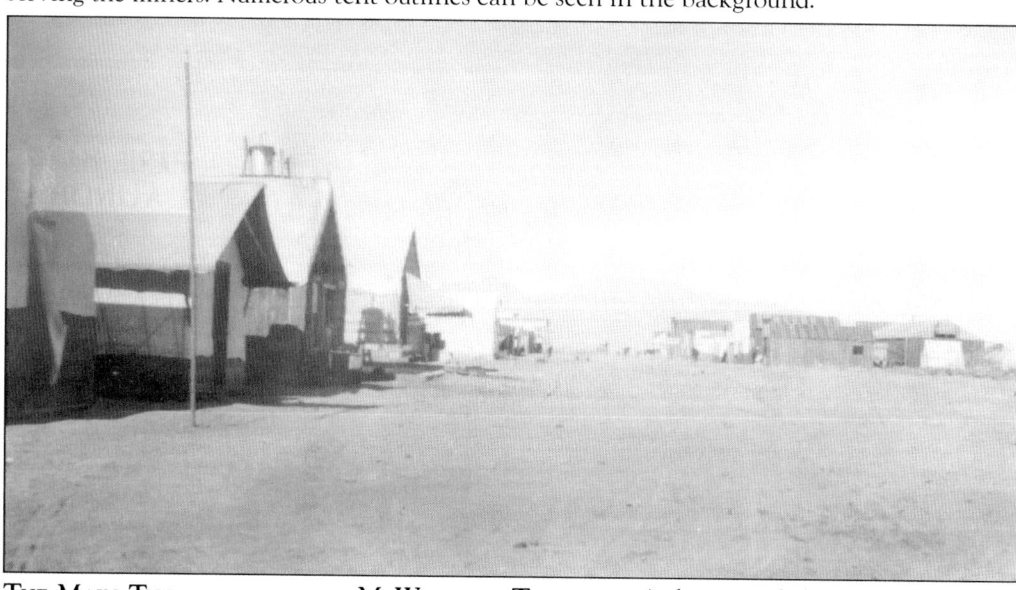

THE MAIN THOROUGHFARE FOR MCWILLIAMS TOWNSITE. A dusty road shouldered by simple wooden structures was actually an improvement from the early campsite in the meadows by spring wells. Still, when the winds roared, the dust choked even those inside many dwellings. It would be decades before service to this part of town would include regularly dampening of dirt roads.

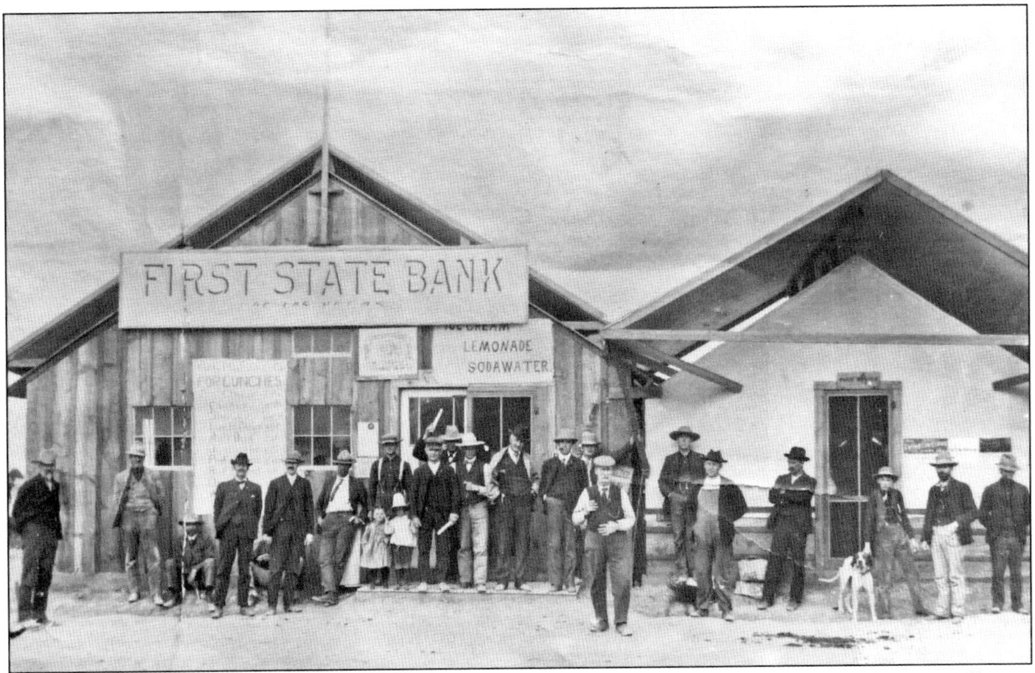

THE McWILLIAMS TOWNSITE BUSINESS CENTER. Early Las Vegans are pictured at the McWilliams townsite, which boasted over 100 buildings, including six general stores, two wholesale houses, three furniture stores, 14 lodging houses, a hotel, warehouses, restaurants, three drug stores, a bank, newspapers, a barbershop, and various trades. A hotel bed still meant sharing a double bed, often with bedbugs.

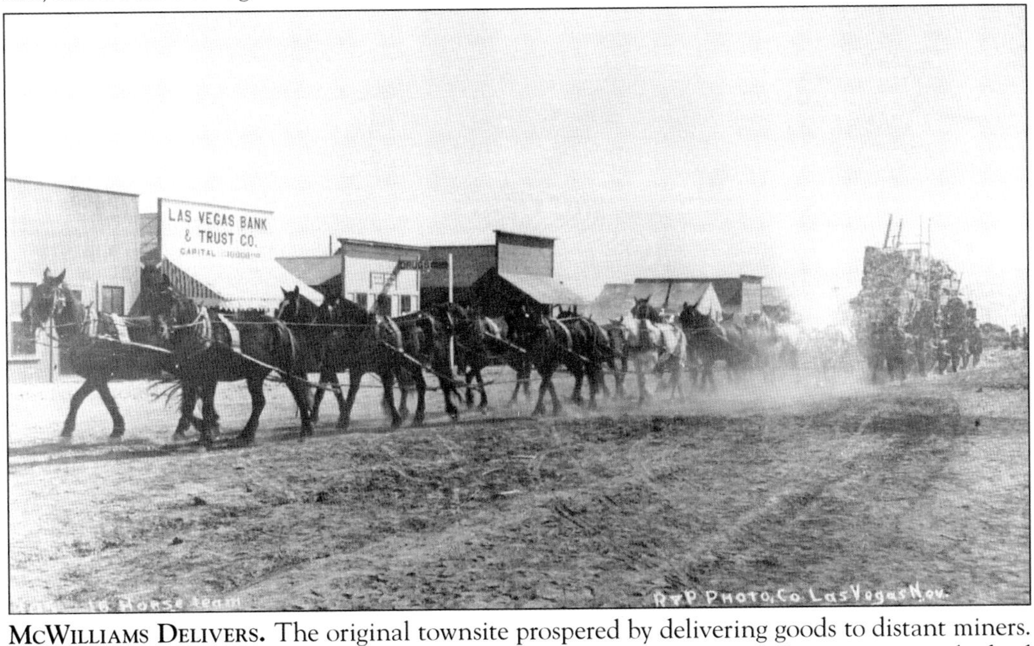

McWILLIAMS DELIVERS. The original townsite prospered by delivering goods to distant miners. 16-horse trains like the one pictured here could carry ample supplies such as mining tools, food goods, and other necessities. They regularly traveled to Goldfield, Rhyolite, and Tonopah. Residency reached 1,500. (Courtesy Nevada State Museum, Las Vegas.)

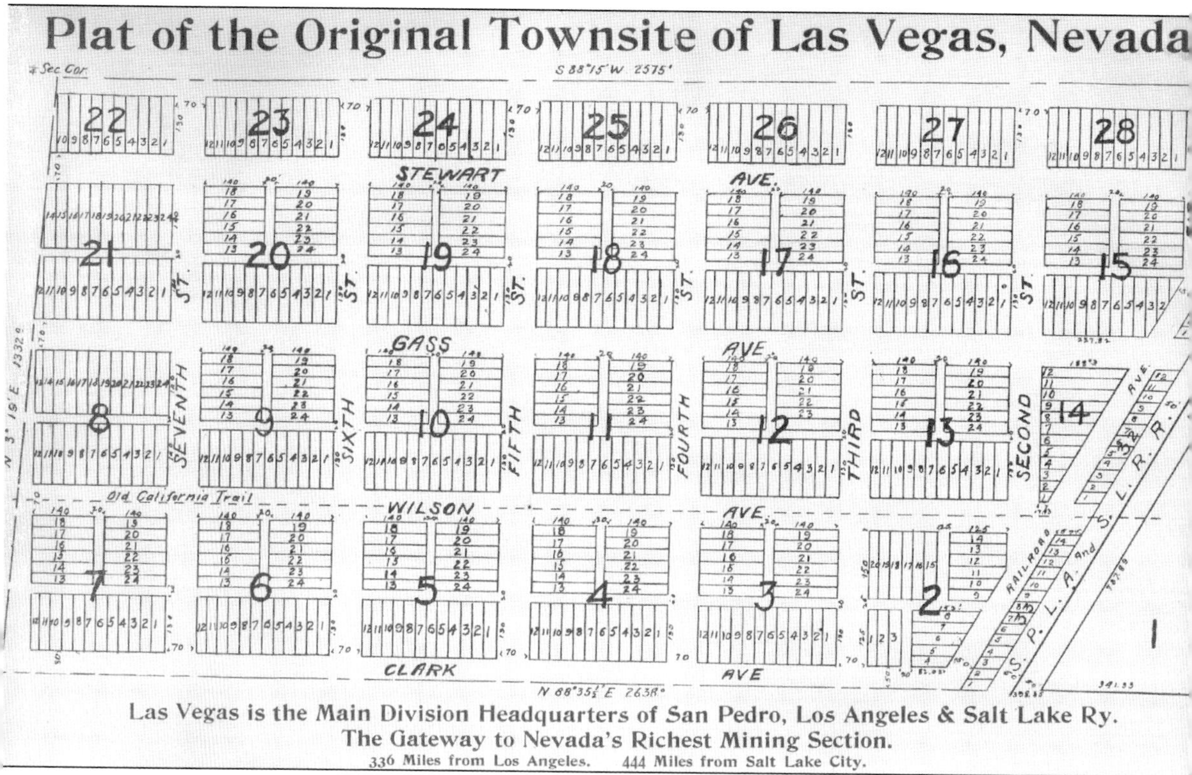

A Carefully Platted Town. McWilliams had his share of critics who scoffed at him accepting little money down and practically giving away property later. Yet there is ample evidence that this surveyor knew something about planning, including a layout of broad avenues. Ironically, even the numbered streets would be taken over by Clark, leaving the Westside roads with alphabet designations.

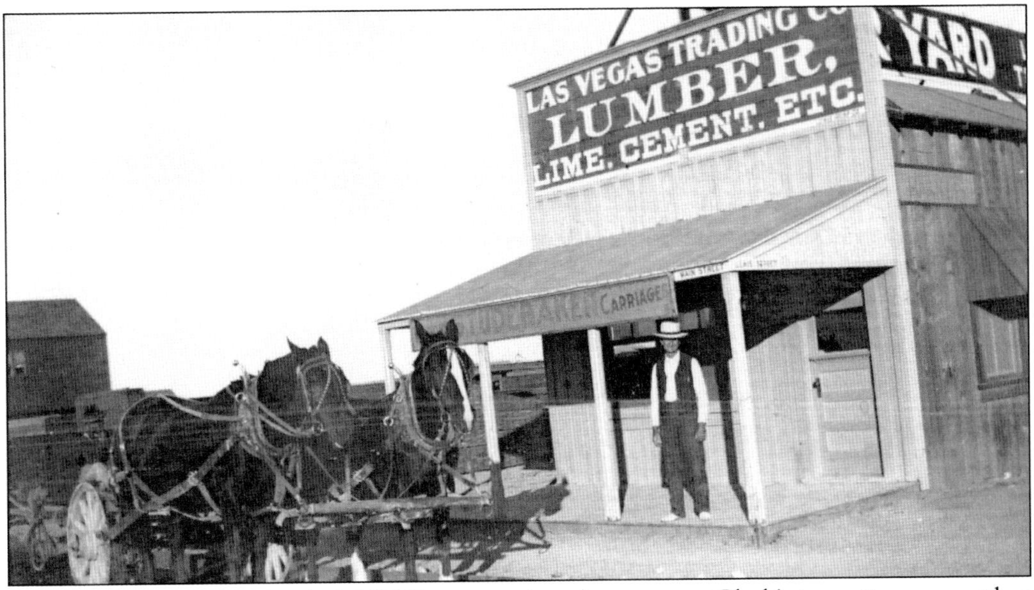

Lumber Supply in Town. As McWilliams continued to prosper, Clark's townsite was mostly a vision. Even historians are unsure where some buildings were situated. This lumber store, which offered a variety of building materials, may have been on either side but signaled a growing Las Vegas.

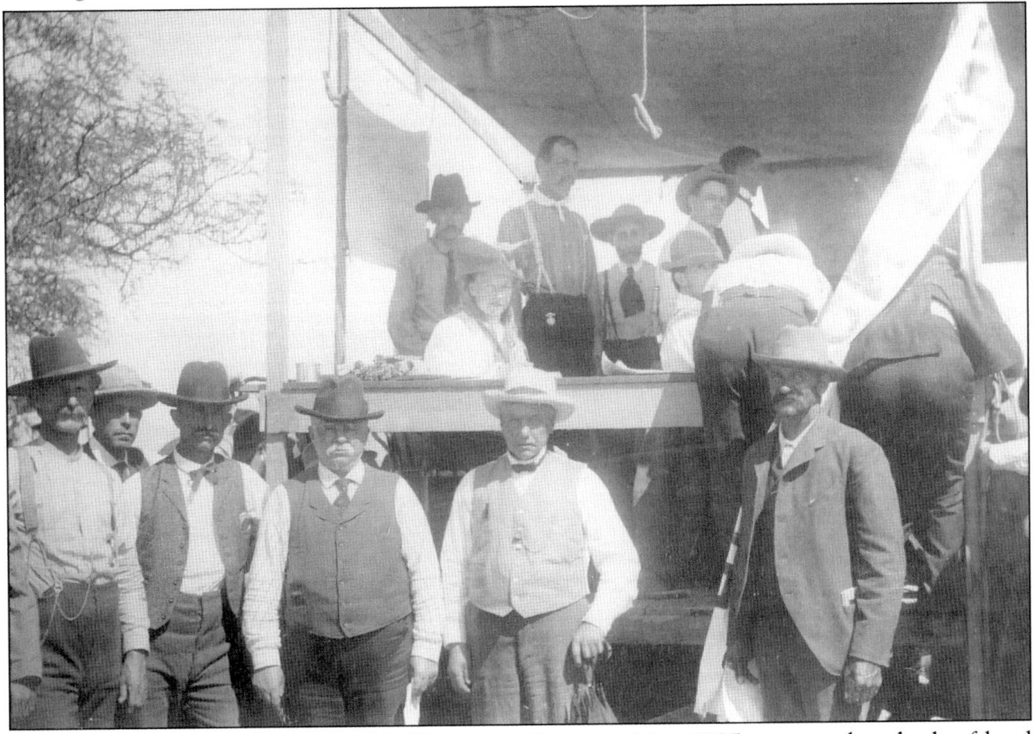

Sen. William Clark Outwits McWilliams. During a May 1905 auction, hundreds of land purchasers braved temperatures of 110 degrees to bid on Clark's land lots. By the day's end, the buying frenzy brought in thousands of dollars. That day also marked what many consider the beginning of the real Las Vegas.

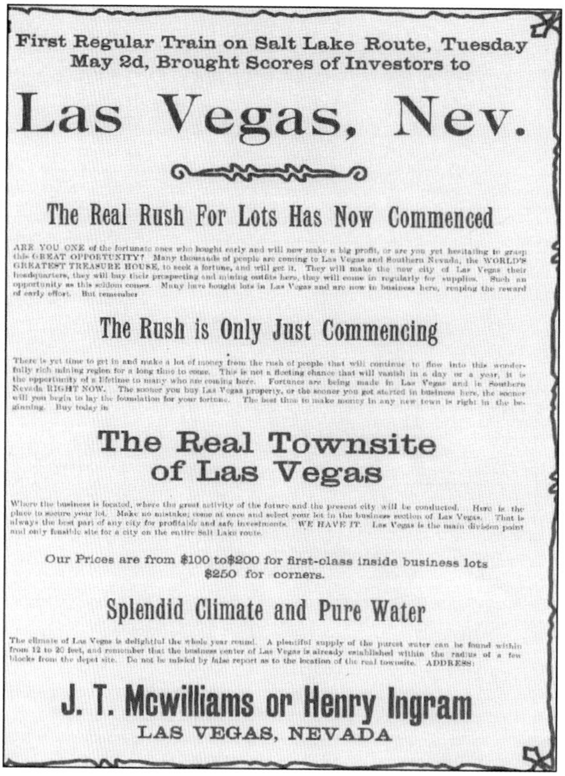

First Regular Train on Salt Lake Route, Tuesday May 2d, Brought Scores of Investors to

Las Vegas, Nev.

The Real Rush For Lots Has Now Commenced

ARE YOU ONE of the fortunate ones who bought early and will now make a big profit, or are you yet hesitating to grasp this GREAT OPPORTUNITY? Many thousands of people are coming to Las Vegas and Southern Nevada, the WORLD'S GREATEST TREASURE HOUSE, to seek a fortune, and will get it. They will make the new city of Las Vegas their headquarters, they will buy their prospecting and mining outfits here, they will come in regularly for supplies. Such an opportunity as this seldom comes. Many have bought lots in Las Vegas and are now in business here, reaping the reward of early effort. But remember

The Rush is Only Just Commencing

There is yet time to get in and make a lot of money from the rush of people that will continue to flow into this wonderfully rich mining region for a long time to come. This is not a fleeting chance that will vanish in a day or a year, it is the opportunity of a lifetime to many who are coming here. Fortunes are being made in Las Vegas and in Southern Nevada RIGHT NOW. The sooner you buy Las Vegas property, or the sooner you get started in business here, the sooner will you begin to lay the foundation for your fortune. The best time to make money in any new town is right in the beginning. Buy today in

The Real Townsite of Las Vegas

Where the business is located, where the great activity of the future and the present city will be conducted. Here is the place to secure your lot. Make no mistake; come at once and select your lot in the business section of Las Vegas. That is always the best part of any city for profitable and safe investments. WE HAVE IT. Las Vegas is the main division point and only feasible site for a city on the entire Salt Lake route.

Our Prices are from $100 to$200 for first-class inside business lots $250 for corners.

Splendid Climate and Pure Water

The climate of Las Vegas is delightful the whole year round. A plentiful supply of the purest water can be found within from 12 to 20 feet, and remember that the business center of Las Vegas is already established within the radius of a few blocks from the depot site. Do not be misled by false report as to the location of the real townsite. ADDRESS:

J. T. Mcwilliams or Henry Ingram
LAS VEGAS, NEVADA

ADVERTISEMENT SELLING LOTS, MAY 1905. Even with the overpowering presence of the planned 40-block Clark townsite, McWilliams heartily promoted his lots that touted Las Vegas as the "world's greatest treasure house" and a "foundation for your future," while warning prospective land buyers against the "false report as to the location of the real townsite." His small down payments may have been his downfall, however.

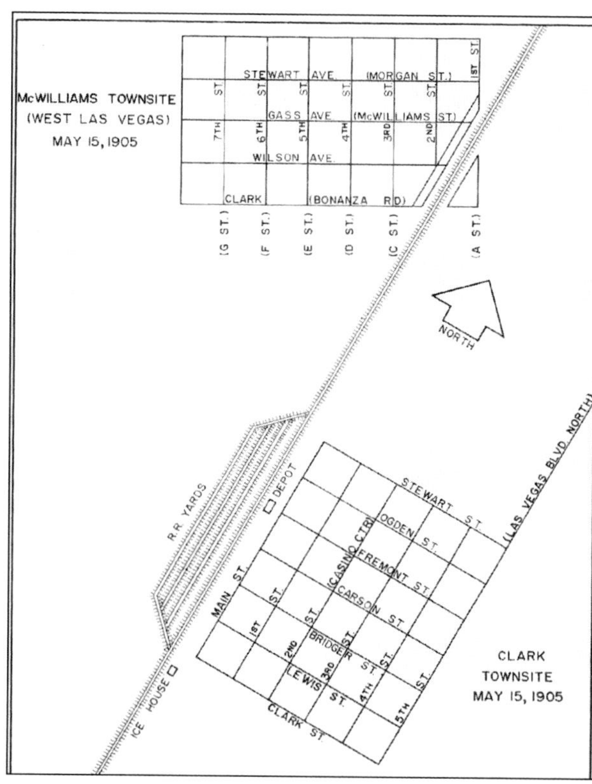

PLAT SHOWING THE TWO TOWNSITES. McWilliams continued his campaign to save his townsite well into 1905, but his frequent, bold advertisements proved no match for the greater powers southeast of the tracks, including an ice plant. Clark's townsite gained popularity largely on speculation and resources. Note the envious position of the main railroad yard near Clark's townsite, later prophetically nicknamed "Glitter Gulch." (Courtesy West Las Vegas Library.)

A Different Kind of Bus. In 1905, a bus referred to a horse-drawn unit of transportation. Here, an ad boasts of free transportation both ways to a Fourth of July celebration for both Clark's and McWilliams's towns. Among the fare are a "Fat man's race" and a "Potato race" for "married ladies only." A baseball game pits Searchlight against Las Vegas. (Courtesy Nevada State Museum, Las Vegas.)

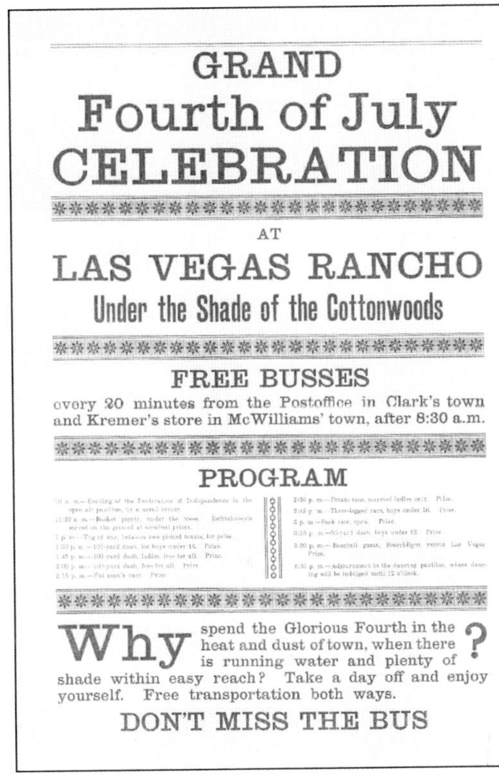

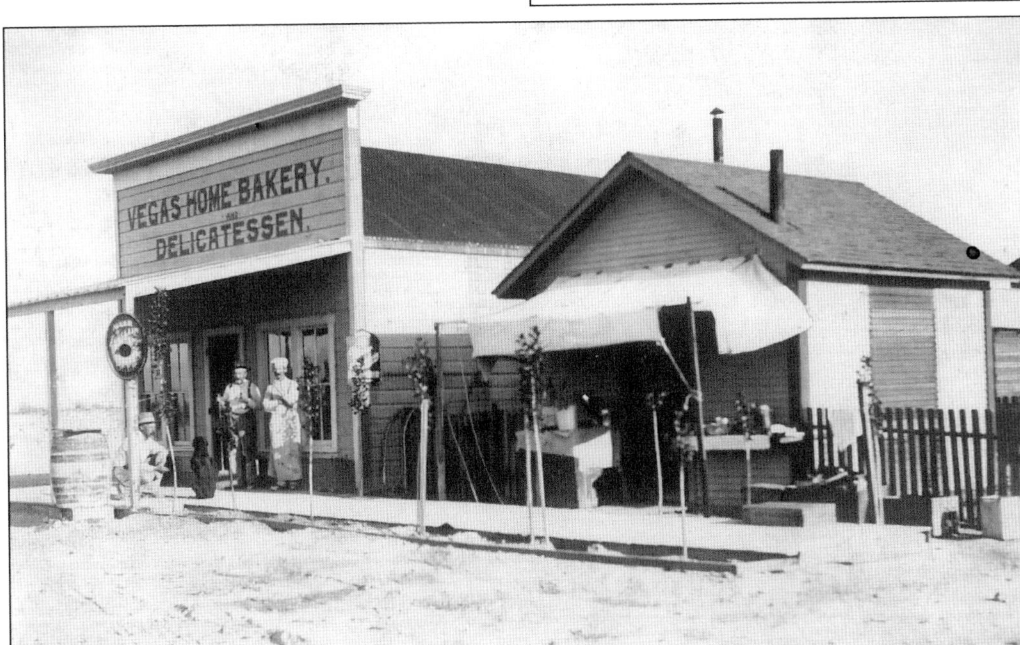

Baked Goods and Delicatessen. For being such a fledging area, many culinary delights were offered in McWilliams's townsite. Moreover, this great attraction would retain its location. When Clark drew people and businesses away from McWilliams's townsite, this bakery's ovens were reportedly too hot and heavy to move.

SAM GAY.

Sam Gay has been a resident of Las Vegas in the early days of Old Rag Town. Shortly after his arrival here he was made night watchman, and served in that capacity until the following election, when he was elected Constable of Las Vegas township and also made Deputy Sheriff under Phil K. Smith, and served during Mr. Smith's term. In 1908 he was again elected Constable and was appointed Deputy Sheriff by O. H. Smith, who was elected Sheriff at the same time that Sam Gay was elected Constable for the second time. He served under Sheriff Smith until the division of Lincoln County, and the newly appointed sheriff, recognizing his incomparable ability as a peace officer, though of a different political faith, appointed him his under-sheriff. This service

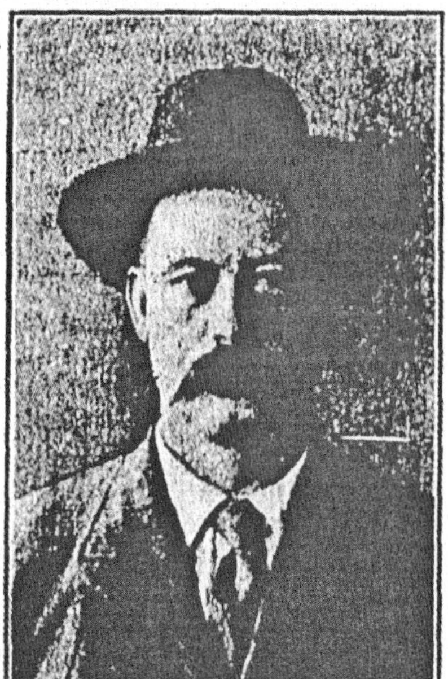

continued until the first of the present year, when for political reasons the Sheriff deemed best to dispense with his services, appointing a Democrat in his place.

Sam Gay's younger days were spent in his home in Massachusetts. At the age of twenty-one he was superintendent of a large stock and dairy farm in Carlisle in that sttae. He came west at the age of twenty-five and the following year held a position as superintendent of the Leach wheat farm at Minoken, North Dakota, in full charge of a ranch of over ten thousand acres. In 1887 he moved to

Early Pioneer Sam Gay. Touted as a great peace officer, Sam Gay could not have known that the later Westside would boast its own unrelated, prominent black Gay family. The big-framed man originated from Massachusetts and was one of the original settlers in Ragtown. As deputy sheriff, he was feared by crooks but enjoyed great popularity. Still, one story is told about the time an entire furnished tent house was stolen while he was nabbing a couple of muggers and an escaped convict. It seems Sam was better at hand-to-hand combat than detective work.

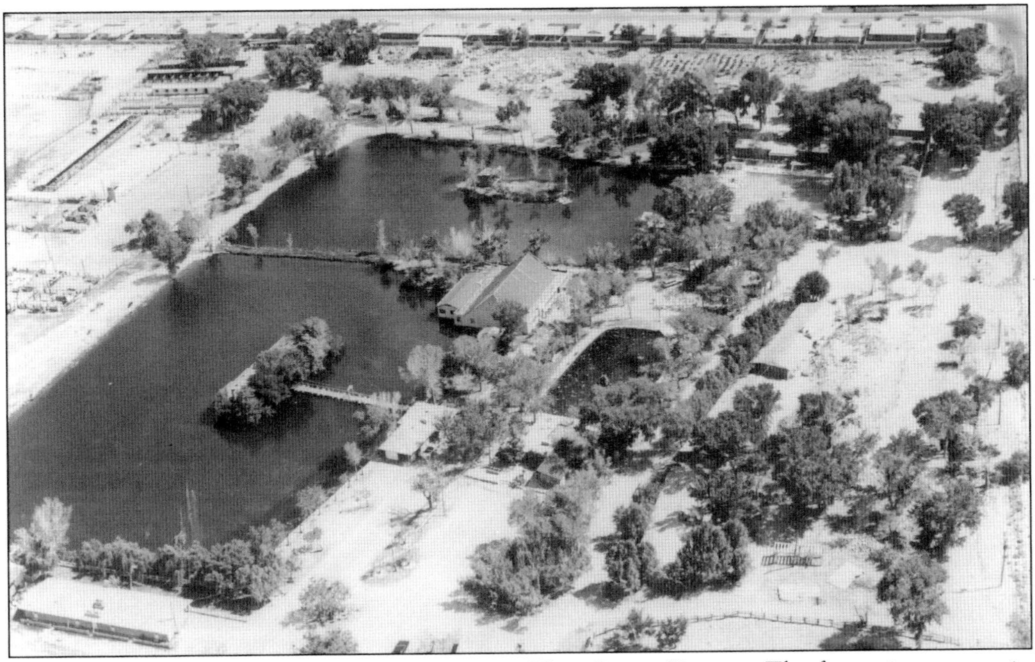

McWilliams's West Las Vegas Expands with Twin Lakes Resort. The first private resort in Las Vegas, on the west side of town, currently abuts the area's western Rancho Boulevard boundary. Built in 1926, the area, later known as Lorenzi Park, boasted many amenities, including park-like grounds, a hotel, a pool, and a beautiful pond.

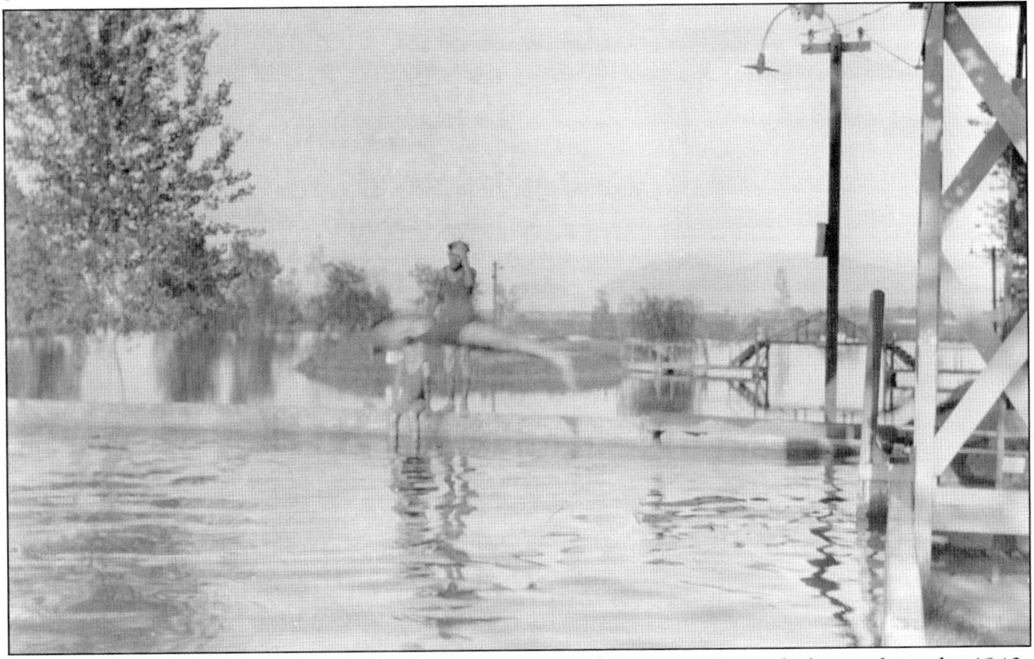

Diving in. The pool was well used. The private resort later served as a dude ranch in the 1940s and again as a hopeful refuge for divorcees in the 1950s. African Americans were not allowed, and some veteran Westside residents skirt mention of Lorenzi Park with the historic Westside, though it is an official site on the West Las Vegas Pioneer Trail.

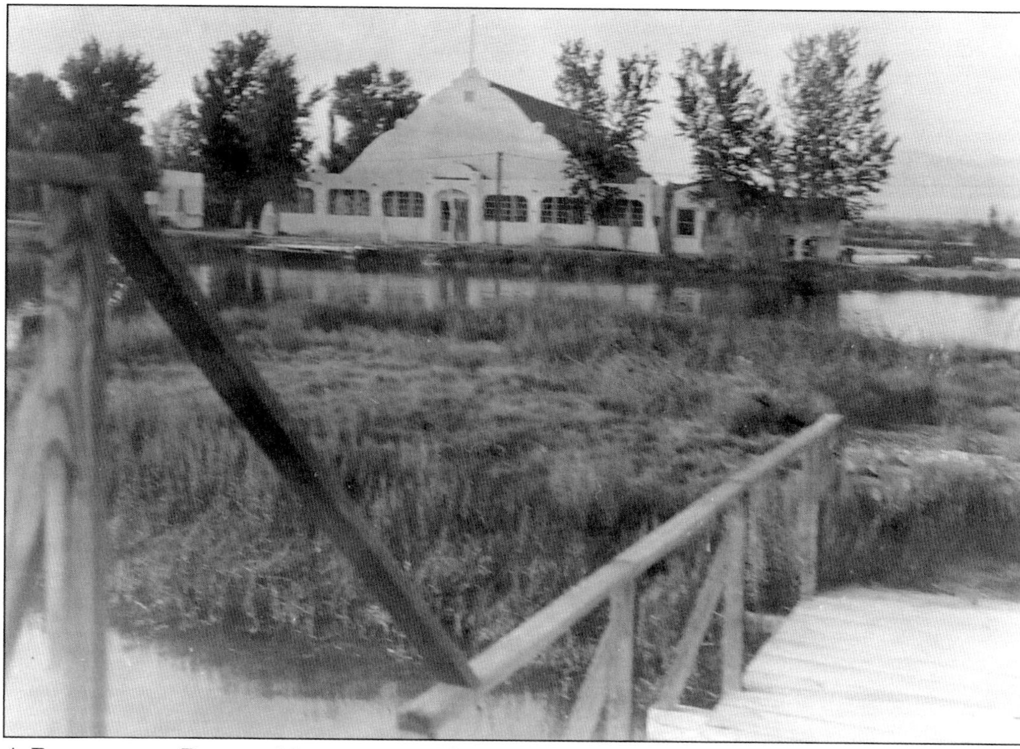

A Picturesque Bridge. Many awaiting divorcees soaked in the serene setting at Lorenzi Park, which offered an expansive tranquil visit during a difficult time. Water, a commodity as precious as gold, was literally the wellspring of its existence. While most people think of Las Vegas as all sand and rock, this early picture of Twin Lakes provides the lush spring vegetation that first drew the railroad. Today, the nearby Springs Preserve surprises visitors with the rich, colorful vegetation that blooms in the area.

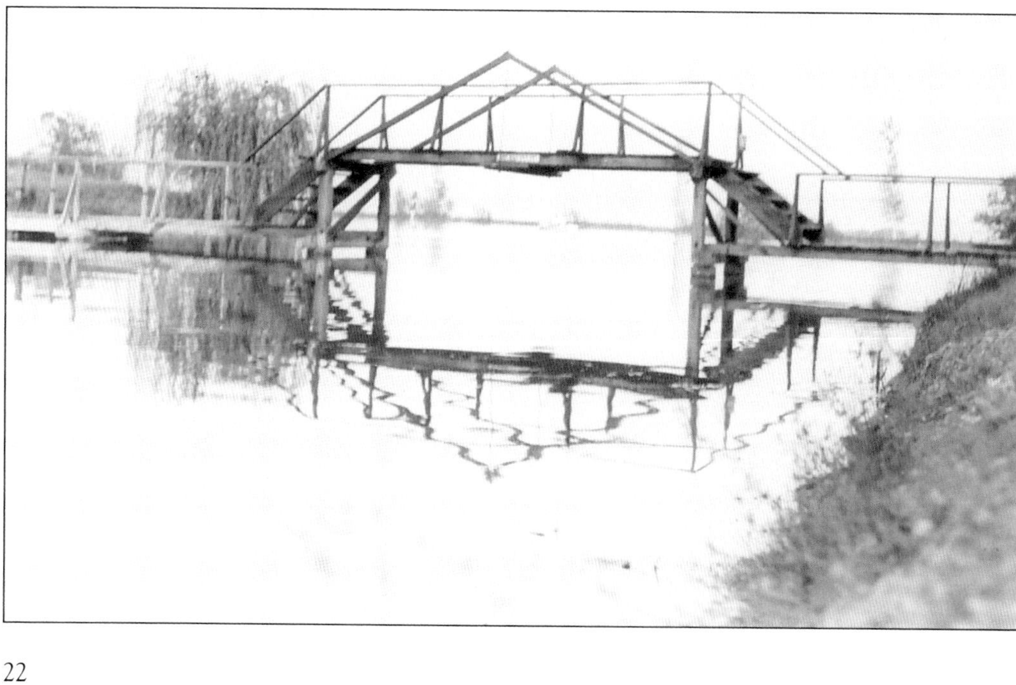

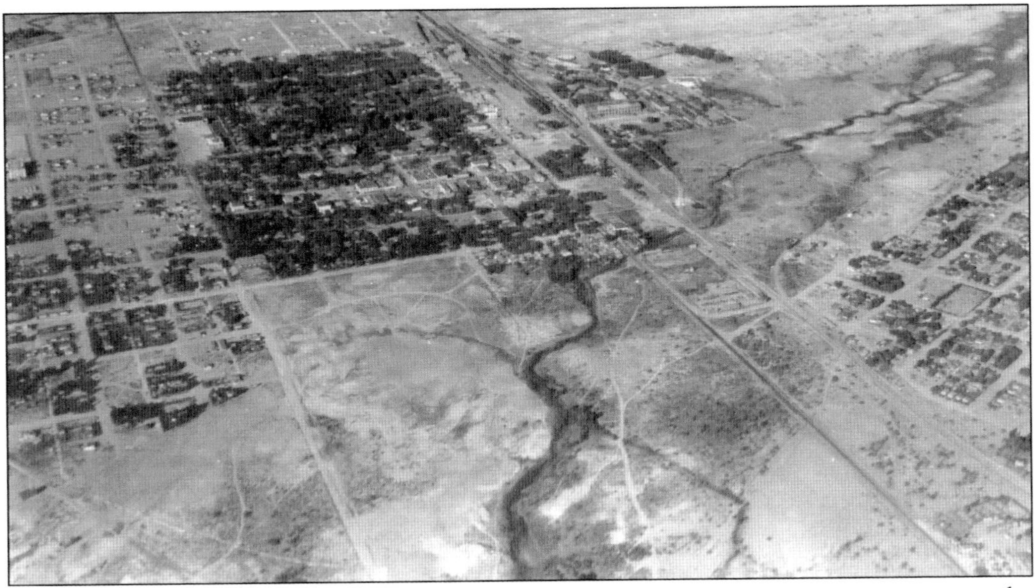

AERIAL SHOTS OF THE WESTSIDE. In the picture above, one can see downtown Las Vegas in the upper left area and the Westside in the lower right quadrant—the opposite of most viewpoints, though developmental differences tell which is which. Below is a 1938 shot of West Las Vegas with railroad tracks visible in the upper portion. Many of the visible rooftops remain unidentified, but a State Museum representative thinks that the white roof may represent the historic Westside School. Note the many vacant lots, which most likely held tents not visible from this view. (Both, courtesy Nevada State Museum, Las Vegas.)

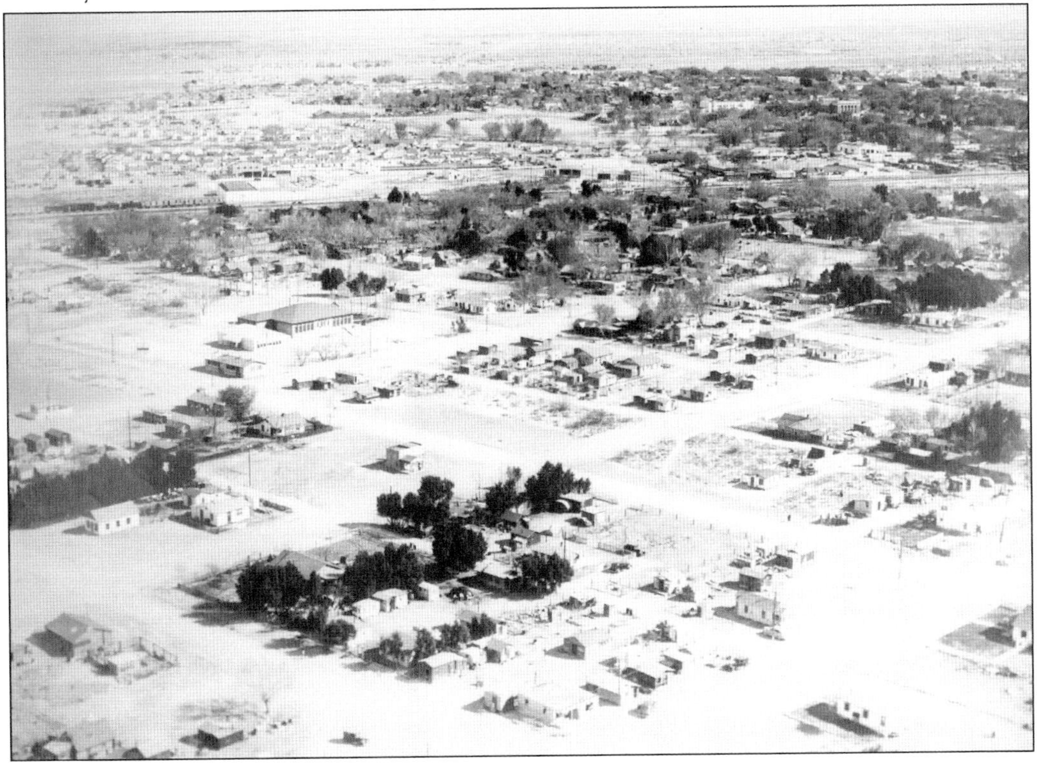

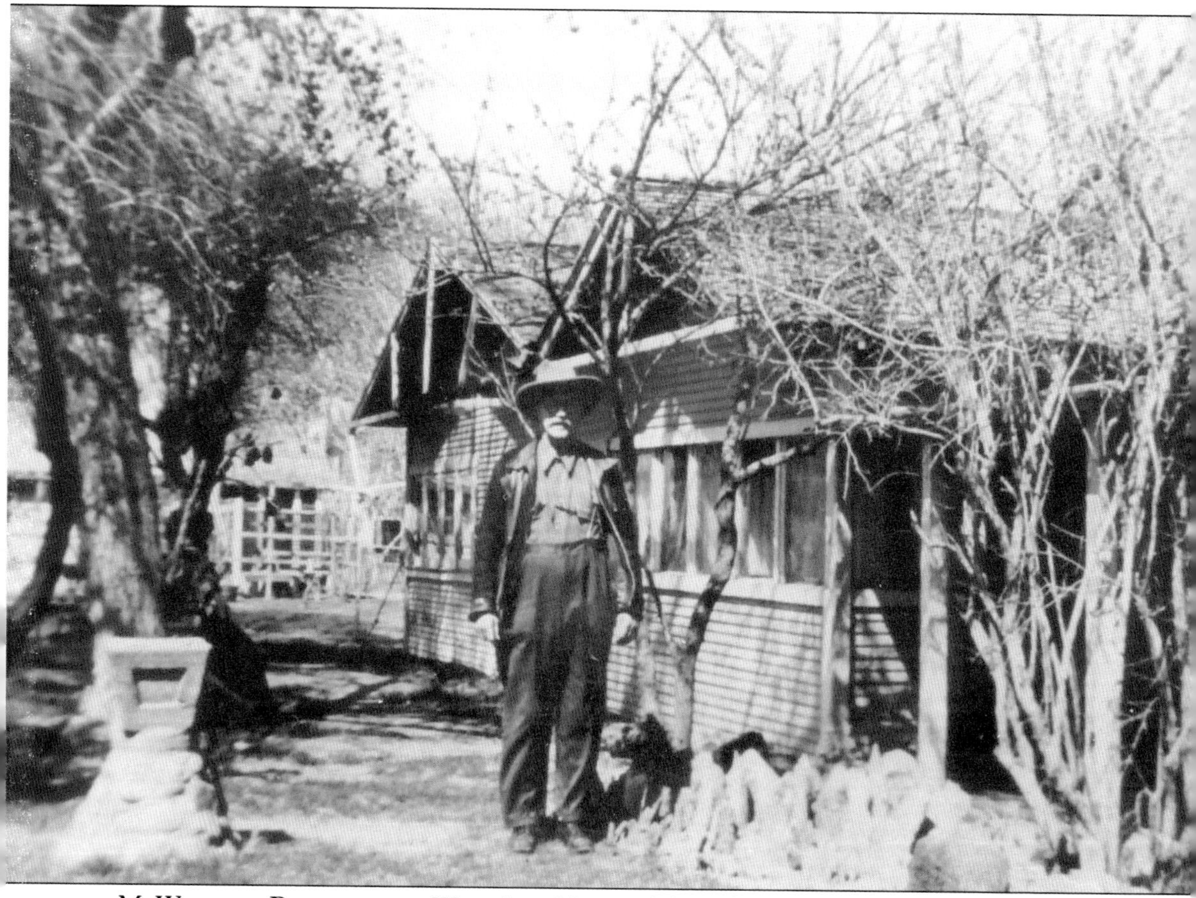

McWilliams Resettled in West Las Vegas. After a hiatus marked with defeat and likely humiliation by a press that quickly labeled his townsite "Ragtown," J.T. McWilliams returned. The publicity about the fire that destroyed the remnants of his dream must have only singed J.T.'s tough Celtic spirits. He maintained his civil engineering practice in his Westside home, where he produced over 3,000 maps of Clark County. Among his other triumphs, J.T. stopped the dumping of cesspool remains into the Las Vegas Creek in 1912. The early environmentalist also frequented Goodsprings and gave away parcels of his land elsewhere, including the water rights, unlike the less magnanimous William Clark.

Two

The Westside Community

Endearing and Enduring 100 Years

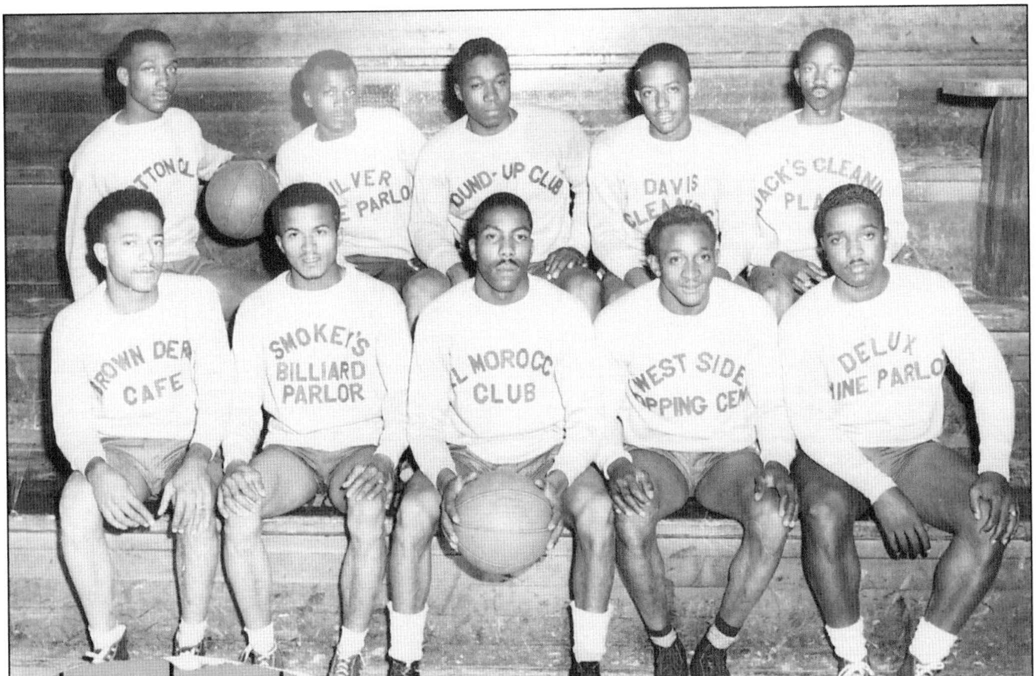

Working as a Team. As the 1940s came to a close and the 1950s loomed, the numerous personalities that emerged in or immigrated to West Las Vegas created well-honed neighborhoods with thriving local businesses and entertainment nightlife. They even joined in play, like this neighborhood basketball team. Local residents recall a mixture of emotions about this time period, when segregation significantly restricted their freedom but compelled them to become a united community. Some perceived the triumphs of the 1960s and 1970s as little more than paper rights in terms of genuine advancements, but the promises of equality unraveled the close-knit ties. The Westside community camaraderie of that earlier time is still elusive but earnestly sought.

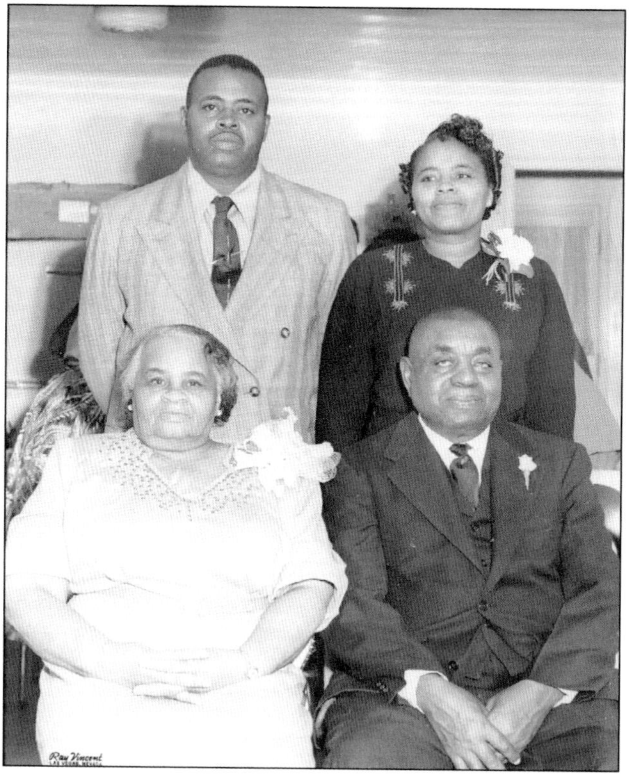

The Ensly Family. This enterprising family owned several businesses, mostly Downtown prior to segregation but later in the Westside. Until the 1930s, African Americans lived a relatively integrated life in Las Vegas. They also frequently lived east of the tracks until Las Vegas boomed and people of color were pushed to the Westside. Although not the first or only prosperous black family, the Enslys are among the most well-remembered pioneers. From the 1930s and even through the 1980s, blacks arrived in Las Vegas from small plantation towns, especially in Mississippi, Arkansas, and Louisiana. Many had worked in cotton fields under a blazing sun from the time they could walk for a few dollars a day and looked forward to work in the shade at $8 a day.

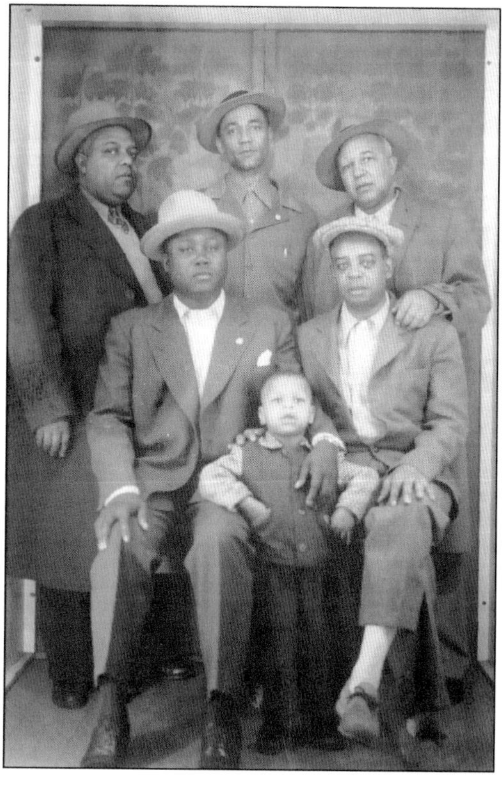

Emigration from Small Plantation Towns. These Southern families provided a unique niche population on the Westside in contrast with other black travelers who resettled from states like Idaho, New York, Michigan, and Utah. Here is an unidentified African American family, possibly from the 1940s, a peak period of black population influx. Prior to this, there were only 150 blacks recorded in Las Vegas, but the gunnery (later Nellis Airforce Base) and Basic Magnesium Plant continued the emigration from the South and other parts of the country. Some came with money; others arrived with a dream.

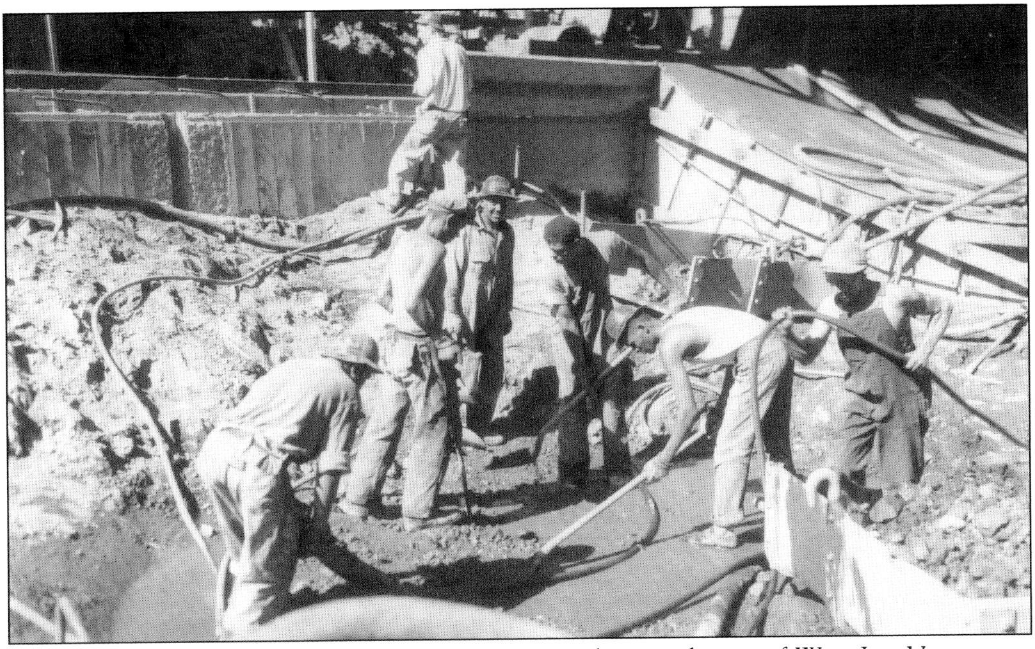

The Boulder (Hoover) Dam Announcement. The population of West Las Vegas grew exponentially as workers, desperate for work due to the Great Depression, swarmed the area in hopes of employment despite the dangers. Yet history records only 44 blacks who worked on the dam, following a two-year battle that brought in 10 blacks in 1932 who worked for 50¢ per hour. Some could rent tents for $5 a week on the Westside while earning four to five times that amount in wages. Older residents recalled that people could have afforded better housing, but none was available.

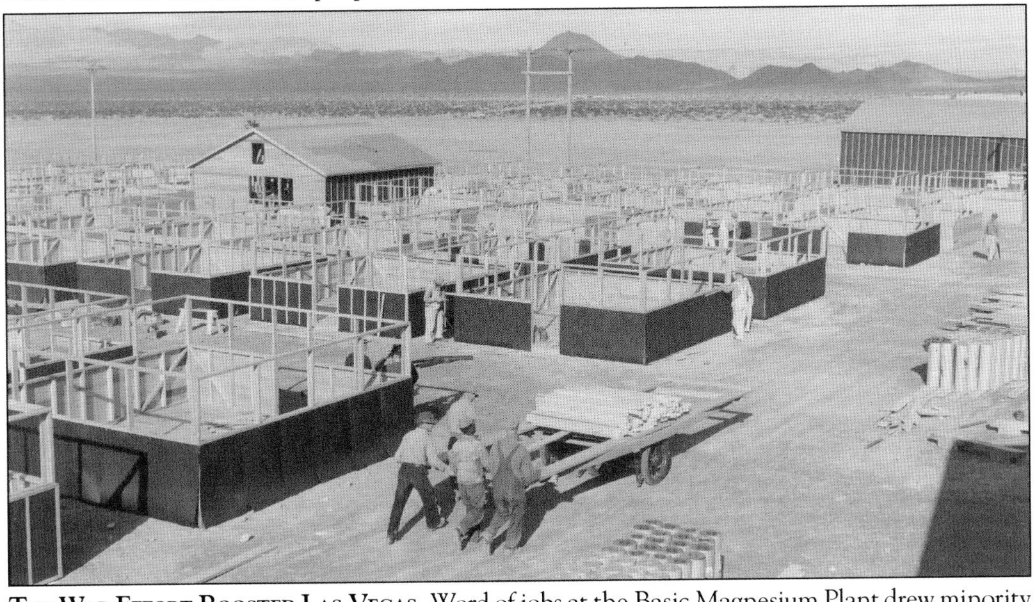

The War Effort Boosted Las Vegas. Word of jobs at the Basic Magnesium Plant drew minority interest. At the time, the relatively few blacks who worked there either lived in Carver Park in Henderson or the Westside. However, prejudiced Southern white workers also came in hordes as a result of the Great Depression, negatively intensifying race relations. Government yielded some jobs under pressure to blacks, but they were still underemployed in the federal works programs.

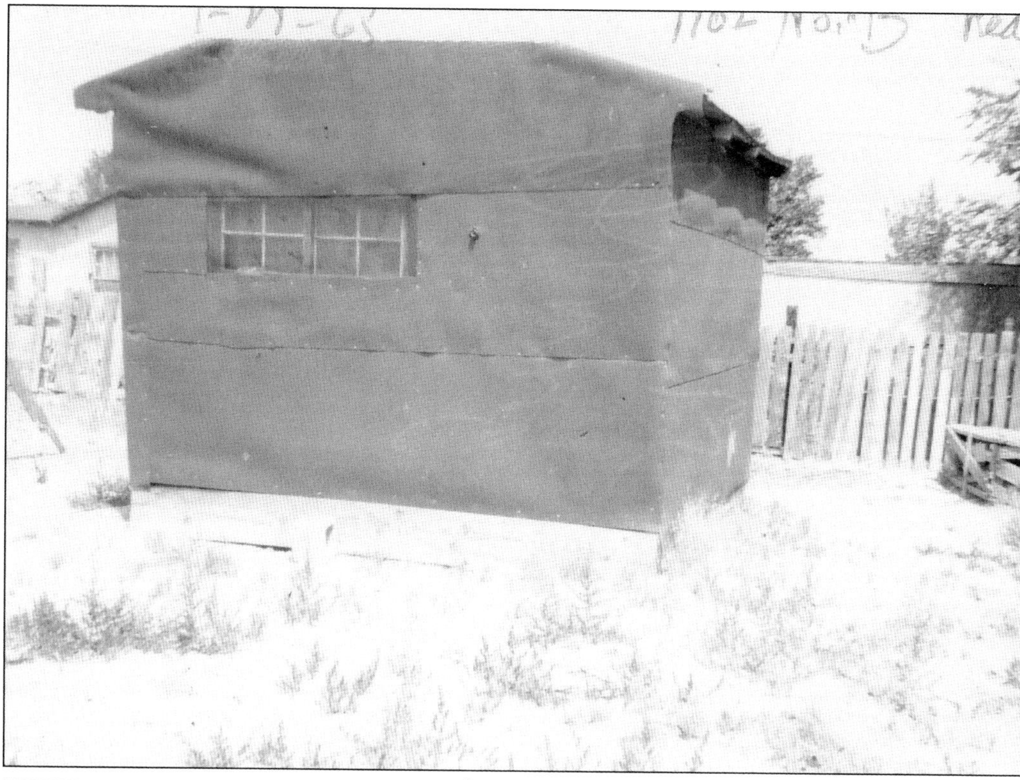

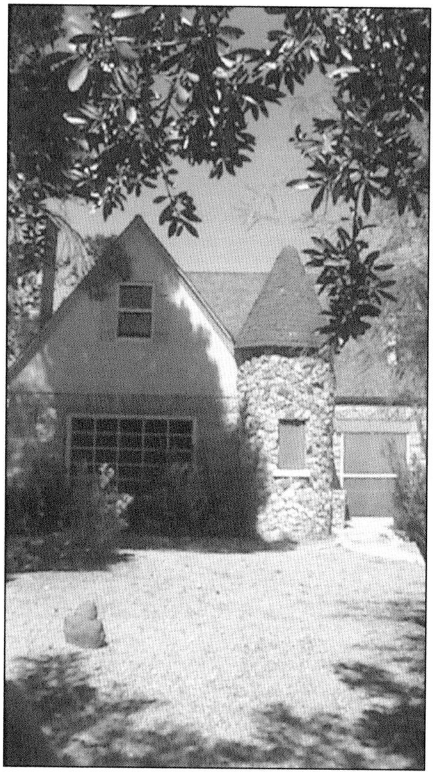

Contrast in Living. The poor condition of housing on the Westside existed through much of the 1940s and was still evident in the 1960s. The area lacked paved roads, electricity, and even indoor plumbing. In severe heat, tar-patched roofs would drip the black sludge inside the home and on to furnishings and occupants. For blacks and poorer Las Vegans, the Westside could not rise above its dishevelment. Because Mayor Ernie Cragin ignored appeals to bring in fire plugs, a sewer system, and lighting, among other improvements, many places were condemned, creating further haphazard housing that fueled yet another cycle of demolished housing. The Christensen House, on the left, was built in 1935 by Lucretia Tanner Christensen Stevens, an African American woman with deep Utah roots. This unique stone Tudor-style house called the Castle seemed mismatched to its later owner, famous cowboy and wrangler Roy Christensen, but proved to reflect the many stories of triumph in the midst of others who struggled more mightily. The two-story mansion is currently used by the Catholic Relief workers. (Left, courtesy Steve Eagle.)

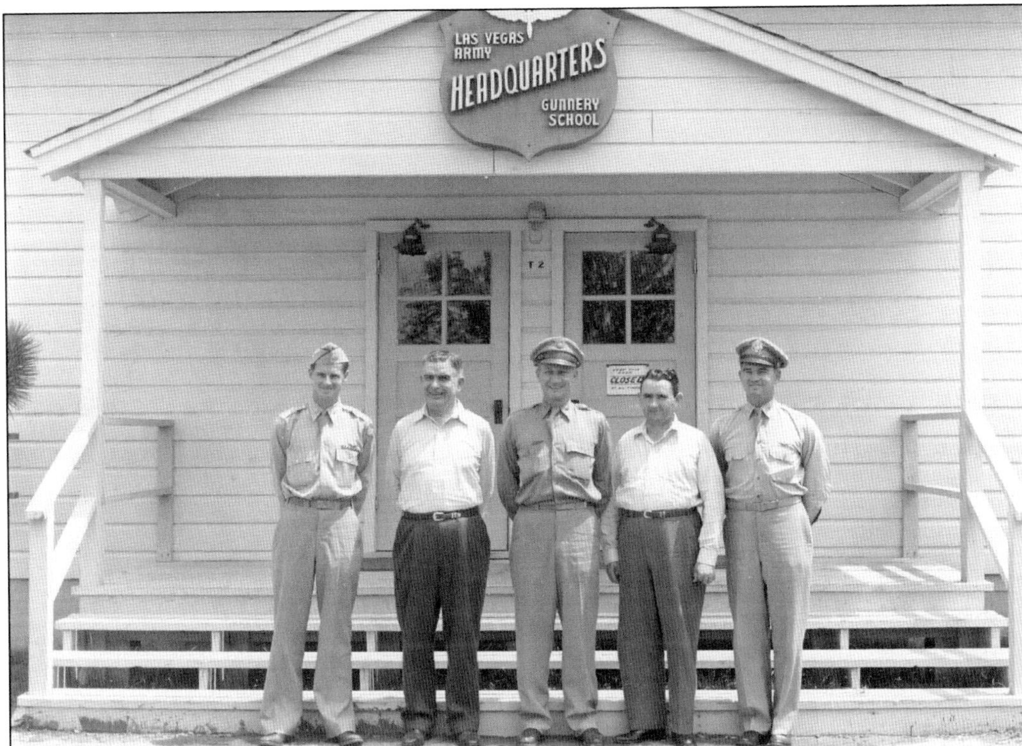

To Appease Southern White Patrons. With the legalization of gambling in 1931, Las Vegas began its own casino development, drawing wealthy visitors from around the country. Mayor Cragin began to impose a system of apartheid with the blacks to appease the still-segregationist Southerners. Although considered an otherwise able leader, the city went Jim Crow under his watch. Seen above, the controversial mayor is second from the left. Despite some isolated accounts of virtual imprisonment of blacks in the Westside after sunset, downtown casinos used the relatively cheap labor of these residents. In turn, many of them strove to rise above the bias in position and esteem, and their children grew from their example.

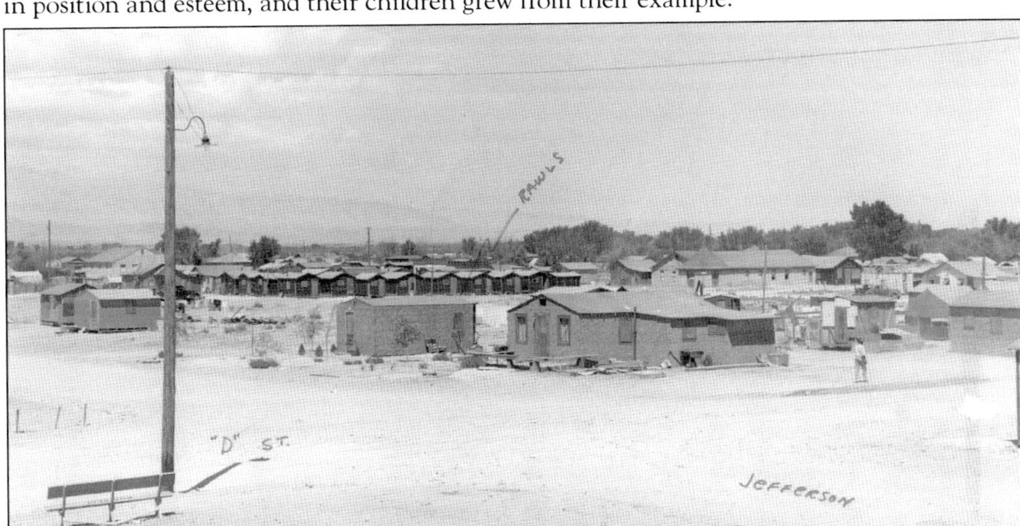

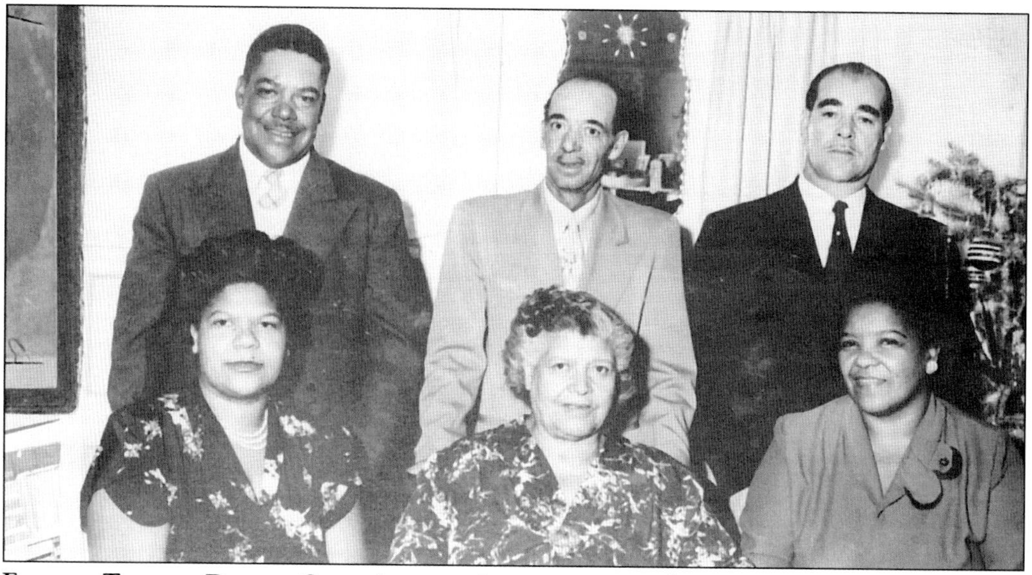

Families Thrived Despite Odds. In spite of circumstances, the Westside thrived regardless of whether families were working, middle, or upper class. Something about their circumstances helped them to unite across economic lines. Jarmilla McMillan Arnold recalls that blacks were all together in one area, and those ties would not loosen even as second and third generations blossomed. Loyalty superseded social status, and they would defend one another against anything considered racist within and outside of the Westside. Here are two unidentified family portraits, both emanating poise and strength. (Both, courtesy Nevada State Museum, Las Vegas.)

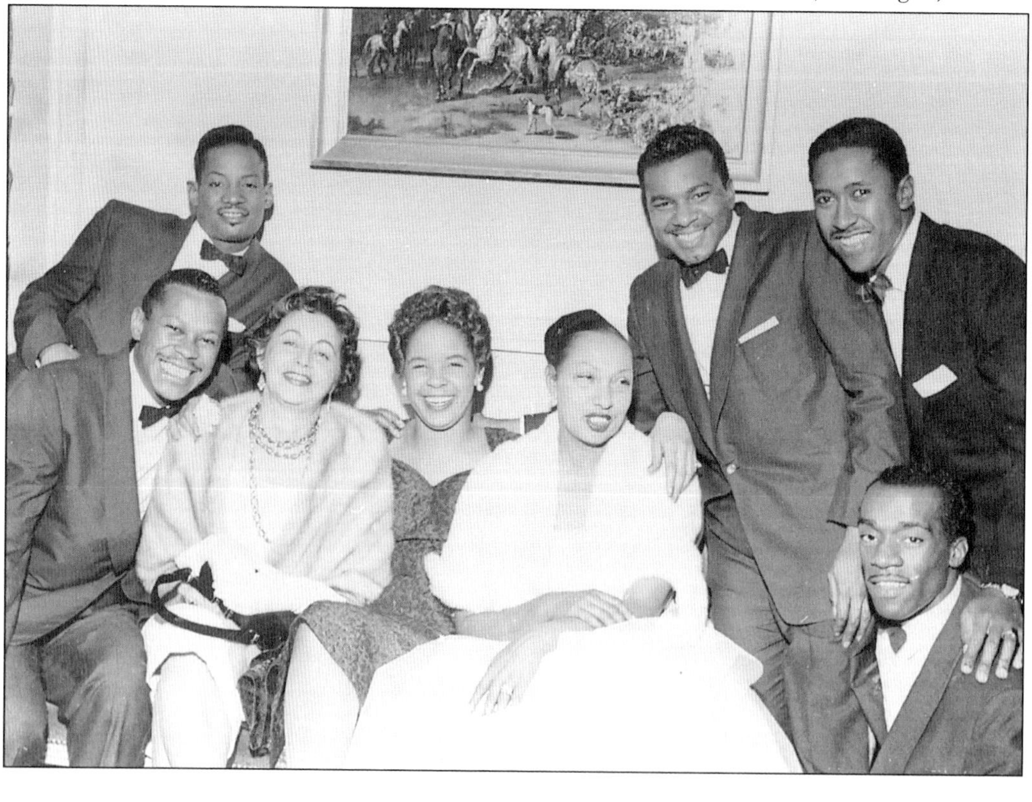

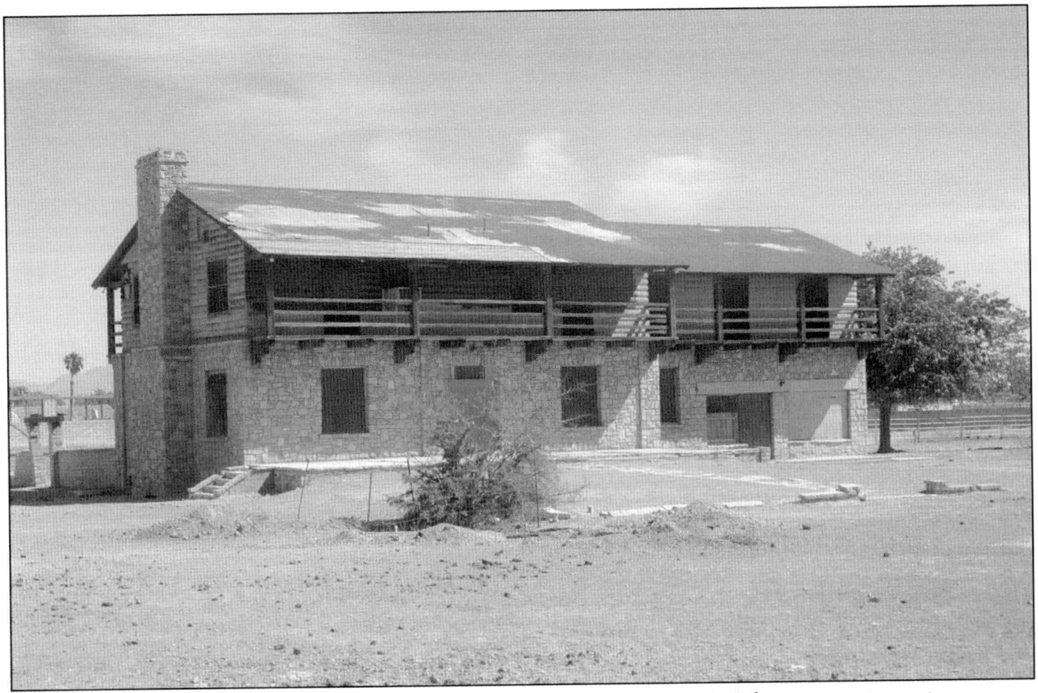

Binion House. Made of native stone and log construction in 1942 by eccentric casino owner and segregationist Benny Binion, this house still stands along the West Las Vegas Pioneer Trail. The Texan boasted a 300-pound black bodyguard by the name of Gold Dollar, but his horse was called by an unspeakable name. Benny favored the odds towards everyday white folks but refused to integrate his casino until "the time was right." Today's Westside residents express mixed feelings about the Binion House being considered part of the historic West Las Vegas area, given Benny's segregationist stance. (Courtesy Steve Eagle.)

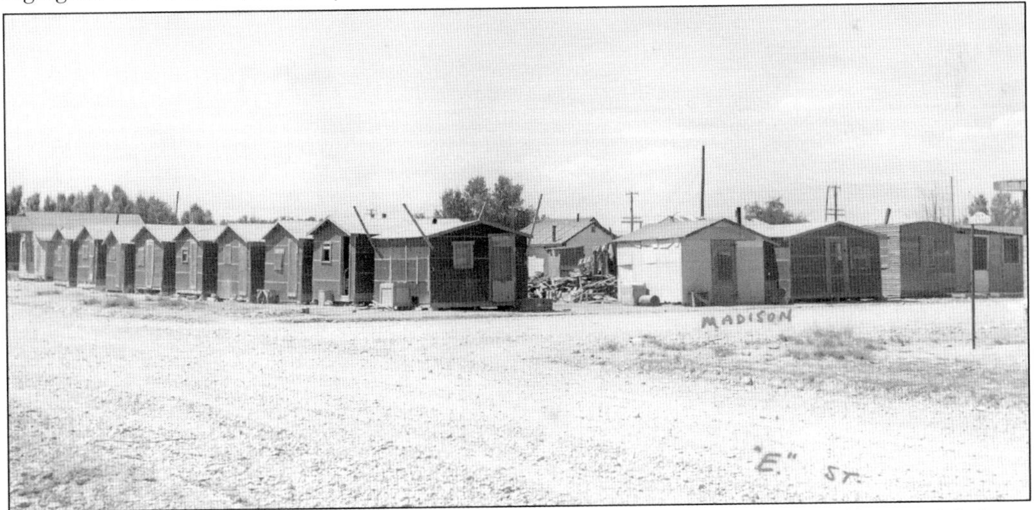

Drop Down Housing. Looking like Monopoly game pieces, these small dwellings at Madison Avenue and E Street lacked poured foundations and may have cost as little as $50 for a 12-by-12-foot living area. Some newer but prefab housing became available in the 1940s and was referred to as drop-down dwellings that lacked foundations. By the 1960s, many of these would be demolished as unsuitable and unsustainable.

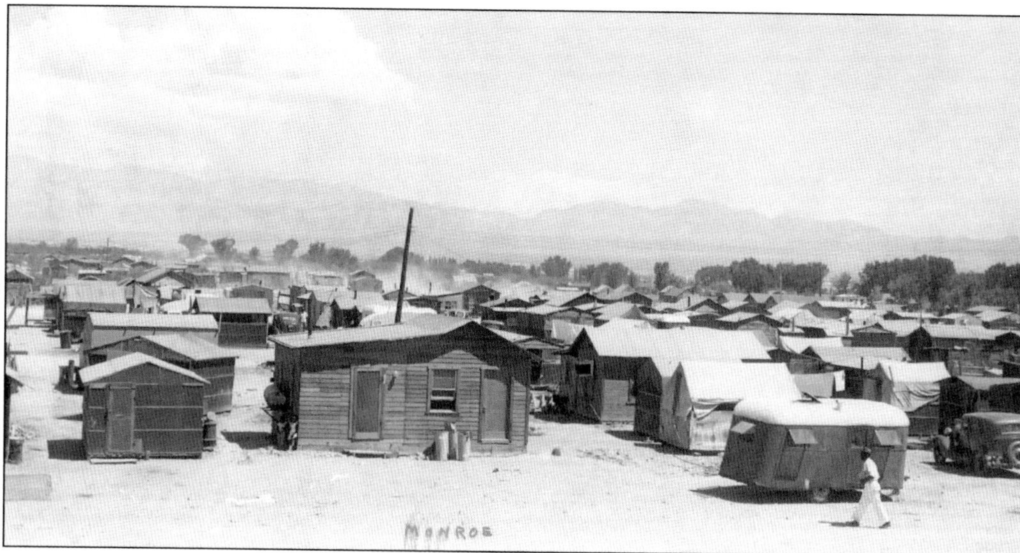

Back to Canvas and Tents. In this view along Monroe Street, one can see a mixture of trailers, flimsy drop-down wooden structures, and even a shaggy tent. Conditions were not much better until after the war. Note the lack of windows and ventilation. A typical cloud of dust swirls in the background. Rain did not help much, as it merely created mud pools. The fact that so many overcame these obstacles is the mark of genuine pioneering.

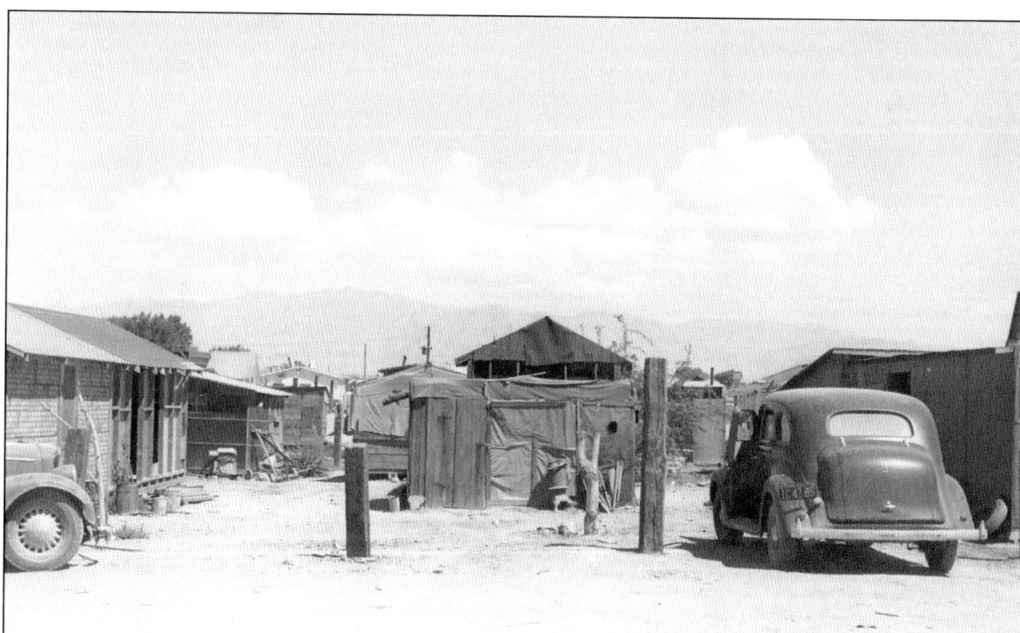

Upgrades in the Midst of Slums. Wartime was both a blessing and a curse for housing, as some tracts were built, but resources remained scarce. Still, residents persevered, and some, like the owner of the house to the left, remodeled and touched up their homes as best they could. Others merely sought day-to-day survival in what were virtually little more than outhouses.

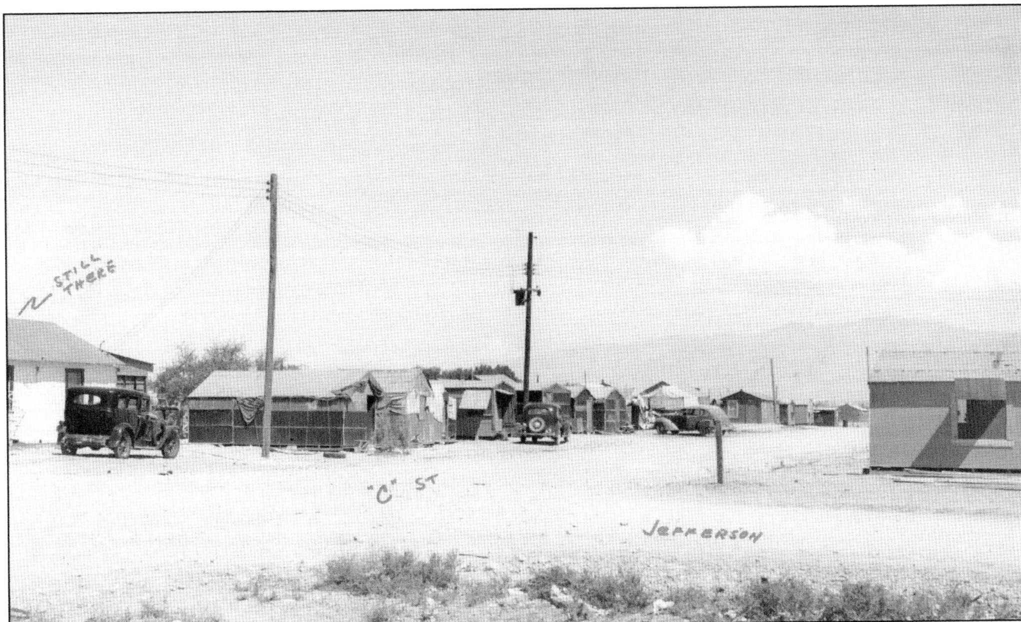

Cars at C Street and Jefferson Avenue. Though residents of West Las Vegas could do little about official home improvements, they proudly drove cars if possible. Although this 1960s photograph indicates that the property still stands, most of these quarters were destroyed a short time later. All that remains of that shameful period are the two-dimensional images categorized in libraries and museums. Few residents have images that date back prior to the 1960s.

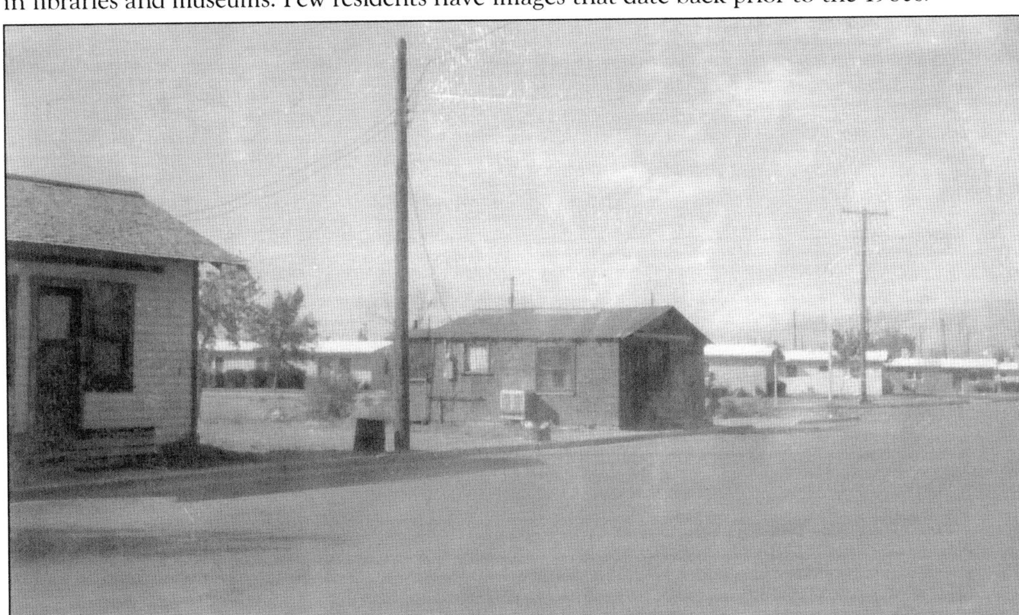

North H Street. These structures begin to show an improved residential situation for those on the Westside, but not remarkably. As late as 1949, the area did not have a public phone, and sewer connections were still in the making. Yet whites in Bonanza Village and nearby areas protested Marble Manor in 1952. This public housing for veterans was developed to ease the housing situation on the Westside and an exploding black population that rose from 664 to 4,302 in the 1940s.

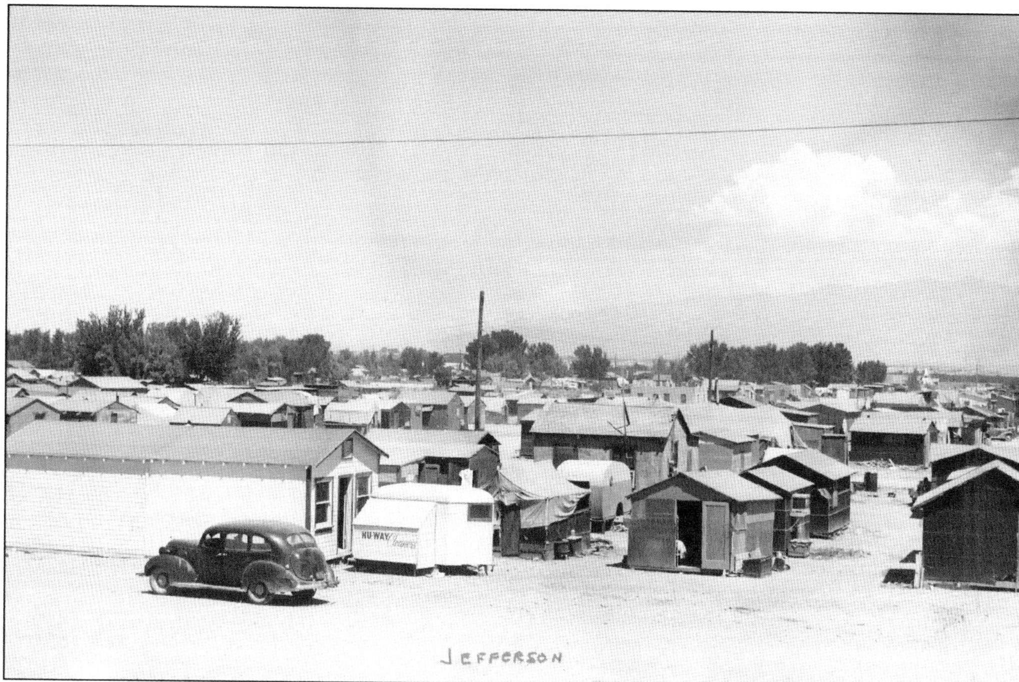

HOUSING DID NOT REFLECT INCOME REALITY. As one local at the time remarked, everyone worked, because if they could not find work, they might as well move on. Note the aluminum siding on some of the housing, along with more modern designs on some of the dwellings. A different view below reminds the viewer of the original McWilliams townsite buildings. The similar wooden fly covers and stilt porch areas could have been duplicates of that era 30 years earlier. The city left the roads unpaved and absent of other upgrades.

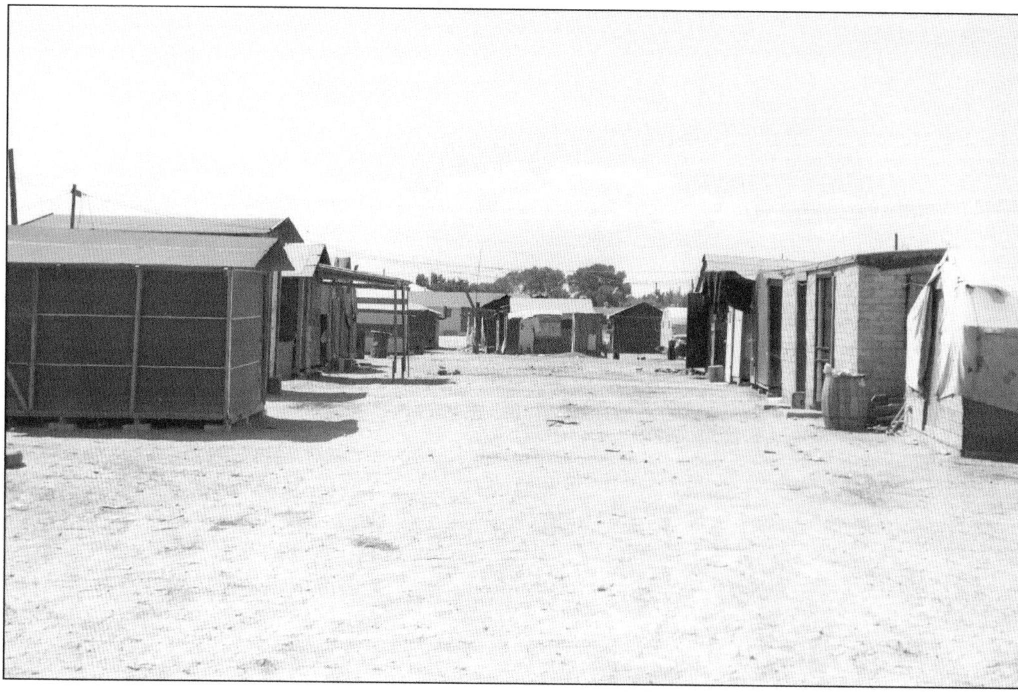

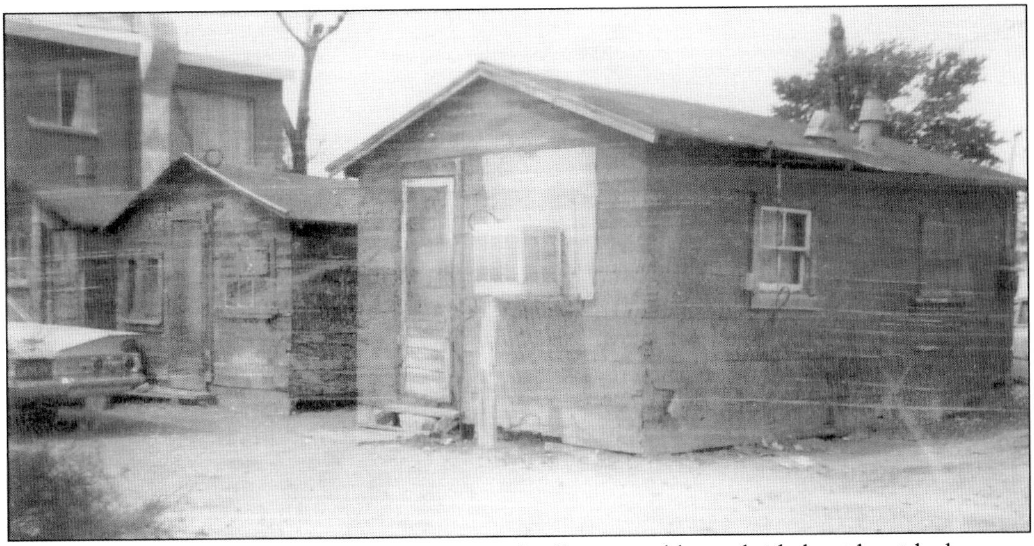

The Good, the Bad, and the Ugly. Certain dwellings would stand side by side with the more contemporary ones, as evidenced here. The 1950s would bring renewed energy to tackle the injustices suffered by Westside residents, but people clung to what they could afford to fix under city radar. Bringing attention to these places only brought about condemnation and demolition in a catch-22 bureaucracy.

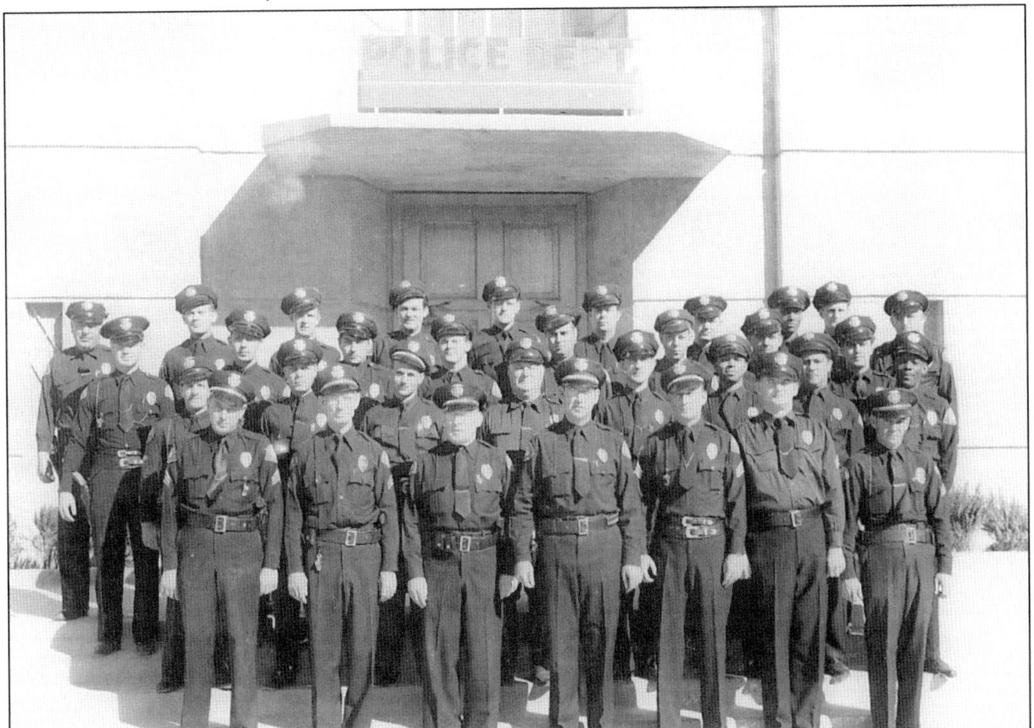

Early Black Policemen. In a crowd of about 40, there are very few policemen of color. In the earliest days of Las Vegas, black policeman could only arrest fellow blacks, not whites. This sometimes earned them disdain in their own neighborhoods, though it was later honored as a first step on the road to fuller integration on the force. (Courtesy Nevada State Museum, Las Vegas.)

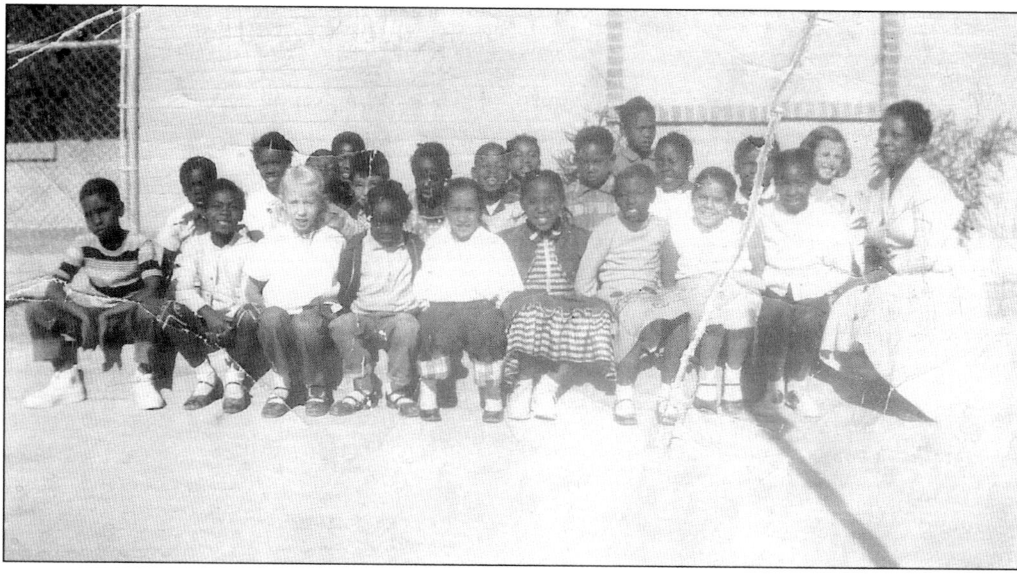

The Oldest Standing School in Las Vegas. The Westside School, built in 1922, started as a two rooms. It eventually grew to enough rooms for educating kindergarten through eighth grade. For African Americans, the Westside School would be the sole educational opportunity until Madison School was built. Still, many blacks had their first experience of any racial integration at Westside School, though the subliminal message was that they were not obtaining a usable education until educators like Mabel Hoggard appeared. Above, Mabel Hoggard sits with her class in 1955. Below is the 1955 graduating class. Many alumni shown in this photograph have passed away, but others jubilantly recalled the happy days at Westside School during a 2010 reunion that was recorded in the *Las Vegas Review Journal.* (Above, courtesy Mabel Hoggard Elementary School, Las Vegas; below, courtesy Brenda Williams.)

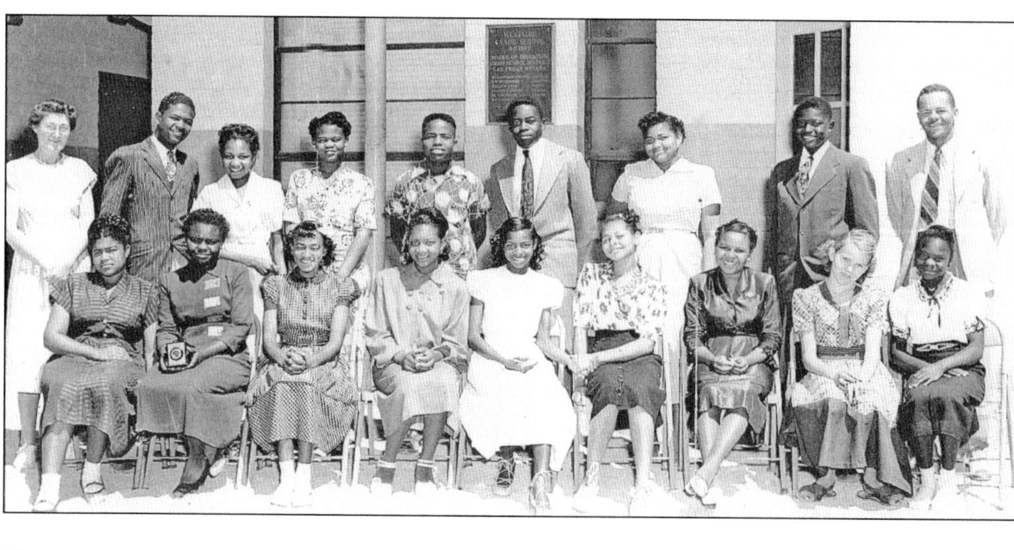

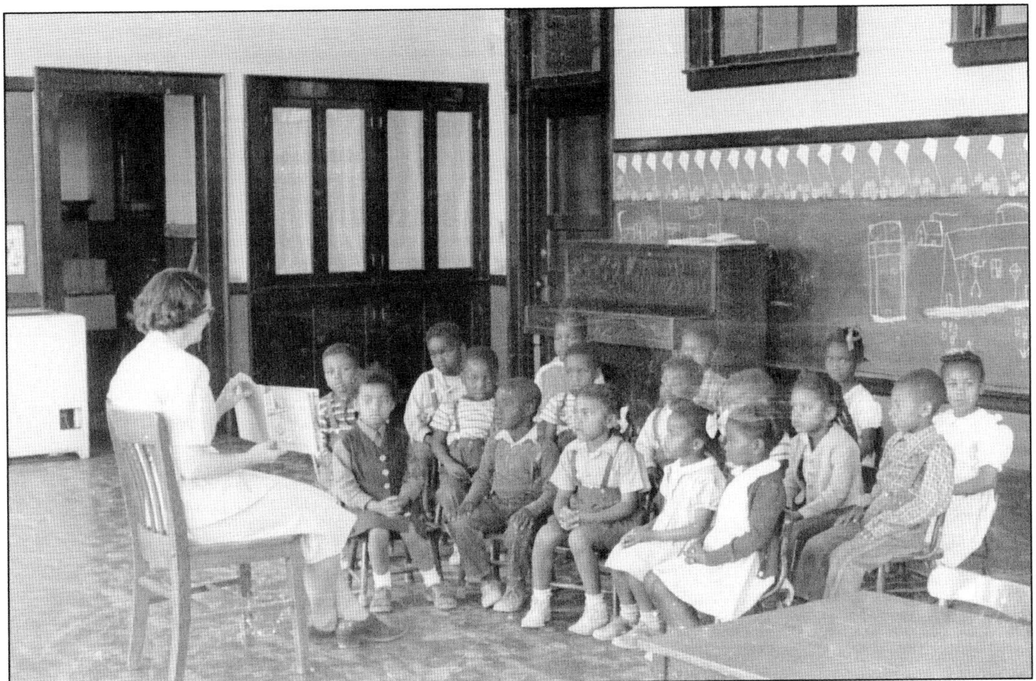

MARGARET WELCH. Welch, a very popular teacher in the early days of Westside education insisted on teaching at Westside School even though she could have had her pick of the other ones across the valley. Her memory was honored at a special reunion in the spring of 2010 as former students recalled her skills and loving nature. (Courtesy Nevada State Museum, Las Vegas.)

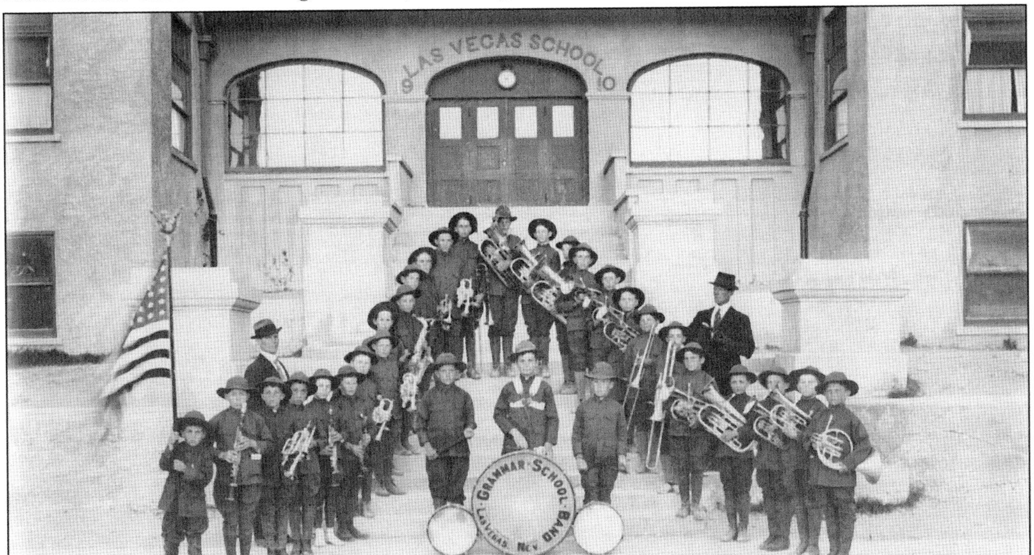

THE INSPIRATION OF MATT KELLY. A 1917 picture of Matt Kelly's school band might be a clue to the naming of one of the Prime Six elementary schools now in the Westside. Still, African Americans would not have attended the school, seen here, after the 1920s. The naming of that elementary school is still unclear, but there is strong indication that it was named after this musician.

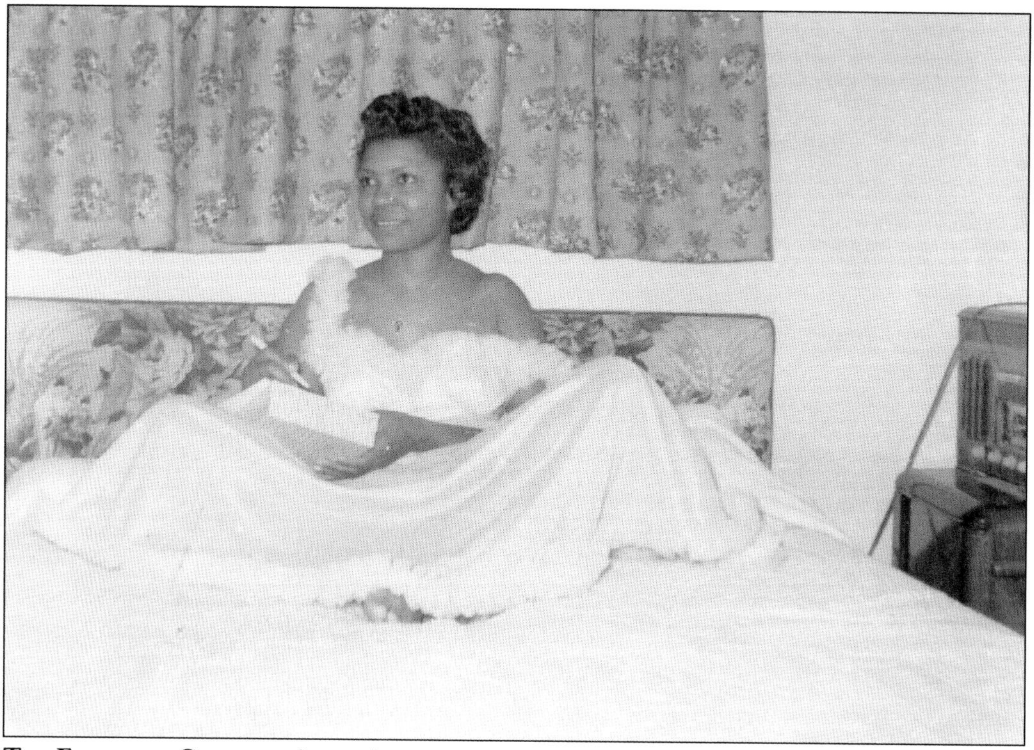

The Exclusive Cadillac Arms Apartments. Longtime resident Edna Mae Williams strikes a lovely pose inside her Cadillac Arms apartment in 1958. She recalls in her 70 years of history from the heart of Westside to Bonanza Village that, despite difficult times, the 1940s and 1950s era was the happiest for the region. Edna Mae remembers posing beside a late-model car near the much-sought apartment complex and noted that "you had to know someone" to secure housing there. (Both, courtesy Edna Mae Williams.)

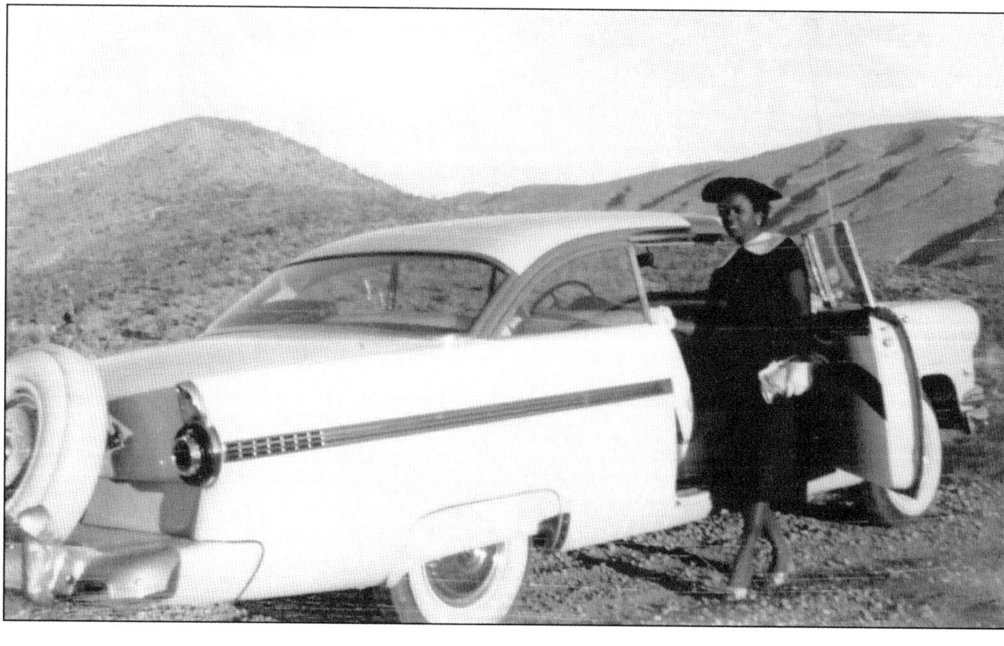

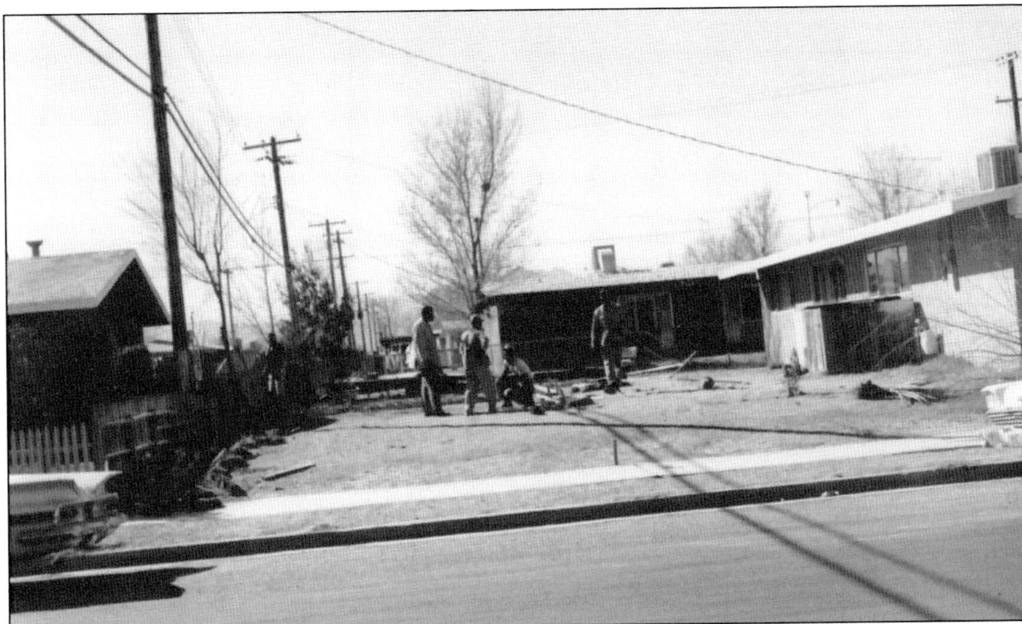

Sunset Manor, First Home for Many. Although Edna Mae Williams was once swindled out of $1,250 in a previous housing matter, she still managed to work two jobs and buy her first home. This exterior view shows the upgrade in design and housing in the Westside. Inside the living room, Edna rests among a 1950s-style couch and pillows. A heart-shaped ceramic dish reminiscent of the era adorns the table. (Courtesy Edna Mae Williams.)

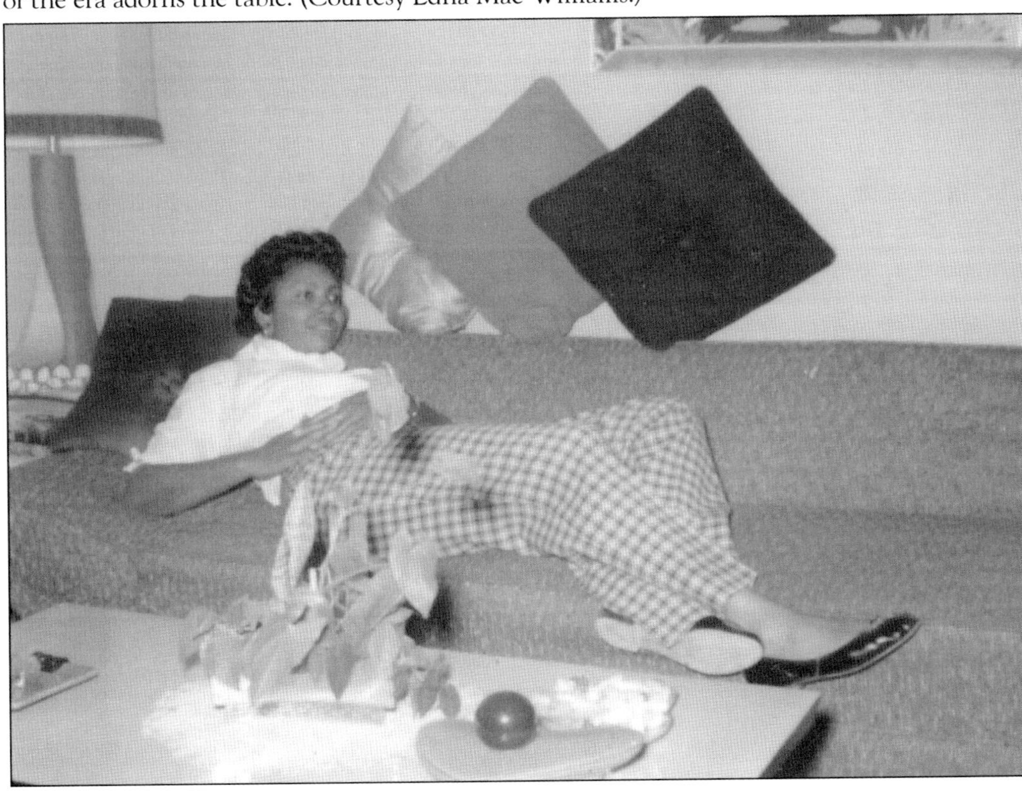

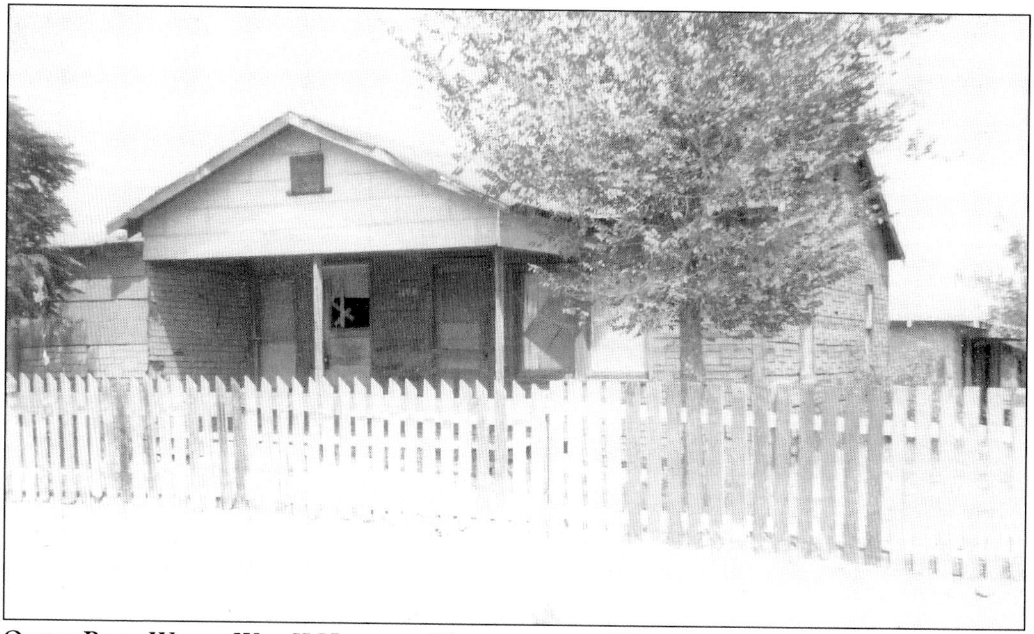

Other Post–World War II Housing. The situation in West Las Vegas eased somewhat for the blue-collar worker, though many still lacked indoor plumbing, heat, and other amenities. As the decade moved along, redevelopment plans were in the offing to replace some of the devastated housing. Here are pictures of two homes that demonstrate some of the classic lines found in other small homes at the time. The house below features a stucco exterior.

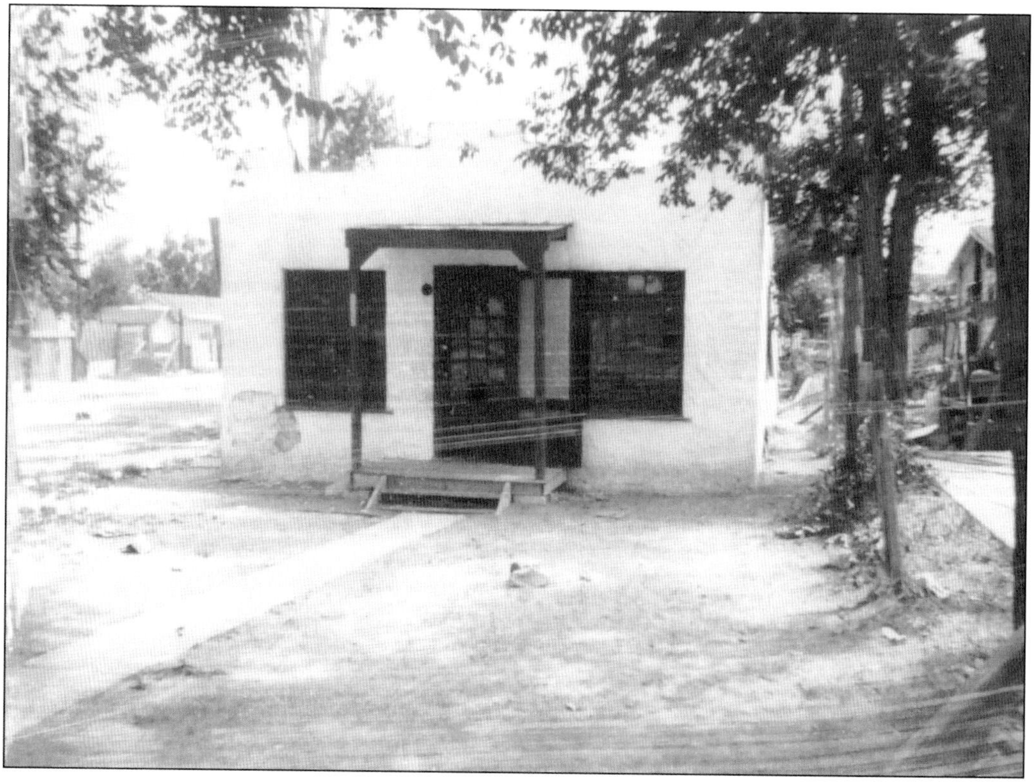

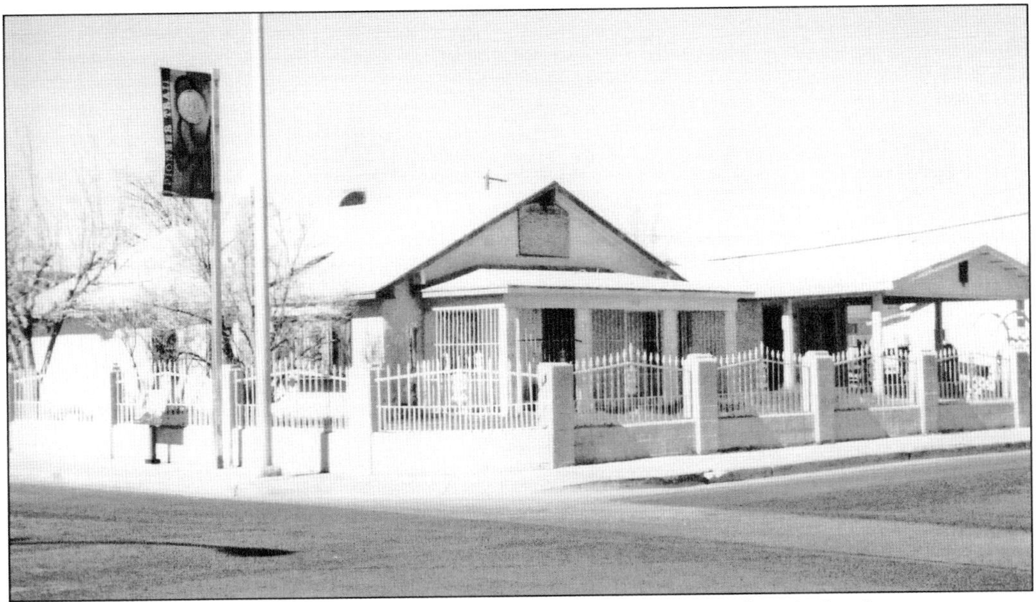

Special Houses Included the Harrison Boarding House. In the 1940s, this precursor to the modern bed and breakfast was the only home for black entertainers who could not stay on the Strip after showtime. Among the stars who slept here were Sammy Davis Jr., his father, and his uncle, Eddie "Rochester" Anderson; Jack Benny's sidekick, Pearl Bailey (also Bob Bailey's cousin); and various well-known groups. Ms. Harrison and the proprietor of the Adams House were known for their homey hospitality. (Courtesy Steve Eagle.)

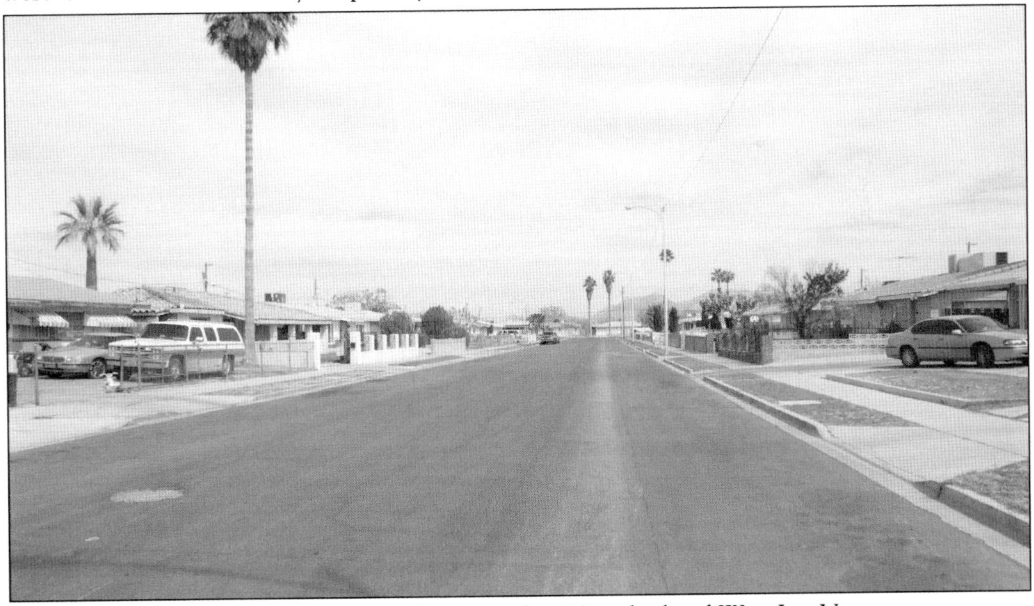

Now Comes Paul Revere Williams. By the early 1950s, the loyal West Las Vegas entrepreneurs and professionals created a demand for middle-class housing. One classic example was the concept of Berkley Square, initially named Westside Park, designed by internationally known black architect Paul Revere Williams and listed on the National Register of Historic Places. The first minority subdivision built in Nevada in 1954, it offered 154 ranch-style homes. This scene shows the famous Wyatt Avenue as it appears today.

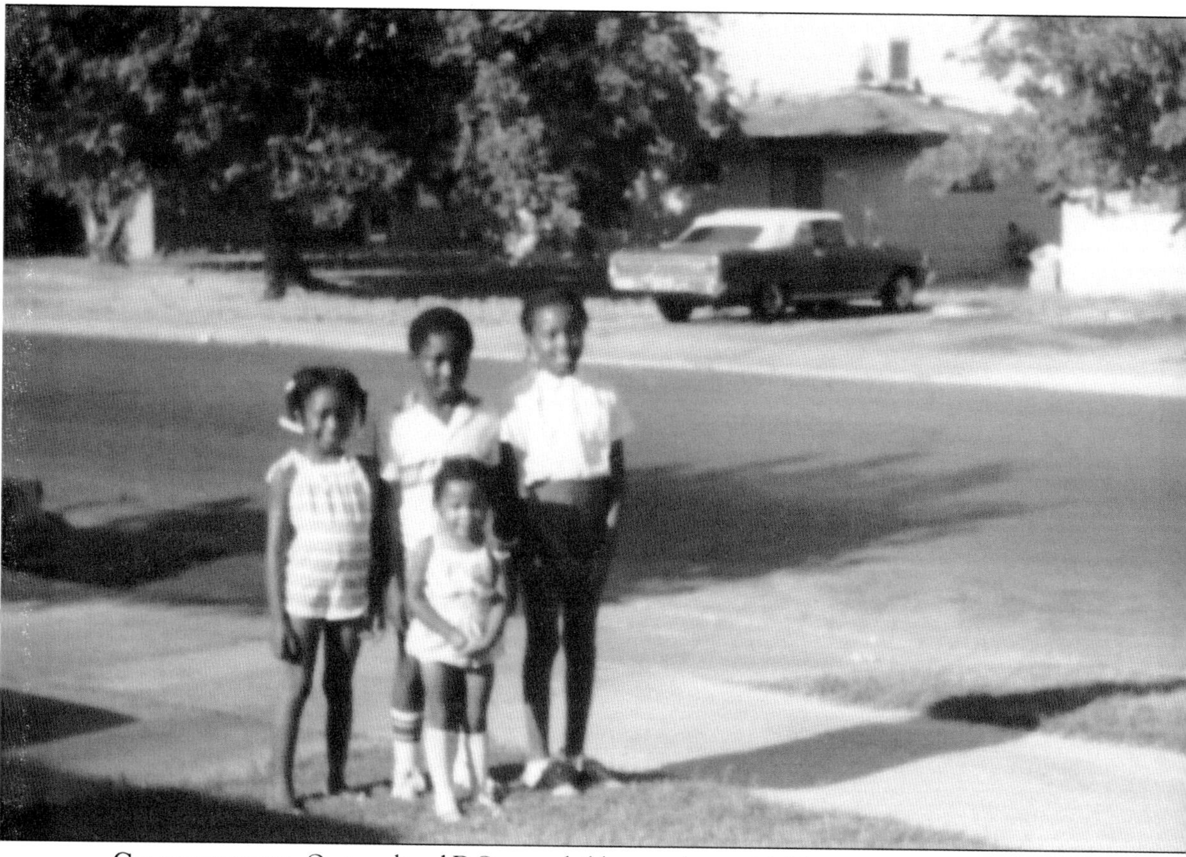

Grandchildren. On tree-lined D Street, children and grandchildren continue to enjoy the fruits of that innovative housing community. Here, three of Agnes Marshall's grandchildren pose in an expansive yard. Agnes recalls many joyful family reunions and a sense of community living in Berkley Square, where she has resided for 55 years. (Courtesy Agnes Marshall.)

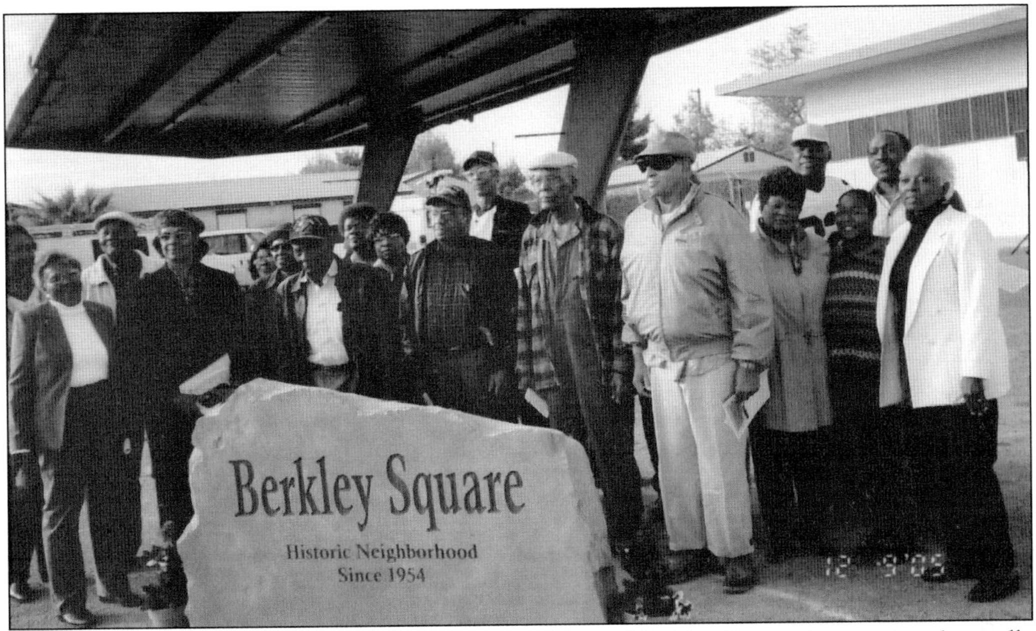

STILL-PROUD RESIDENTS. For nearly 60 years, residents of Berkley Square have pointed proudly to their innovative housing tract, which earned an historic site designation. The tract focused on pedestrian safety and minimal cross traffic with curved streets and culs-de-sac. Typical of Las Vegas, sandstone monuments often serve as markers for unique areas. Above, a group of residents poses for Agnes Marshall. (Courtesy Agnes Marshall.)

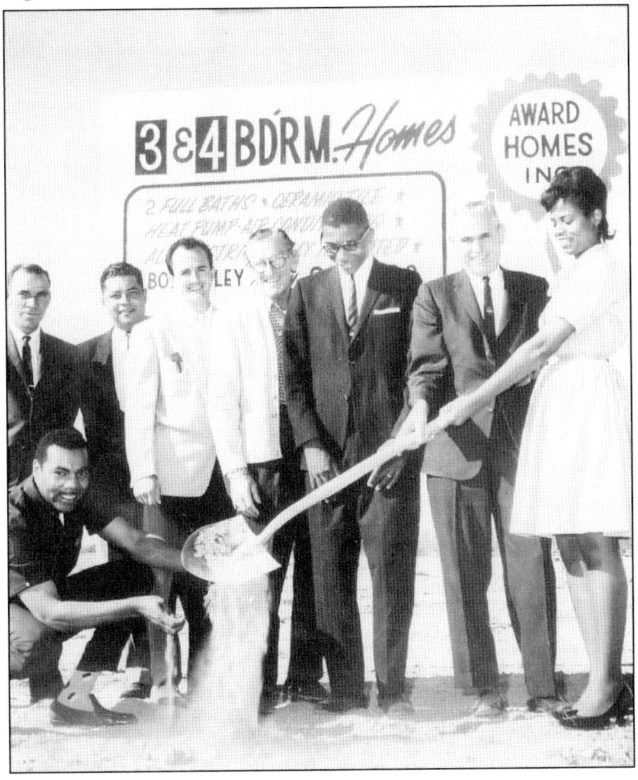

COMMUNITY MEANT ALL. Though some in West Las Vegas emerged as leaders in various enterprises, such as Bob Bailey, everyone came together to build a better community. In this image, Mayor Oran Gragson lends a hand, along with two people believed to be David Hoggard and Marion Bennett, to start a new development. This photograph may have been taken at a deluxe apartment complex on H Street. (Courtesy Nevada State Museum, Las Vegas.)

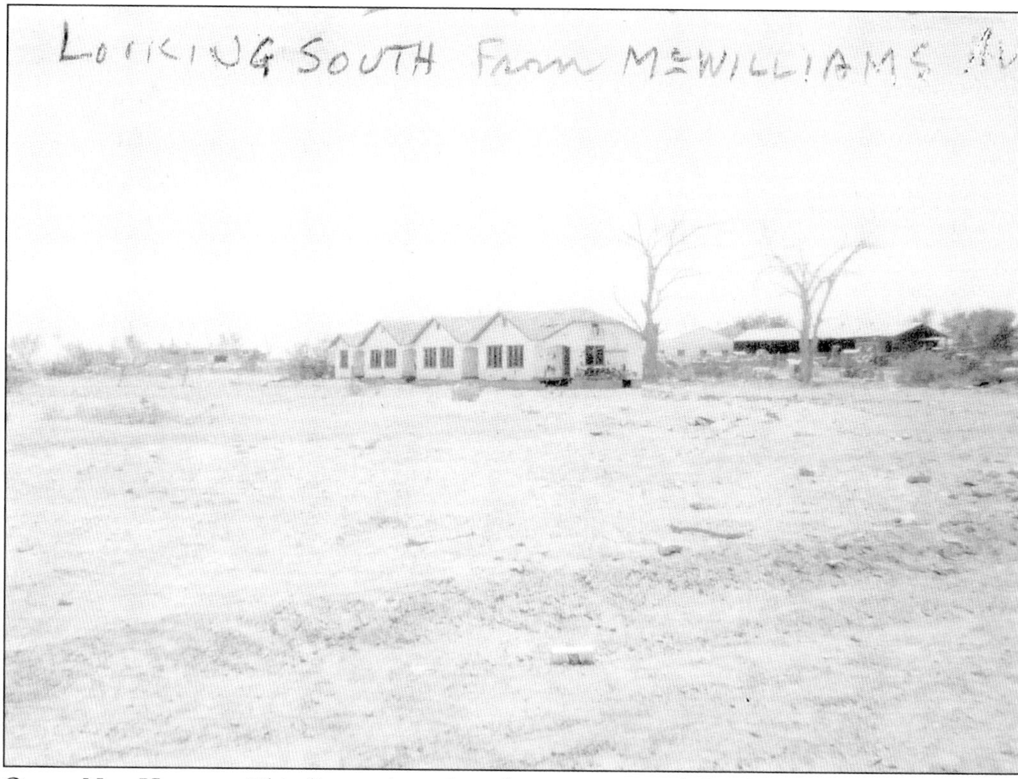

Other New Housing. This distant shot of new housing appears behind the famed Moulin Rouge, located at 900 West Bonanza Road. The only identifier is its location to the hotel and casino, but it was likely near Washington Avenue west of what is now Martin Luther King Boulevard.

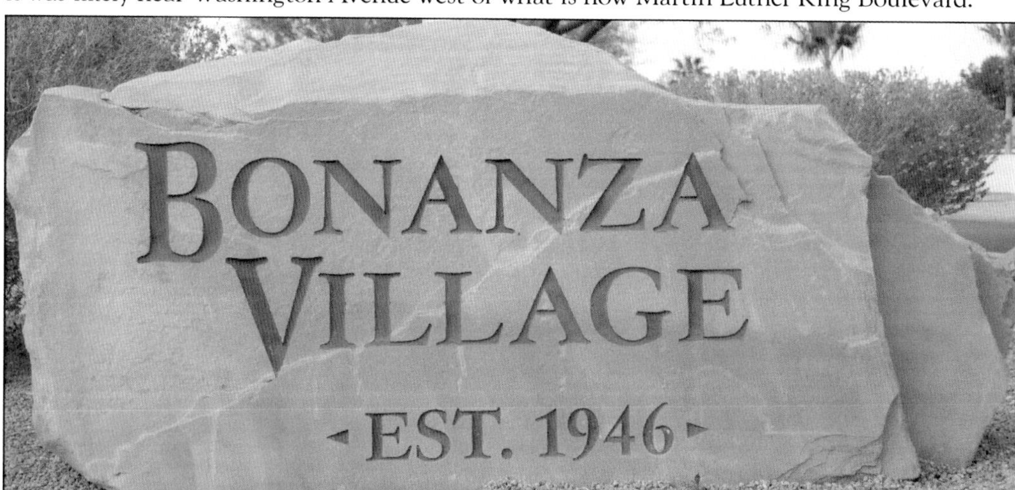

Bonanza Village Goes Ebony. As African Americans gained more success and achieved firsts in many civil and government arenas, they began to seek better housing. Katherine Joseph was the first. Bonanza Village, once an all-white community, gradually became the setting for the upper-middle-class blacks. These quarter-acre lots zoned for horses provided the right niche for those who enjoyed the fruits of their labor but desired to remain loyal residents of the Westside.

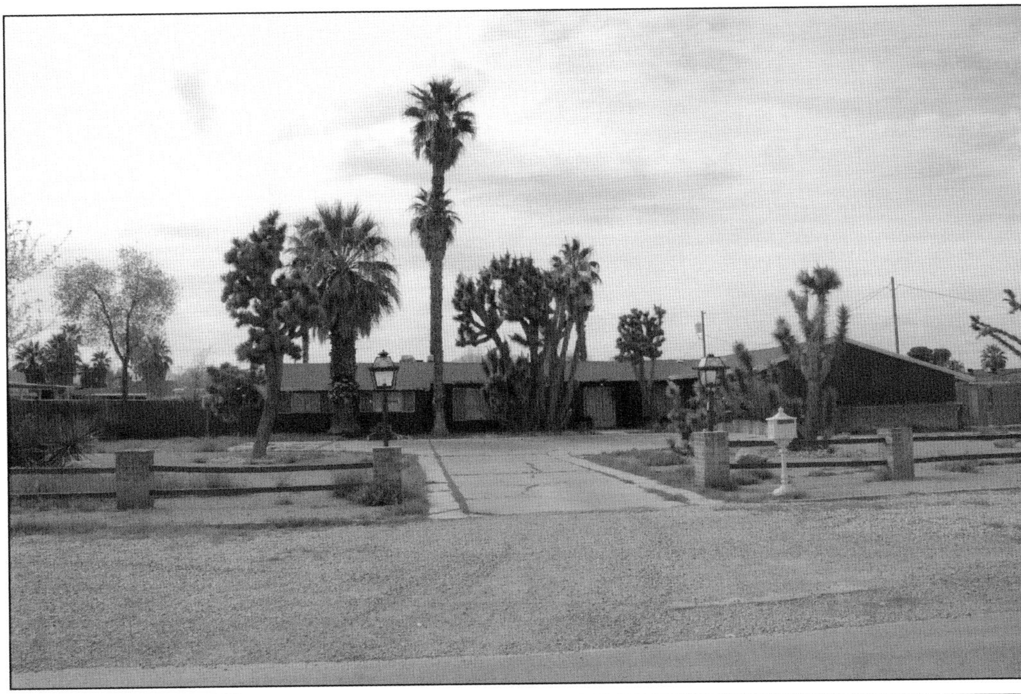

WEST'S EXPANSIVE HOME. Dr. Charles West eventually relocated to Bonanza Village, greatly expanding his elbow room, until his death in 1984. Here, his ranch-style home still rests on a huge one-third-acre lot. His son resided in the home until his own passing in the early 2000s. At right, looking south from Bonanza Village, one can see the famous Las Vegas Stratosphere and the Wynn Hotel complex.

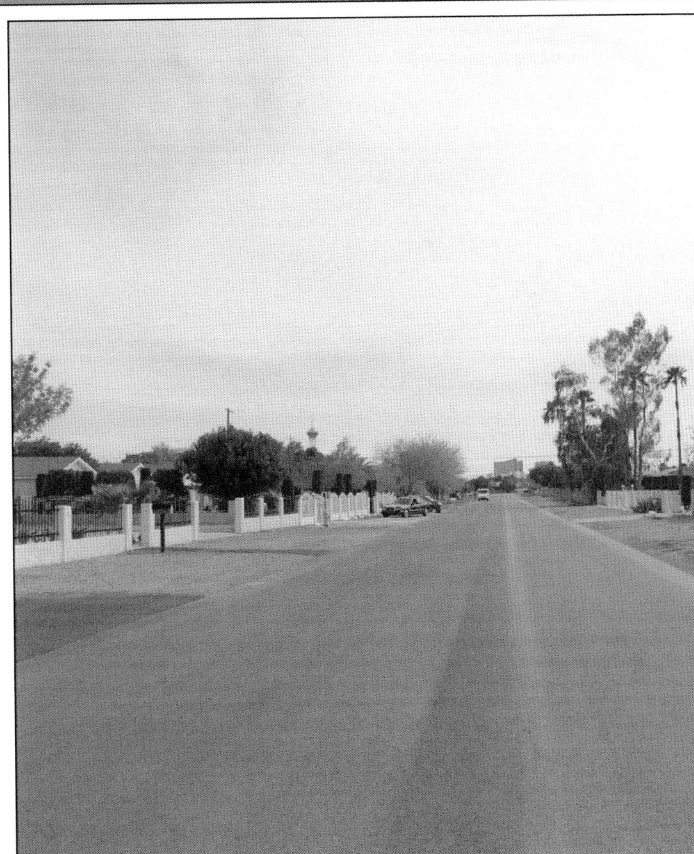

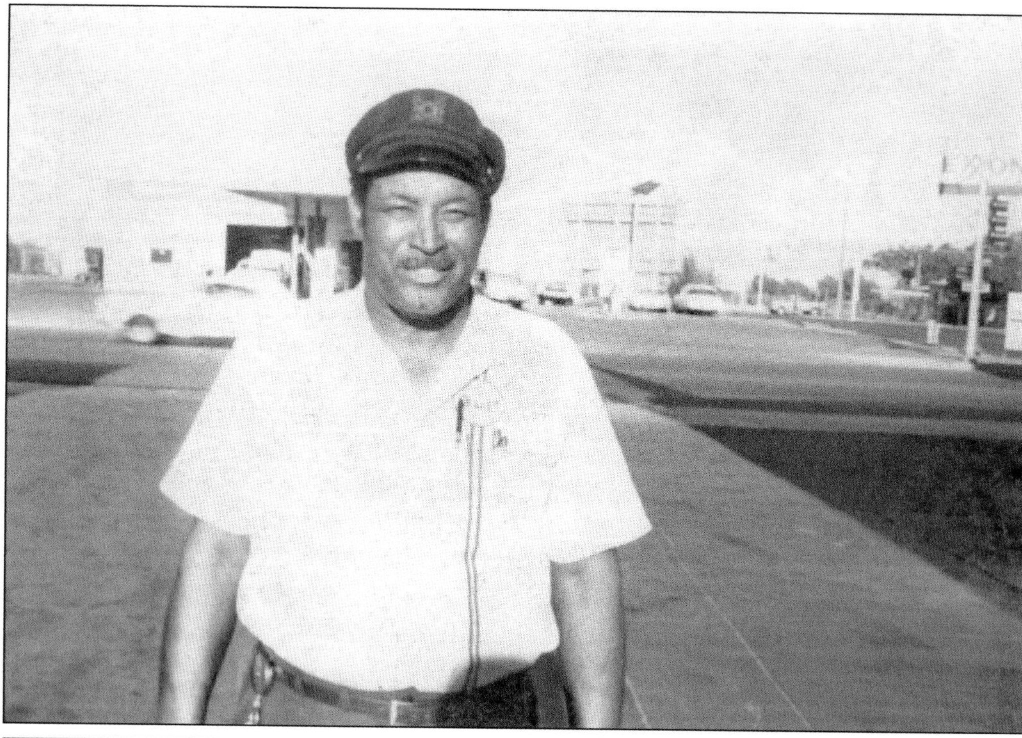

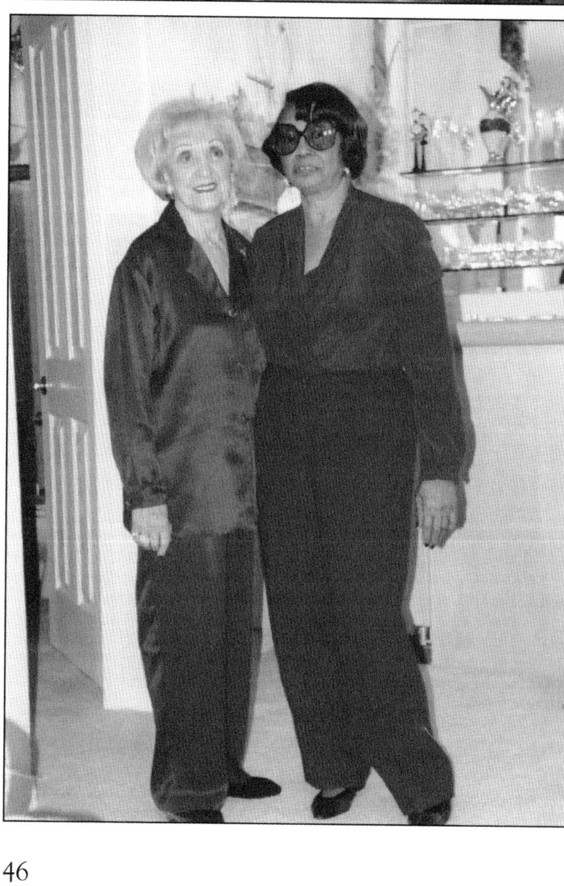

The Local Businesses, Gas Stations. Joe Whittacker owned a gas station on Owens and D Streets in the 1960s. Small businesses were quite successful when blacks populated the Westside, and everyone patronized each other's establishments. (Courtesy Edna Mae Williams.)

Toni Clark of the Desert Inn Clarks Feted Edna Williams. In a seemingly unlikely scenario for the 1950s, Wilbur and Toni Clark, developers of the Desert Inn Hotel, befriended West Las Vegan Edna Mae Williams. Even when widowed 20 years later, Toni, the daughter of an Italian street sweeper, continued the relationship, bestowing upon Edna photographs and other memorabilia marking their long-term acquaintance. Edna still speaks about their rapport with great pride today. (Courtesy Edna Mae Williams.)

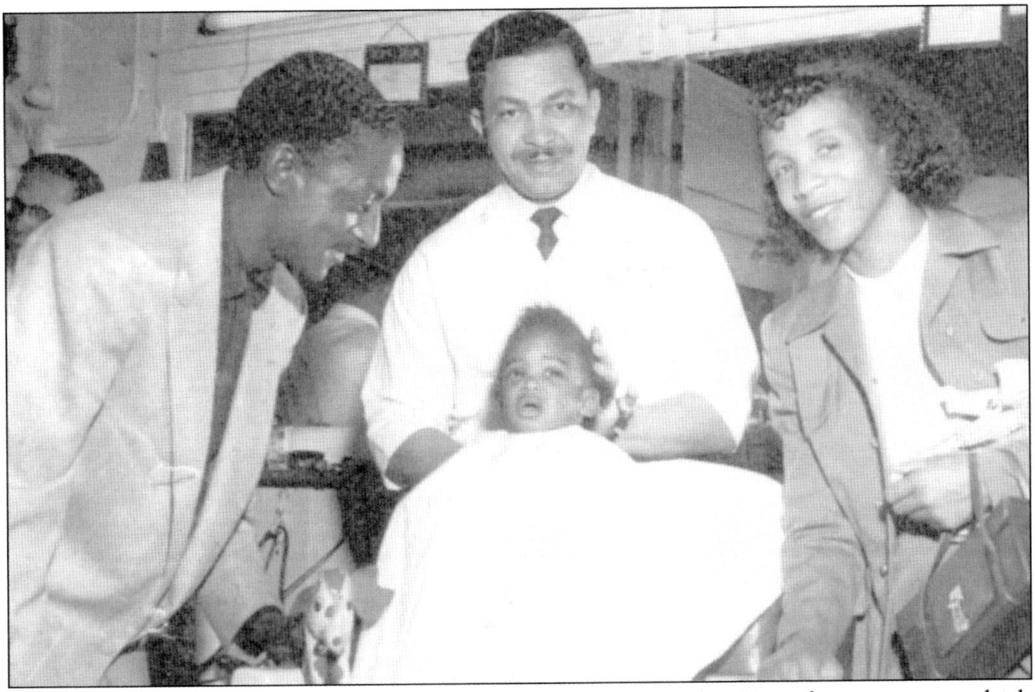

SELF-SUSTAINING BUSINESS THRIVED. Though stung by racism, the Westside community, which was then mostly African American, built very successful businesses, including grocery and clothing stores, barbershops, hair salons, liquor stores, and other retail establishments. The Sportsman Barbershop was one such place. Seen here, Johnus Geran finishes a young boy's first haircut. (Courtesy Trish Geran.)

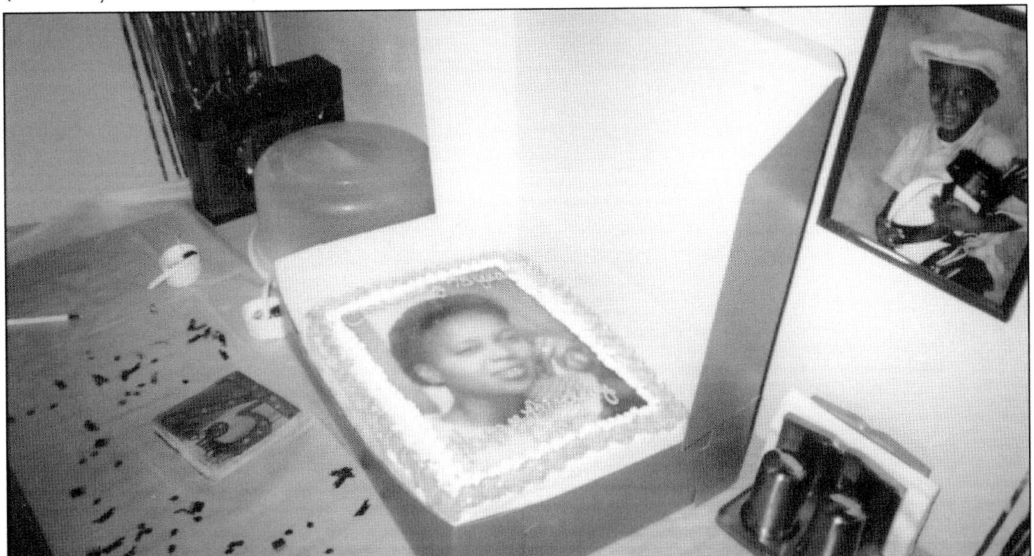

THE 1950S STILL BRING HOPEFULS. Agnes Marshall represents many of the mid-20th-century arrivals who sought warmer climates and better opportunities despite the segregation, which many considered equally harsh elsewhere. Here is a cake photograph of Agnes when she was 15 and living in Louisiana. She later moved to Salt Lake City before settling in Las Vegas. (Courtesy Agnes Marshall.)

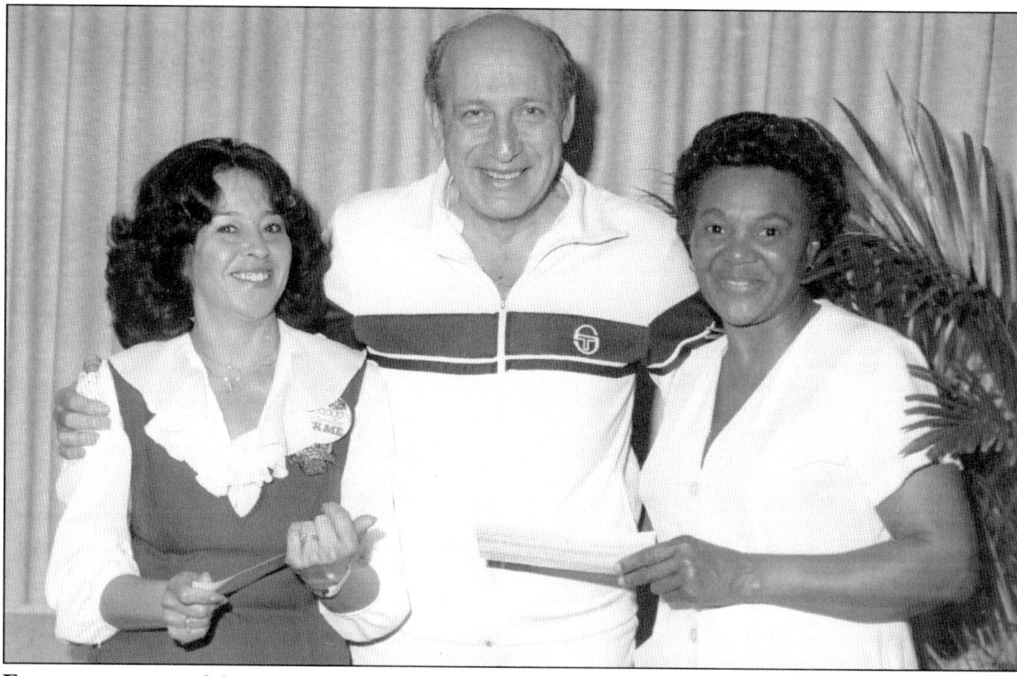

Employee of the Month. Agnes Marshall, who worked for the Riviera for over 30 years in the pantry area, is seen here being rewarded by the hotel for exemplary work. Though African Americans rose in the esteem of their bosses, the negative impact of segregation would take several more decades to overcome, and prejudices were still to be found in many quarters. However, black employees slowly began to rise in corporate ranks and are heralded today as esteemed elders of the Westside. (Courtesy Agnes Marshall.)

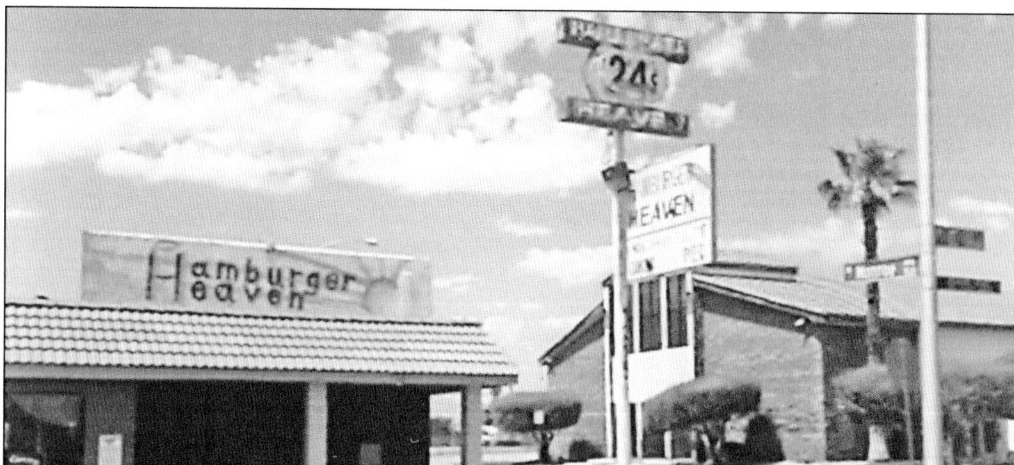

Bringing Heaven to the Community. Many businesses thrived as the Westside experienced growth with more prosperous residents. Hamburger Heaven, where a hamburger could be bought for a little loose change, was one of the more popular informal hangouts during the mid-century. Change in ownership did not dampen enthusiasm until 2010, when the establishment was finally closed and torn down.

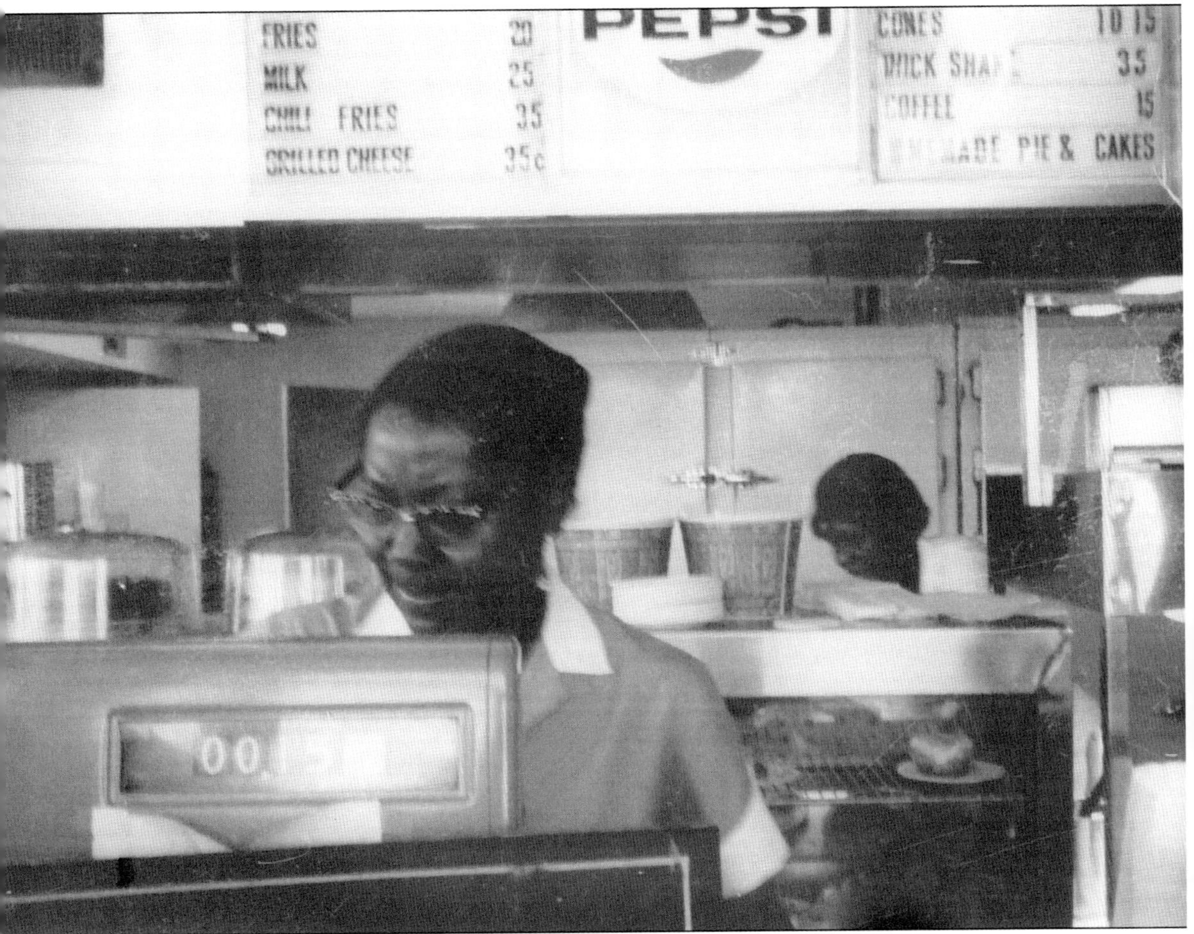

The Ebullient Miss Kathy. Hamburger Heaven's memorable owner served out-of-this-world food and boosted the sense of family. According to locals, Mr. and Mrs. Johnson's potato pie would make you "slap your face," and the egg custard was unparalleled. As a hearkening back to the 1960s when hamburgers were still only 25¢, the site of Hamburger Heaven remains a reminder of that era hundreds still fondly recall.

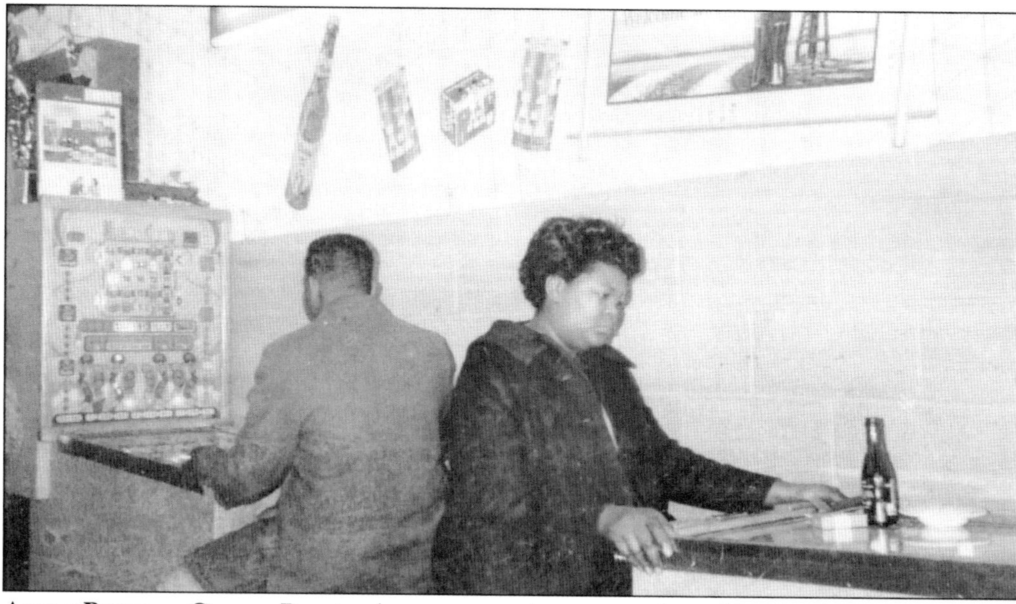

ADULT BUSINESS GROWS. Despite the numerous, innocuous places like Hamburger Heaven and Bravos Family Store, which served the best glazed donuts for a dime, adults still desired their spirits. Liquor stores like Bruno and Snowden Liquors grew in popularity. The Snowden family was well known in the area, and in a succeeding generation, Anthony Snowden would later become the first African American to run for mayor. Still, some rued the presence of these shops. Later, numerous church sites would rise, wiping out many liquor stores or the chance of their establishment.

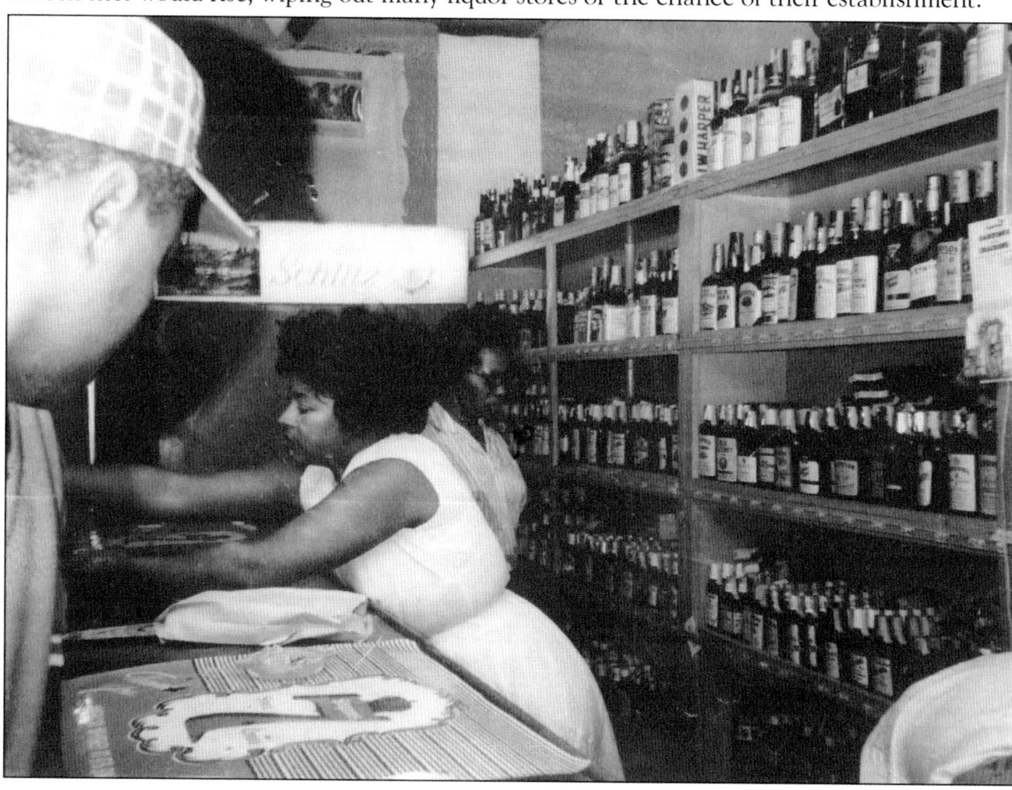

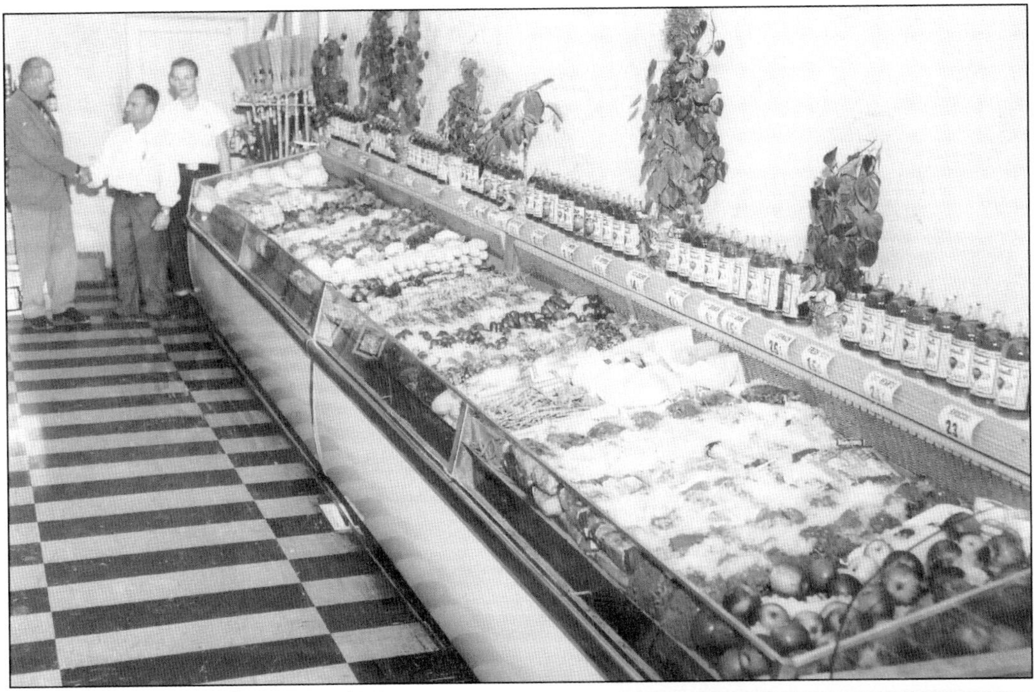

Gilbert's Grocery Store at 400 West Bonanza Road. The fresh food aisle proudly displayed here was in the popular Gilbert's Grocery Store near Snyders Malt Shop in the mid-20th century. Residents recalled the Gilbert brothers decades after the grocery store closed. Some remembered Ranch Market on Van Buren Avenue, where O.J. Simpson bagged groceries, and the Dixie Meat Market on H Street, among others.

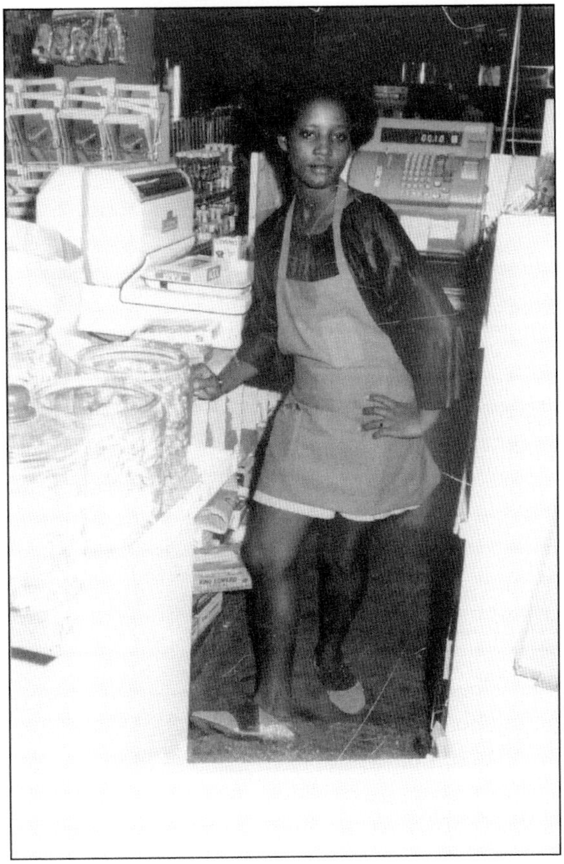

The Ever-Present Community Store. There was always some type of community store, though prices were often high. Here, a clerk poses at the cash register at Dixon Community Store. Later, Jimmy's Market would thrive for a while in the Westside. Eventually, Mario's at Martin Luther King and Lake Mead Boulevards would become the most well-known community shop.

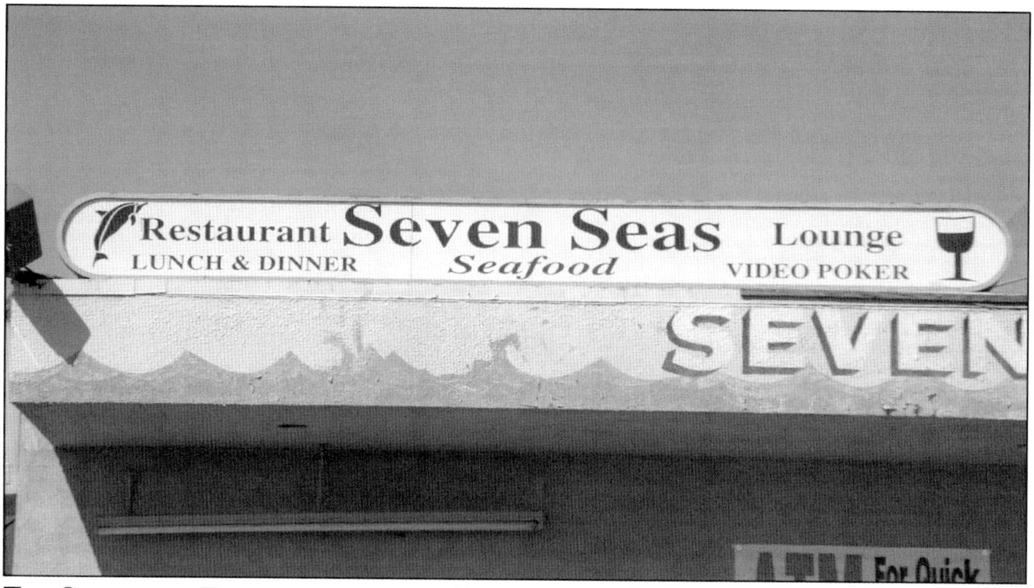

The Community Expands along with Restaurants. Seven Seas has been a staple of the Westside community for nearly 50 years. Initially established as a food mart, it was located on the expanded western side of the area. The popular eatery and bar still draws new and old patrons for meetings and entertainment on the weekends. Owner Louis Conners, like many veteran business owners, can be found across various settings, working to renew the area.

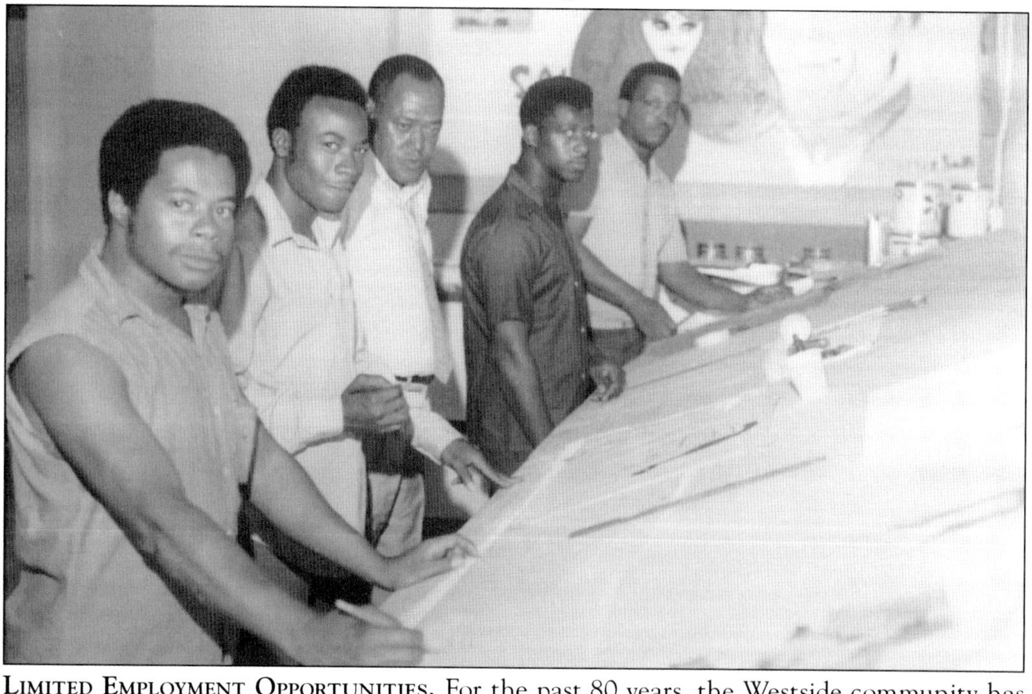

Limited Employment Opportunities. For the past 80 years, the Westside community has continuously struggled for equal opportunities. More often than not, the leveling plane was a government program with uneven results. The Equal Opportunity Board (EOB) office provided training in the late 20th century. Still, there was often an absence of viable job offers. In the photograph above, a few learn the art of sign painting.

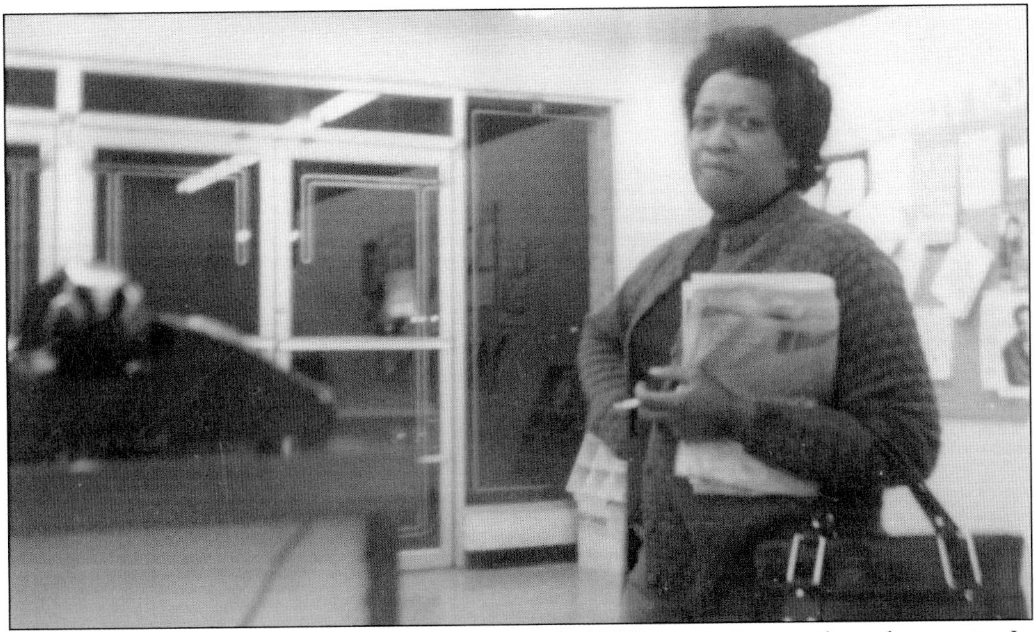

Help Always around the Corner. An unidentified EOB counselor stands ready to assist. In the Westside, many civil rights leaders supported their community in the way of professional assistance, though government funding often fluctuated.

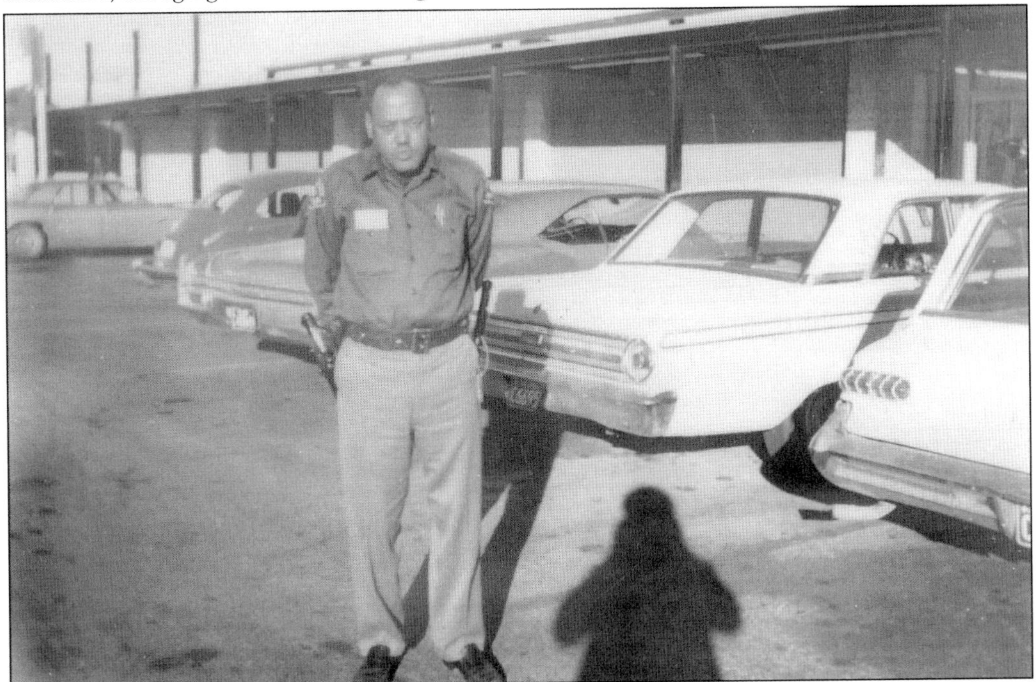

Friendly Security. Seen here, a security guard poses in front of the EOB office. Unfortunately, given great frustration and denial of employment despite increasing desegregation policies, the area youth in the 1960s rebelled against an unjust system. Even federal projects that provided for minority hiring often went unmet due to loopholes in worker qualifications. This circumvention remains today in redevelopment areas.

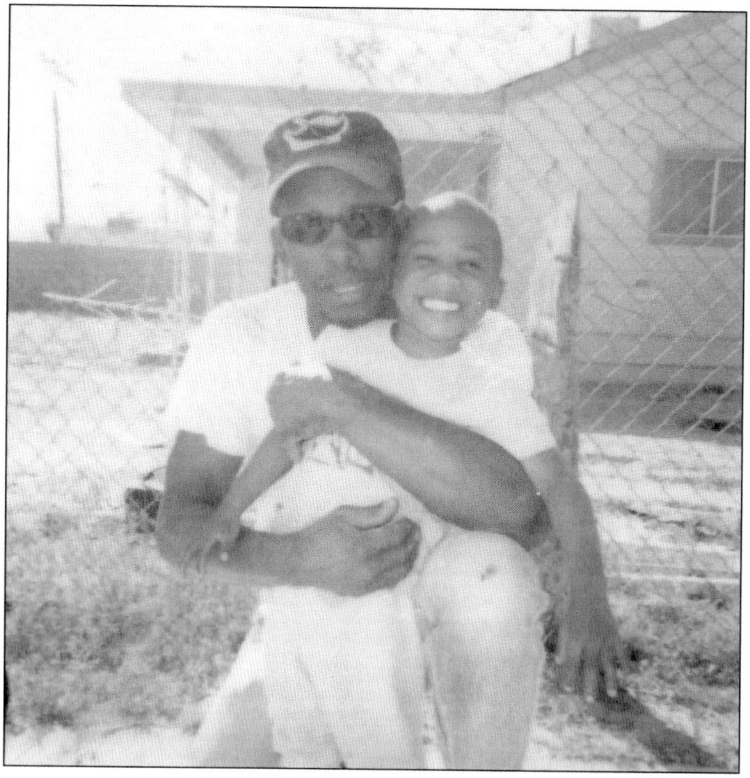

Everyday People. At left is the familiar face of local musician Leonard Brown, pictured with his godson Zachery Allen. Brown played at numerous casinos and nightclubs, including the Town Tavern, the Cotton Club, Love's, the Brown Derby, and the Cove. Below is Mosley Johnson, most remembered for her association and employment with Redd Foxx. Mosley Johnson's aunt Connie worked for B.B. King. (Both, courtesy Nancy Forman.)

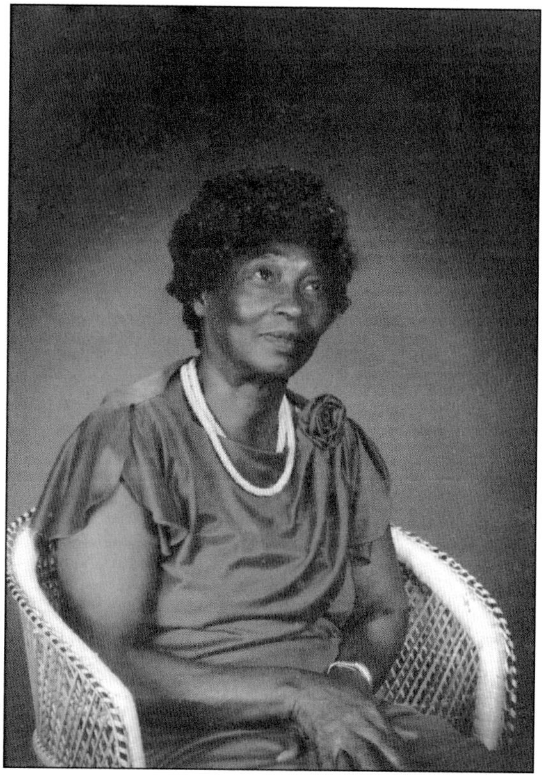

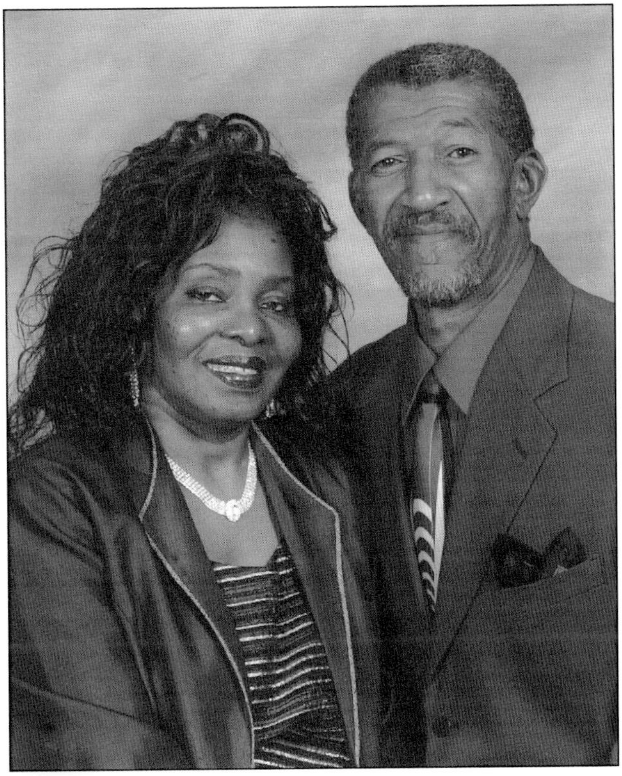

Several Generations. It is unusual to find families who have resided in Las Vegas for more than 40 or 50 years without children, grandchildren, and even great-grandchildren in the area. Mimi Smith and her husband, Samuel, seen in the photograph at right, followed in their parents' footsteps. Below is Mimi's mother-in-law, Bernice Wilson, who worked at the El Rancho in the pantry for several decades. Mimi and her family have been Las Vegas residents for over 60 years. (Both, courtesy Mimi Smith)

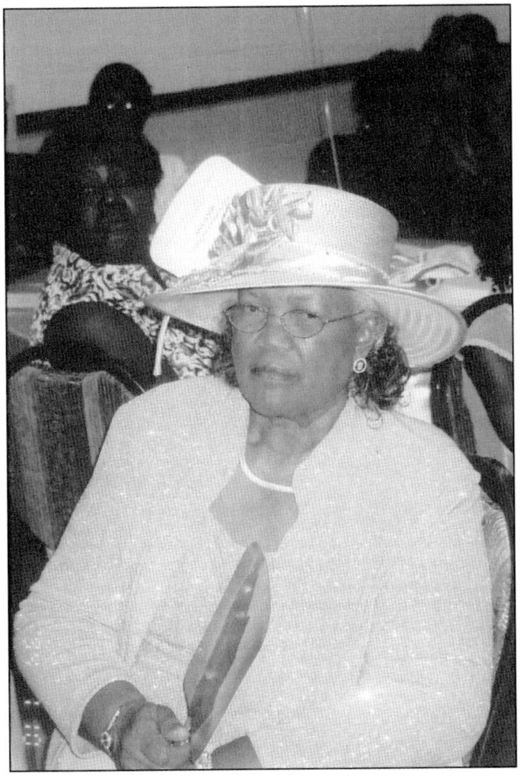

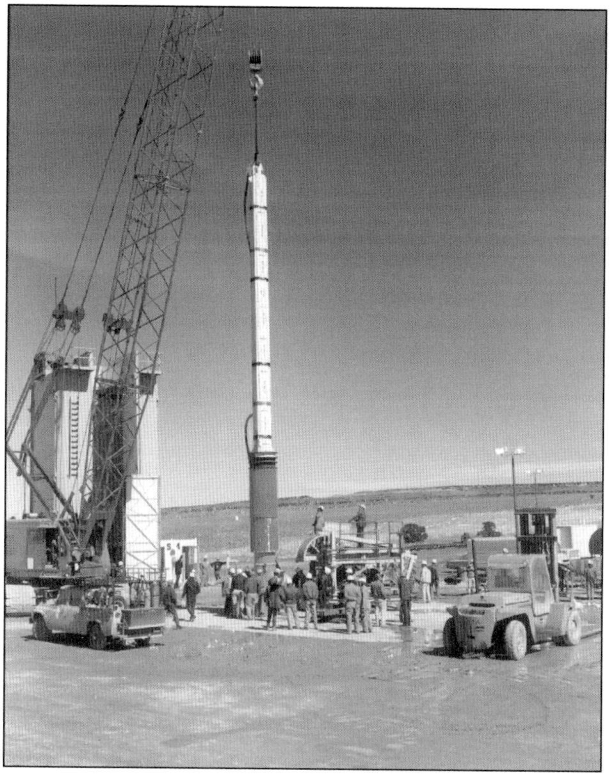

Atomic Site. Other African Americans came to Las Vegas for jobs at the gunnery or Basic Magnesium, but soon there were atomic site opportunities. Unfortunately, many who drove west from the effects of the Great Depression to seek sustainable jobs discovered that the new age of warfare brought long-term consequences of radiation. Along with whites, few were compensated for overexposure, even to this day.

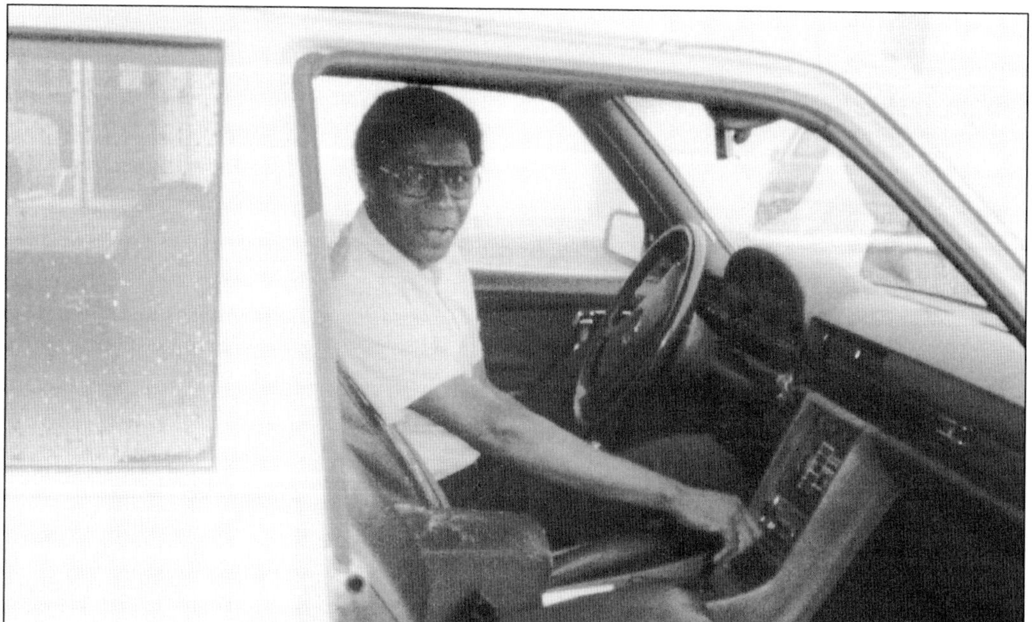

A Chat with Local Minister. Rev. Marion Bennett, a popular minister at Zion United Methodist in Las Vegas Heights, civil rights advocate, former state assemblyman, real estate leader, and noted community leader, has been a well-known face in the community for decades and generally accessible and visible in the Westside. (Courtesy Edna Mae Williams.)

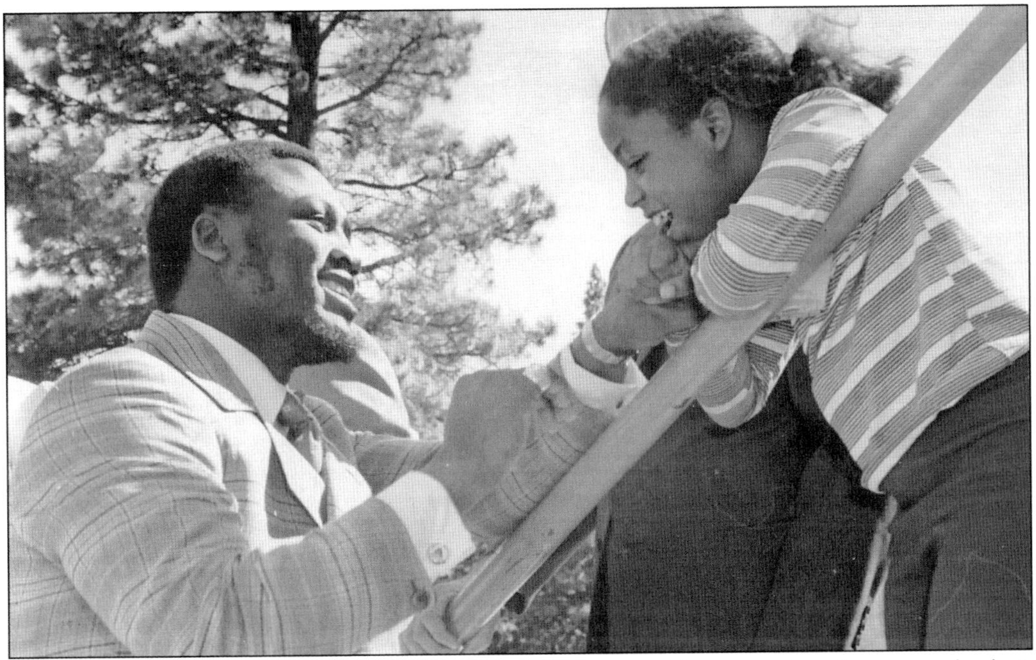

Boxing Champion Joe Frasier Greeting a Youngster. Many sporting figures made their presence known on the Westside as well. It was an everyday event to see a black champion boost the youths' spirits. The Westside of yesteryear was a special haven for black people who resided or visited Vegas, as they were unwelcome in other parts of the city for many decades.

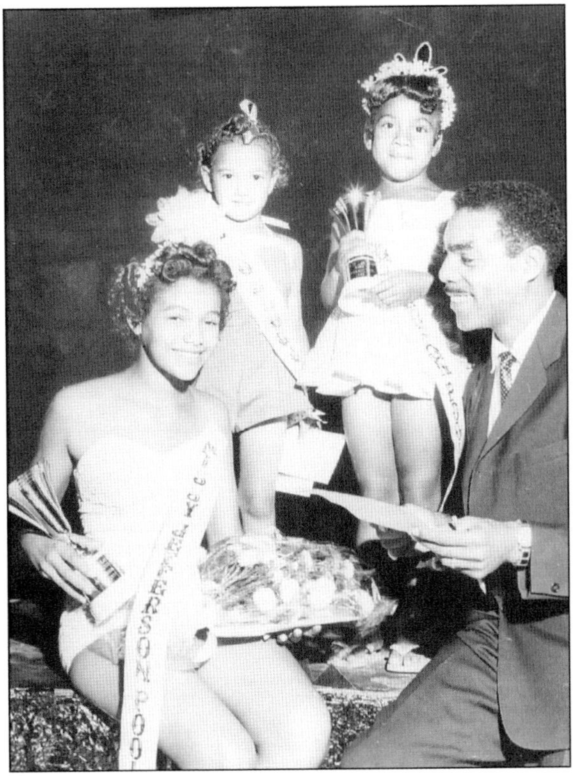

The Youth at the Jefferson Center. Swimming, dancing, and other activities filled the young people's time. In this photograph, Bob Bailey honors Miss Jefferson Pool with younger regal court members beside her. On a somber note, black teens in the 1950s who sought entertainment away from the Westside were often disappointed. Jarmilla McMillan Arnold still remembers the sting of having to sit on the left side of the movie theater, against the wall. (Courtesy Nevada State Museum, Las Vegas.)

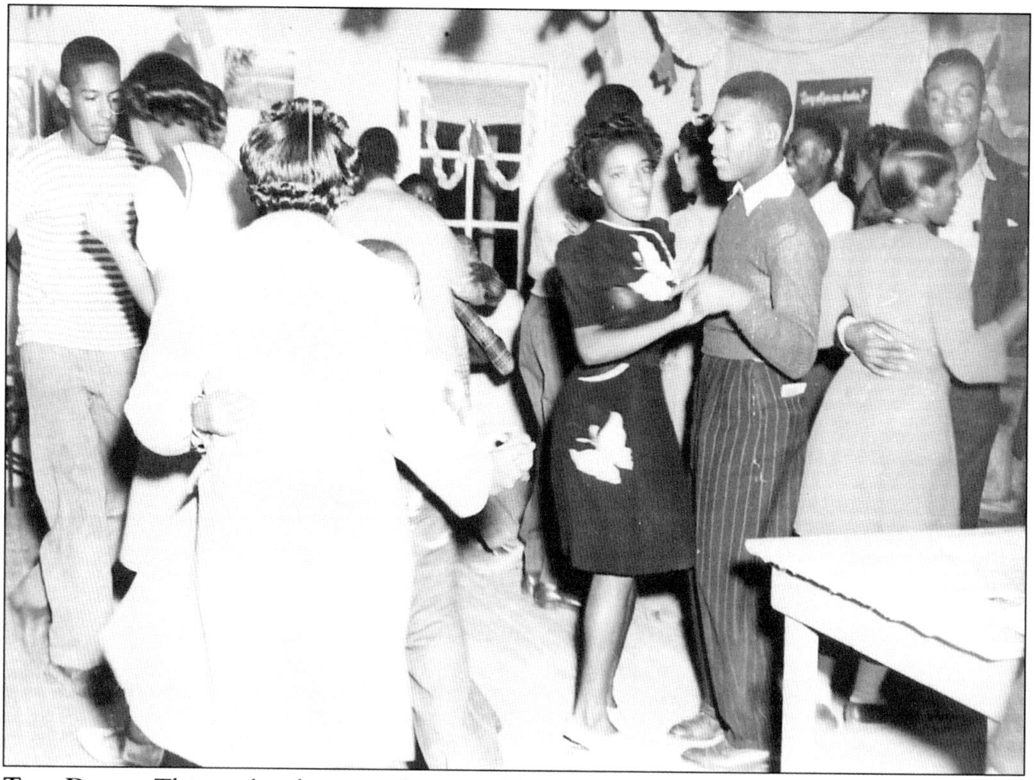

TEEN DANCE. This weekend get-together most likely took place at the Jefferson Center, the hub for youth during the late 1940s and early 1950s. Older residents recall many happy memories of those times and rue that there are not similar centers today. Sadly, there is no remnant of the Jefferson Center, unless some attics hold old photographs not yet discovered. (Courtesy Nevada State Museum, Las Vegas.)

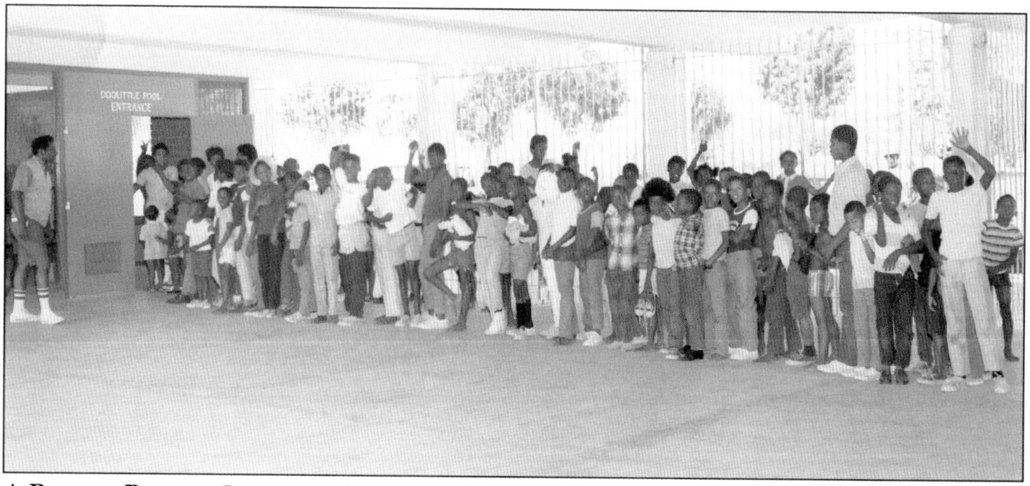

A POOL TO REPLACE JEFFERSON CENTER. When the center closed, youth on the Westside had no place to swim. The opening of the Doolittle Community Center swimming pool on J Street near Lake Mead Boulevard changed that. In these images, one can see the crowd waiting to get in. The center also offers many other amenities today, including a state-of-the-art basketball court, as well as exercise, computer, and game rooms.

Three

The Eminent and the Elected

Overcoming Demise with Dignity

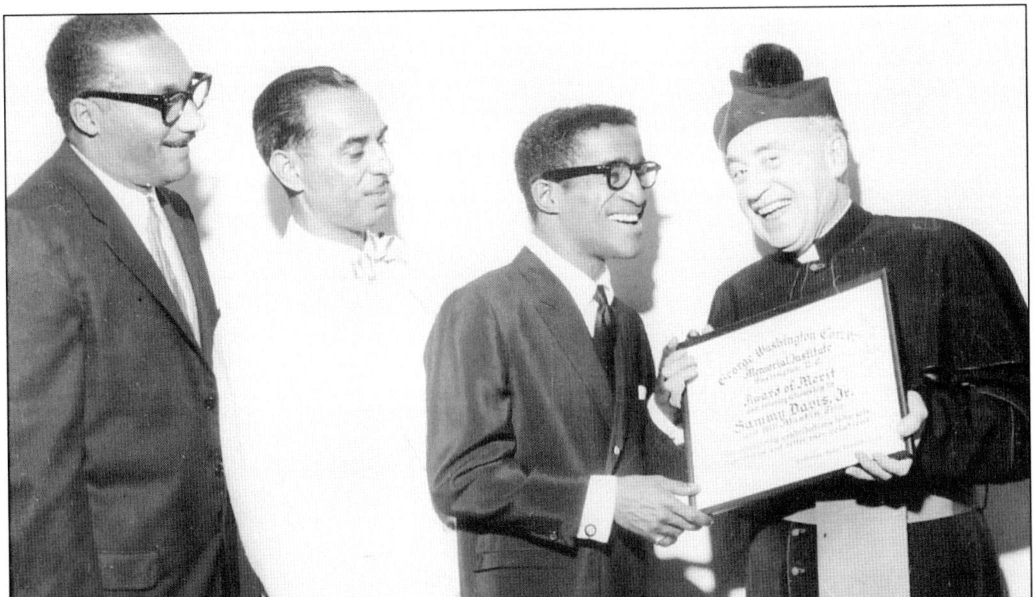

Sammy Davis Jr. Receiving Accolade. Dr. James McMillan (far left) and Dr. Charles I. West (second from left) look on as the noted singer receives the George Washington Carver Award of Merit from a Catholic cleric on behalf of the Will Mastin Trio. Whether doctor, lawyer, businessman, casino operator, or minister, almost all West Las Vegas leaders could be found at many forums poring over the issues of the day. As such, they were everyday Westside community members, even while stepping up and out as leaders. They would promote civil rights, publish newspapers, lead marches and movements, or enter broadcasting to raise consciousness related to racial relations and decades of exclusion and persecution. Several entered politics or other civil service areas historically blocked to blacks. Many African American firsts rose from West Las Vegas. (Courtesy Nevada State Museum, Las Vegas.)

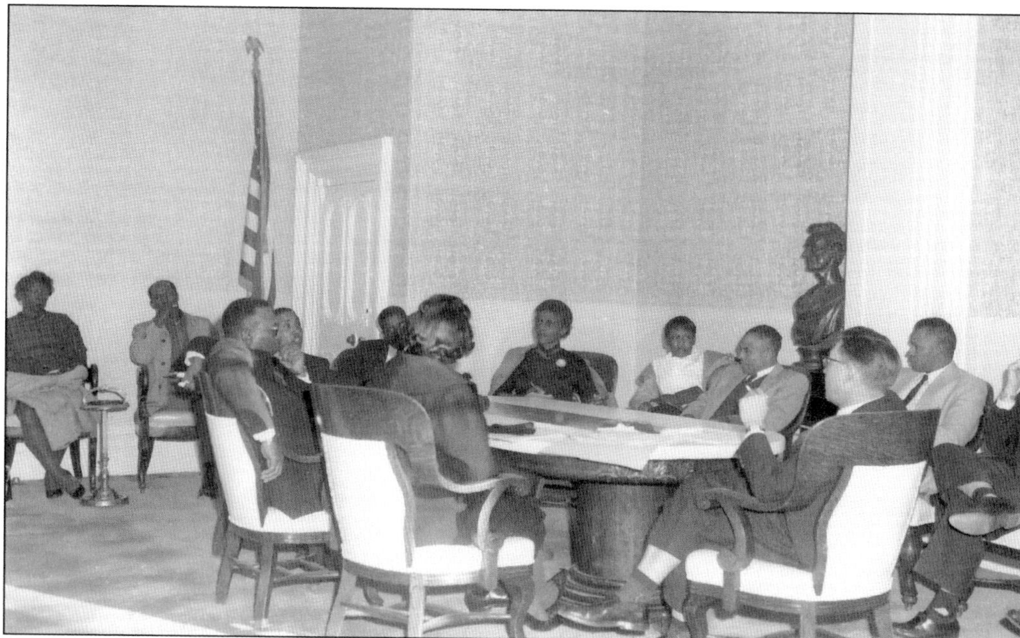

Civil Rights in Everyone's Blood. In this photograph, "Moon" Mullins, Donald Clark, Alice Smith, and eight others meet at the federal Grant Sawyer Building. Donald Clark rose to notability in the 1960s, chaired the Clark County Economic Opportunity Board, and was a county commissioner in the 1980s.

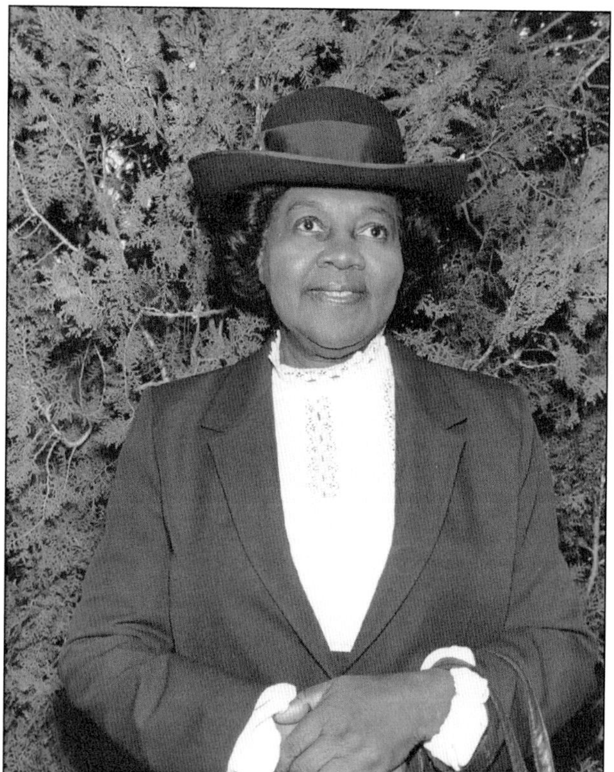

An Early Pioneer in Civil Rights. Lubertha Johnson came originally from the South through Chicago before landing in Las Vegas. This spunky lady opened a grocery store in West Las Vegas and hired African Americans. Though she left for a time, she returned more determined than ever to advance racial equality. She was the only woman present at the Moulin Rouge when desegregation was announced for the Strip.

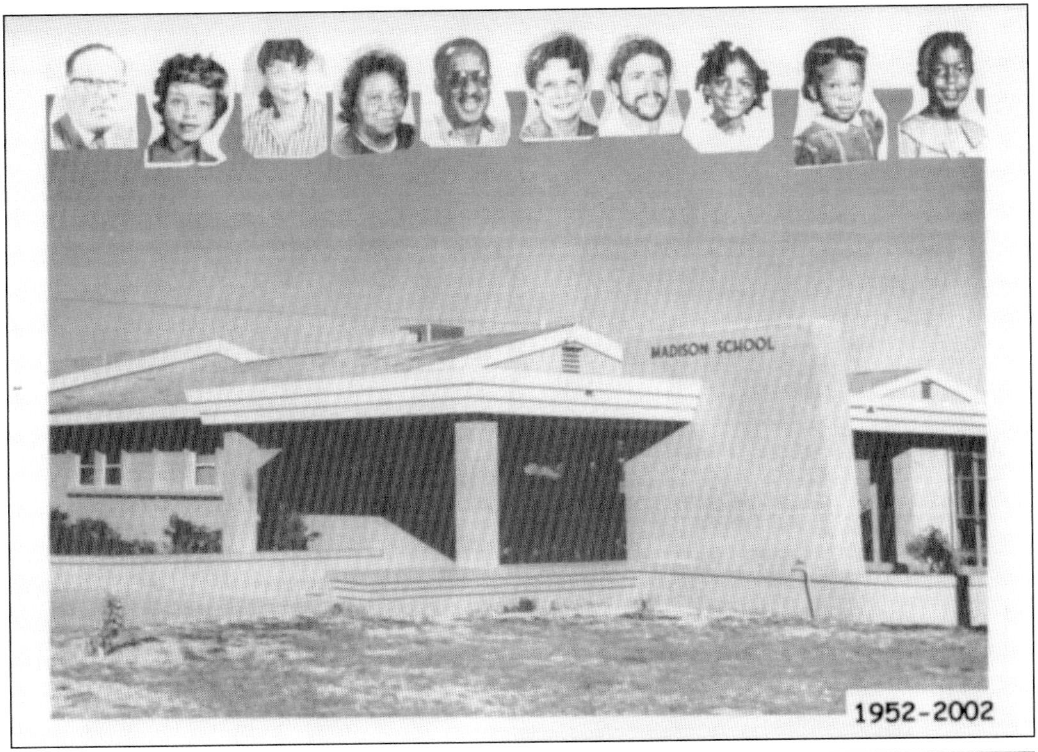

MADISON SCHOOL. Like its pioneer black educators, Madison School was held in high esteem for advancing the opportunities of Westside children. The second school after the historic Westside School, Madison was the first founded specifically for this expanded community in the early 1950s. It has since been replaced by Wendell P. Williams Elementary School.

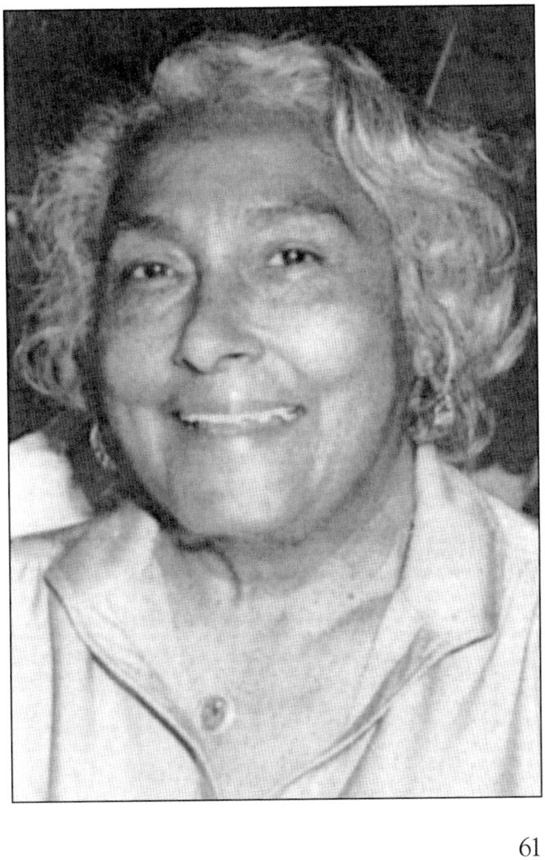

ENTREPRENEURIAL FIRST LADY. Lucille Hughes arrived in Las Vegas when there were less than a few hundred African Americans in 1931. She and her husband, Albert, opened a grocery store on Jackson Avenue that remained in business for 53 years. An avid church attendee, Lucille spent much of her free time helping raise funds for various charities.

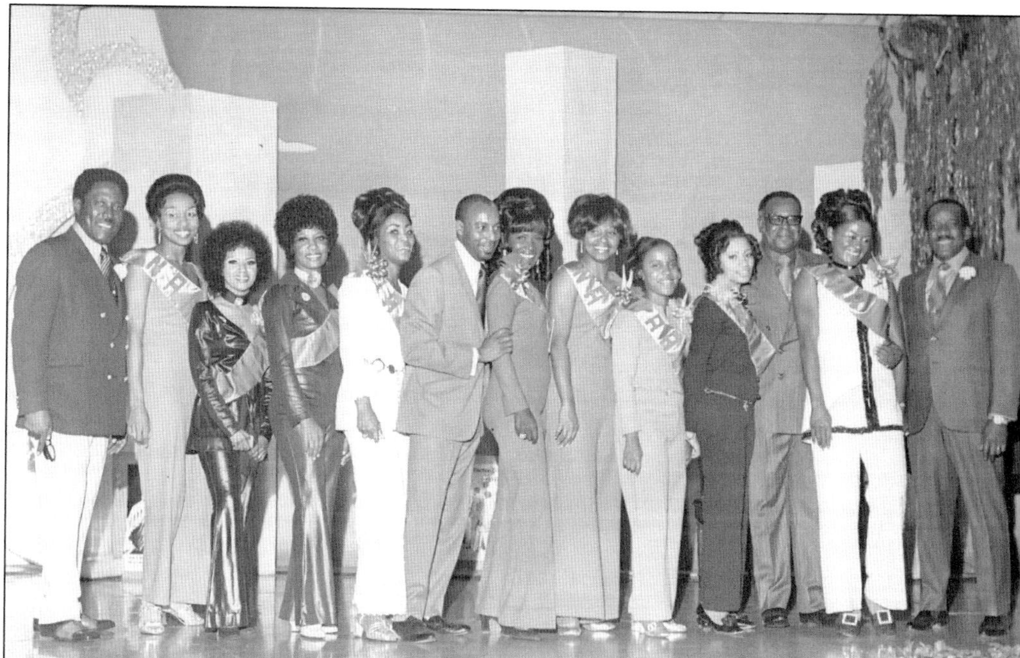

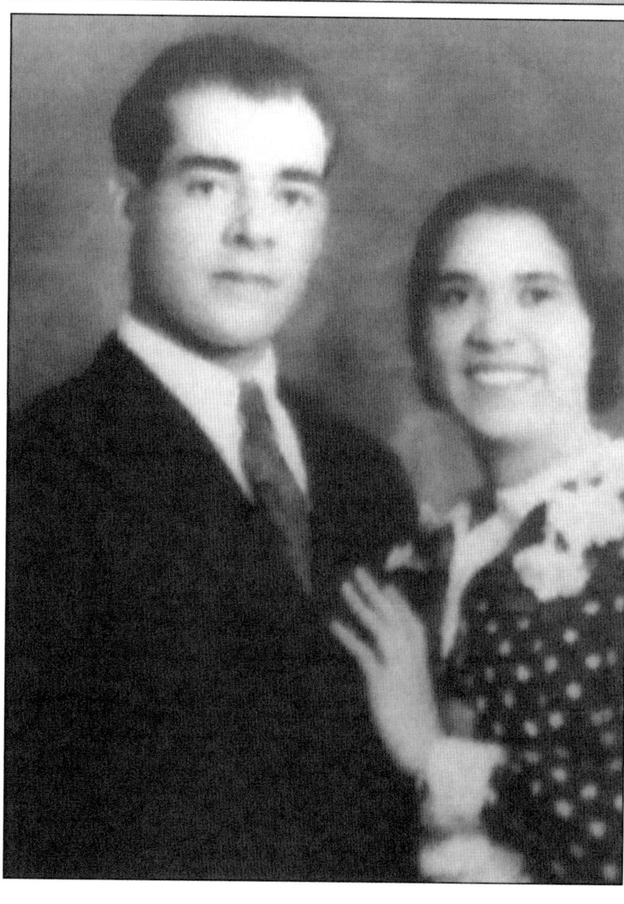

A 1960s Celebration. Although Katherine Joseph cannot recall exactly what this event was or where it took place, she recognized H.P. Fitzgerald on the right end. H.P. was the first black person appointed principal in Clark County. A city park and school bear his name. Katherine Joseph is standing seventh from the right. (Courtesy Katherine Joseph.)

The Christensens. An early photograph, likely taken in the 1930s or 1940s, shows the Christensens, a pioneer family of West Las Vegas who kept alive the dream of a castle home. Roy Christensen would become known as a black cowboy who often lent his talents and horses for Western-themed events, such as Helldorado Days.

Early Photograph of Sarann Knight Preddy. This classic image of Sarann Knight Preddy, taken in her early years, graces the Pioneer Trail sign outside the Christensen House, along with another picture taken during a special fashion show once held there. Sarann arrived in Las Vegas in 1942 and soon became an astute business woman and gaming expert. She had experience in almost every public field, whether it was real estate, entertainment, politics, or civil rights.

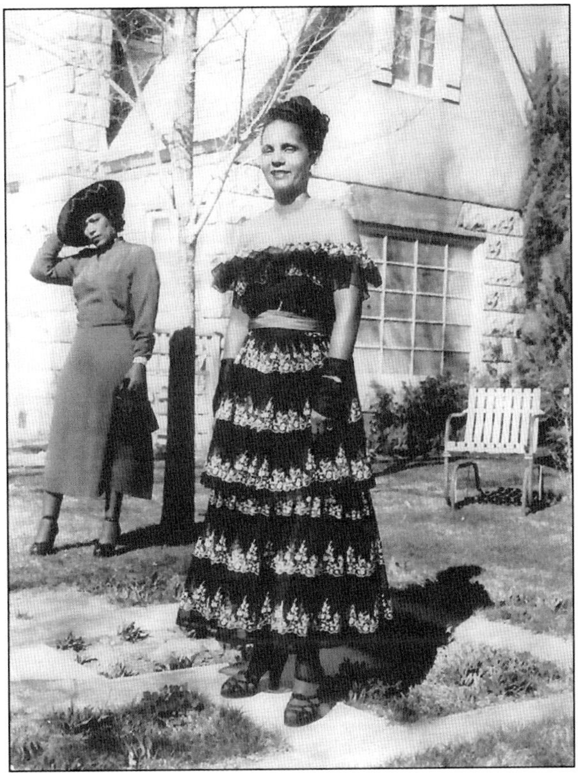

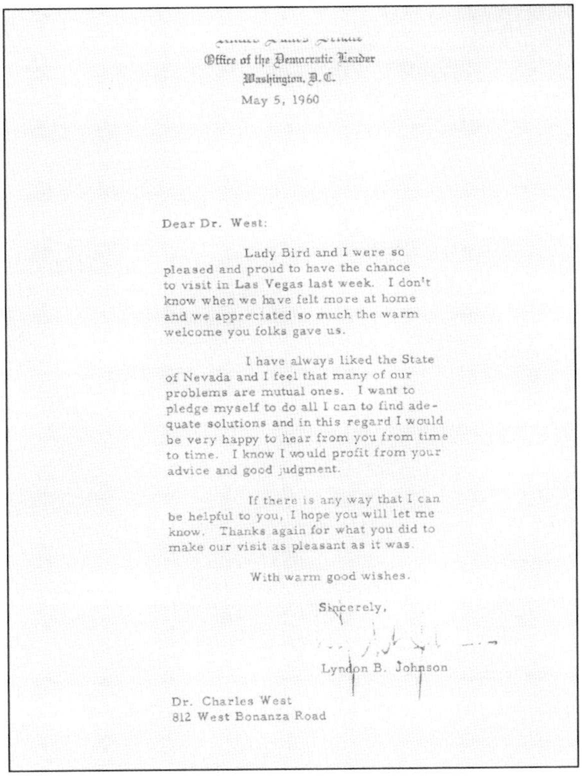

Office of the Democratic Leader
Washington, D.C.
May 5, 1960

Dear Dr. West:

Lady Bird and I were so pleased and proud to have the chance to visit in Las Vegas last week. I don't know when we have felt more at home and we appreciated so much the warm welcome you folks gave us.

I have always liked the State of Nevada and I feel that many of our problems are mutual ones. I want to pledge myself to do all I can to find adequate solutions and in this regard I would be very happy to hear from you from time to time. I know I would profit from your advice and good judgment.

If there is any way that I can be helpful to you, I hope you will let me know. Thanks again for what you did to make our visit as pleasant as it was.

With warm good wishes.

Sincerely,

Lyndon B. Johnson

Dr. Charles West
812 West Bonanza Road

The First Licensed Black Doctor in Nevada. Dr. Charles I. West moved to Las Vegas in the 1950s. With vibrancy and business insight, he eagerly transformed the image of the Westside for blacks in several areas besides medicine. Coming from a prominent family back east, Dr. West displayed social acumen and held invaluable professional connections that built up the Westside. He frequently corresponded with Washington, as evidenced in this letter from then-senator Lyndon Johnson. (Courtesy West Prep Academy, Las Vegas.)

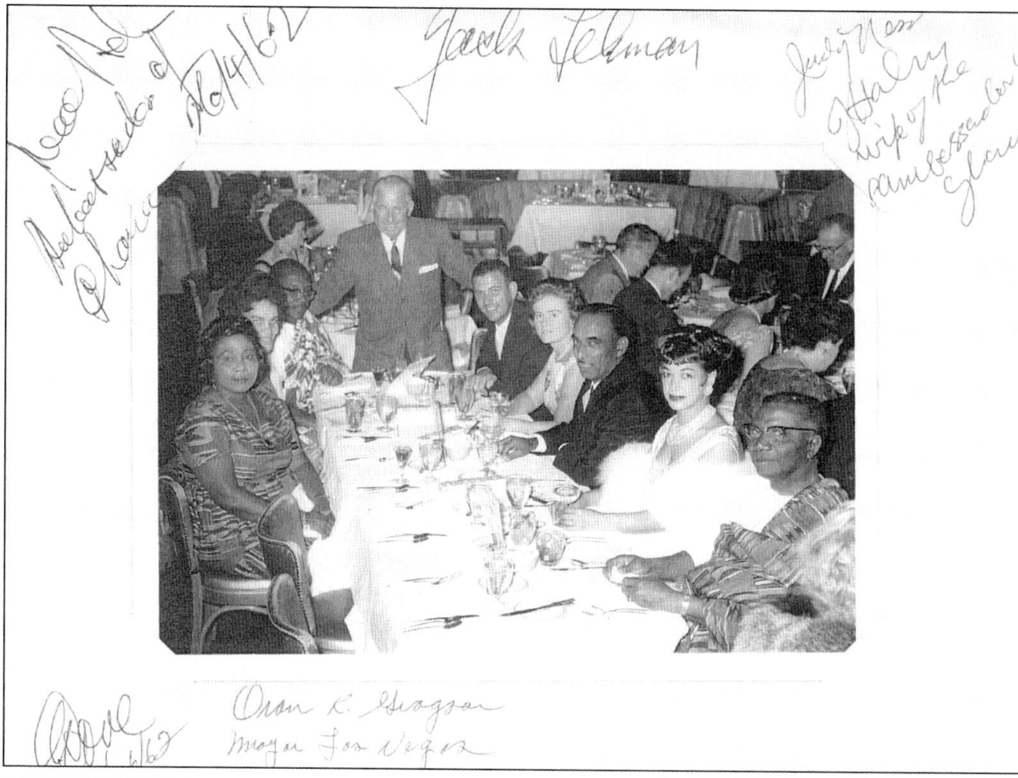

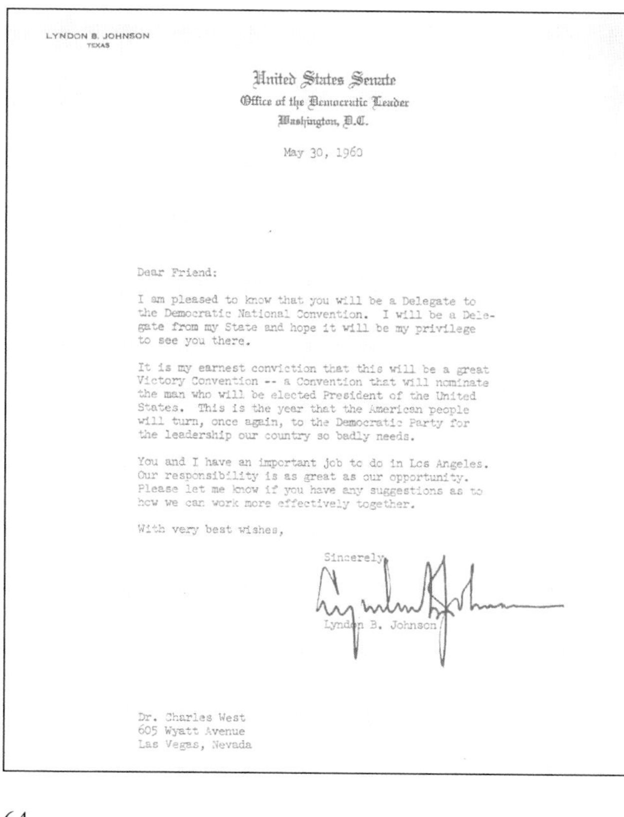

LYNDON B. JOHNSON
TEXAS

United States Senate
Office of the Democratic Leader
Washington, D.C.

May 30, 1960

Dear Friend:

I am pleased to know that you will be a Delegate to the Democratic National Convention. I will be a Delegate from my State and hope it will be my privilege to see you there.

It is my earnest conviction that this will be a great Victory Convention -- a Convention that will nominate the man who will be elected President of the United States. This is the year that the American people will turn, once again, to the Democratic Party for the leadership our country so badly needs.

You and I have an important job to do in Los Angeles. Our responsibility is as great as our opportunity. Please let me know if you have any suggestions as to how we can work more effectively together.

With very best wishes,

Sincerely,

Lyndon B. Johnson

Dr. Charles West
605 Wyatt Avenue
Las Vegas, Nevada

International Connections. Dr. West entertained internationally known guests as well. On one occasion, he touted the president of Ghana at the Moulin Rouge during a special dinner and later held a reception for him and his entourage at his Berkley Square home. (Courtesy West Prep Academy, Las Vegas.)

A More Personal Invitation. Less than a month after the first letter, Sen. Lyndon B. Johnson writes again, this time to congratulate Dr. West on being a Democratic National Convention delegate. This time, it is written to his home address on Wyatt Street in Berkley Square. (Courtesy West Prep Academy, Las Vegas.)

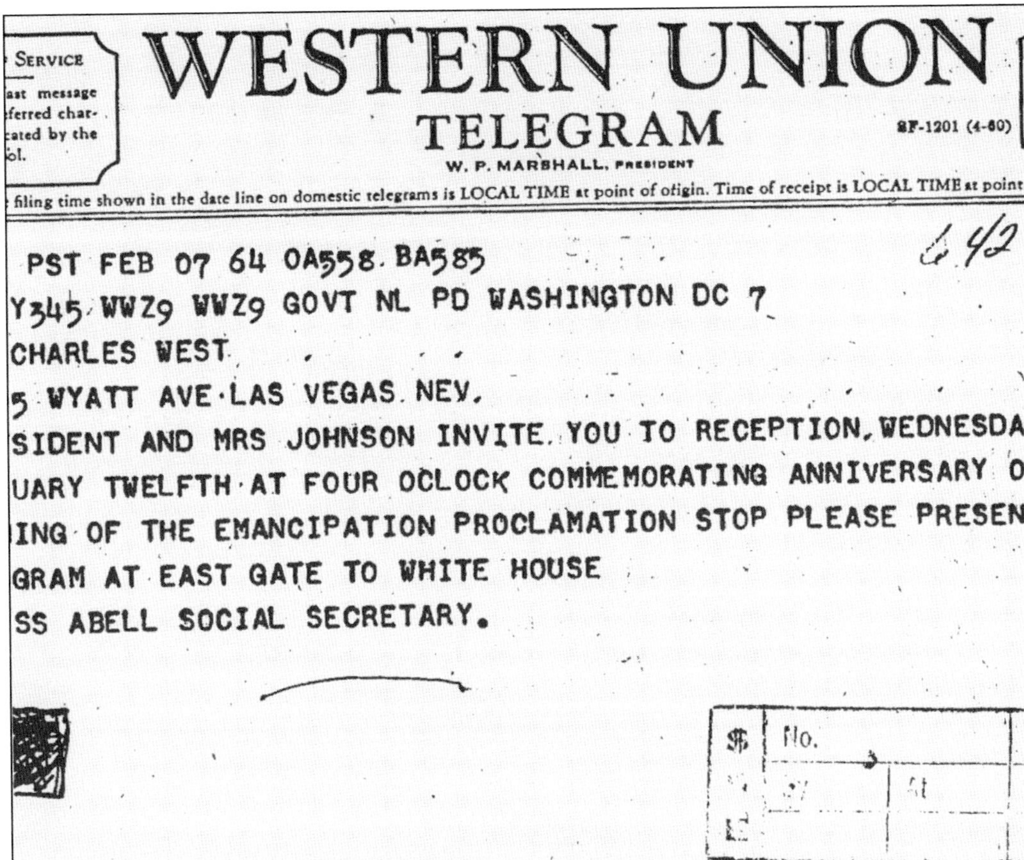

SERVICE
ast message
ferred char-
cated by the
ol.

WESTERN UNION
TELEGRAM
W. P. MARSHALL, PRESIDENT

8F-1201 (4-60)

filing time shown in the date line on domestic telegrams is LOCAL TIME at point of origin. Time of receipt is LOCAL TIME at point

PST FEB 07 64 OA558 BA585

Y345 WWZ9 WWZ9 GOVT NL PD WASHINGTON DC 7

CHARLES WEST

5 WYATT AVE LAS VEGAS NEV

SIDENT AND MRS JOHNSON INVITE YOU TO RECEPTION WEDNESDA
UARY TWELFTH AT FOUR OCLOCK COMMEMORATING ANNIVERSARY O
ING OF THE EMANCIPATION PROCLAMATION STOP PLEASE PRESEN
GRAM AT EAST GATE TO WHITE HOUSE

SS ABELL SOCIAL SECRETARY.

President Johnson Remembers. Four years later, President Johnson sent a telegram to Dr. West, inviting him to the White House to celebrate the anniversary of the Emancipation Proclamation. Dr. West brought prominent attention to the Westside, though the greater influence was often disregarded by Nevada and Las Vegas powers. (Courtesy West Prep Academy, Las Vegas.)

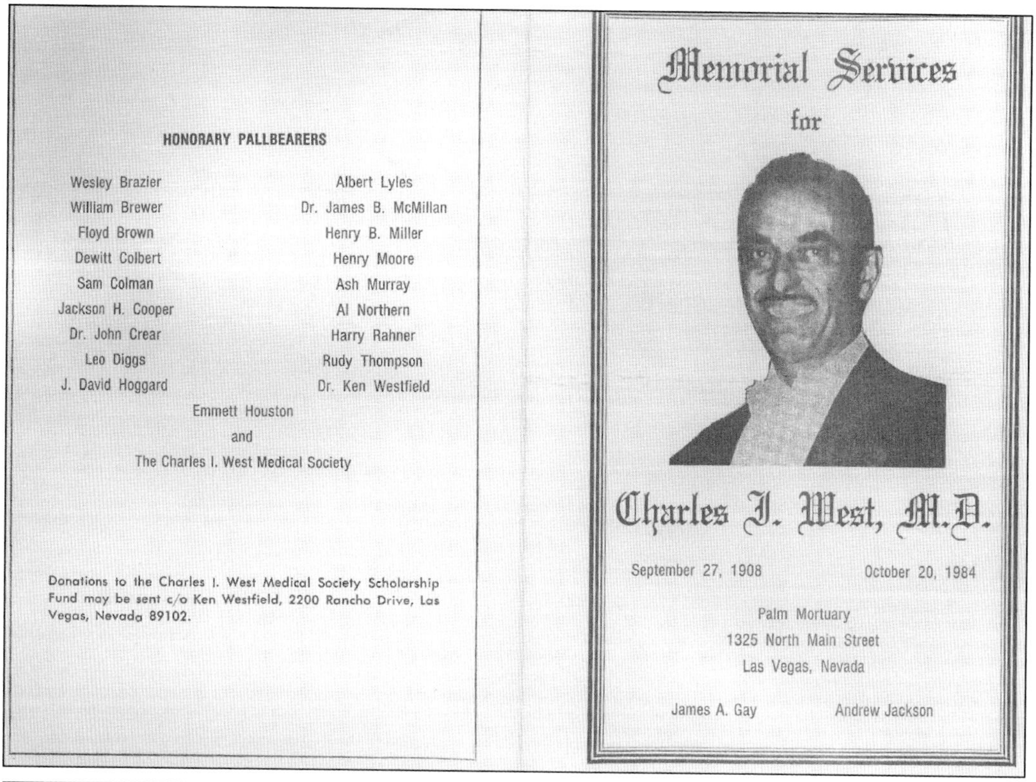

HONORARY PALLBEARERS

Wesley Brazier	Albert Lyles
William Brewer	Dr. James B. McMillan
Floyd Brown	Henry B. Miller
Dewitt Colbert	Henry Moore
Sam Colman	Ash Murray
Jackson H. Cooper	Al Northern
Dr. John Crear	Harry Rahner
Leo Diggs	Rudy Thompson
J. David Hoggard	Dr. Ken Westfield

Emmett Houston

and

The Charles I. West Medical Society

Donations to the Charles I. West Medical Society Scholarship Fund may be sent c/o Ken Westfield, 2200 Rancho Drive, Las Vegas, Nevada 89102.

Memorial Services

for

Charles I. West, M.D.

September 27, 1908 October 20, 1984

Palm Mortuary

1325 North Main Street

Las Vegas, Nevada

James A. Gay Andrew Jackson

FAREWELL TO DR. WEST. The obituary reveals the many distinguished persons who came to bid farewell to the good doctor who once took house calls and could bring down a house with his persistent drive to ensure equality for blacks. Though he sat through countless meetings to articulate human rights, he would not stand wordlessly at injustice. (Courtesy West Prep Academy, Las Vegas.)

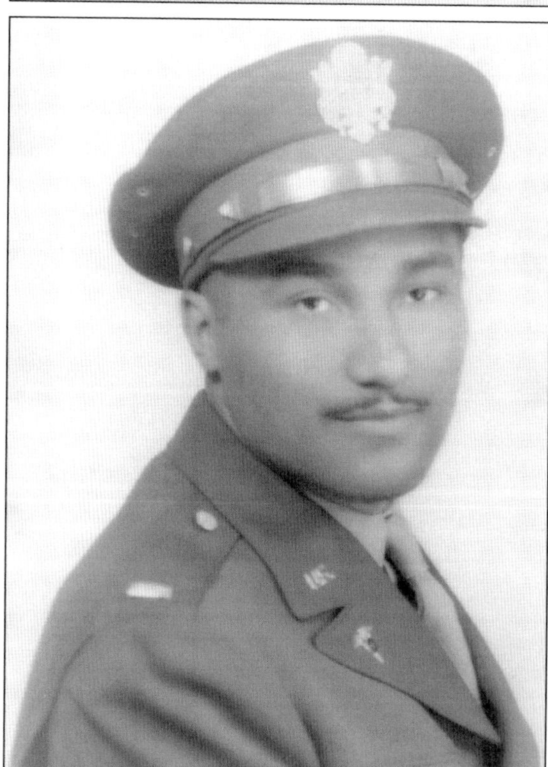

THE FIRST LICENSED BLACK DENTIST IN NEVADA. Despite the need to challenge the state for his license after excelling on the dental boards, James T. McMillan moved to West Las Vegas at the encouragement of Dr. West. He is seen in uniform prior to his Las Vegas battles. Dr. McMillan proved equally earnest and determined in his battles for racial equality; like many of his counterparts, he became involved in several different boards that positively affected the daily lives of African Americans in Las Vegas. (Courtesy Marie McMillan.)

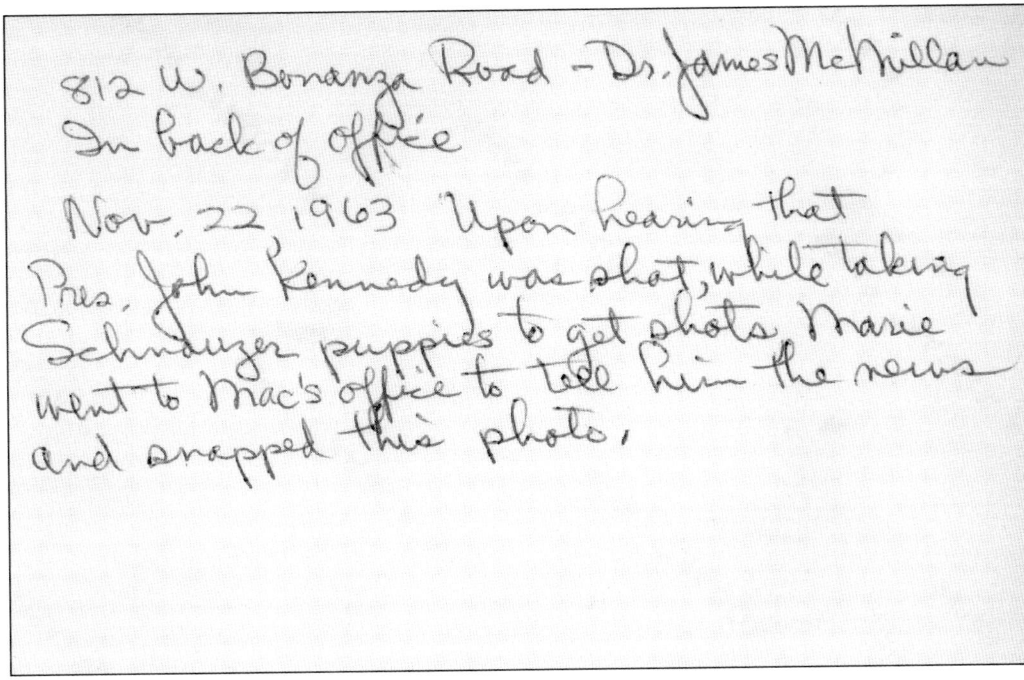

812 W. Bonanza Road - Dr. James McMillan
In back of office
Nov. 22, 1963 Upon hearing that
Pres. John Kennedy was shot, while taking
Schnauzer puppies to get shots, Marie
went to Mac's office to tell him the news
and snapped this photo.

The Day of Kennedy's Assassination. Marie McMillan took this snapshot of her husband, an uncharacteristically quiet Dr. McMillan, after being told that John F. Kennedy had been assassinated. She has kept the note describing the day since 1963. He looked numb, likely stunned by the loss of the popular president. (Both, courtesy Marie McMillan.)

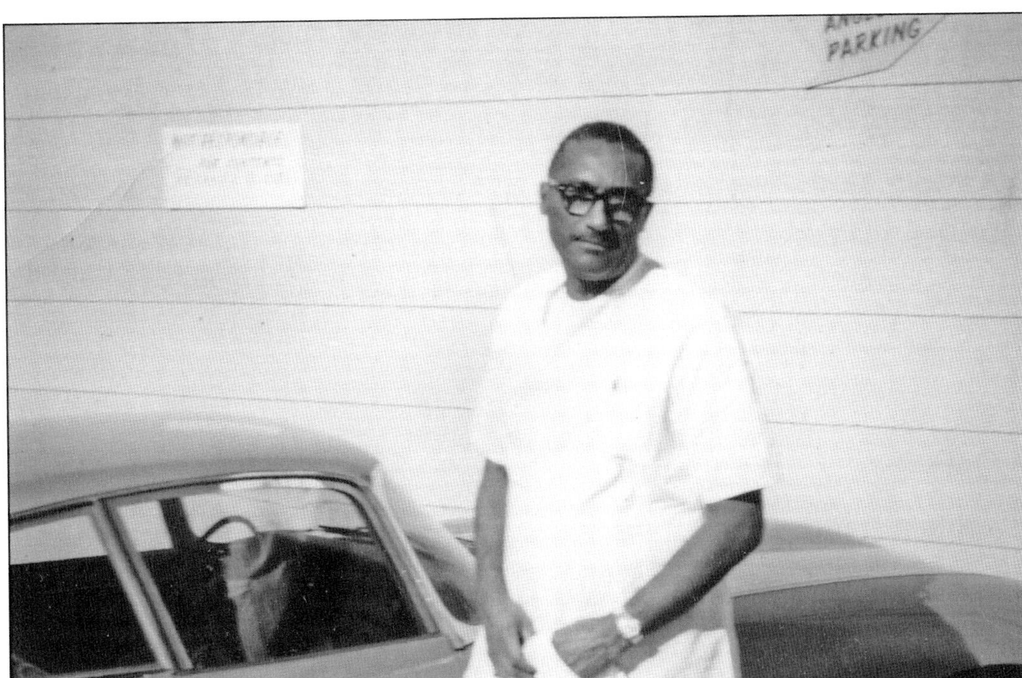

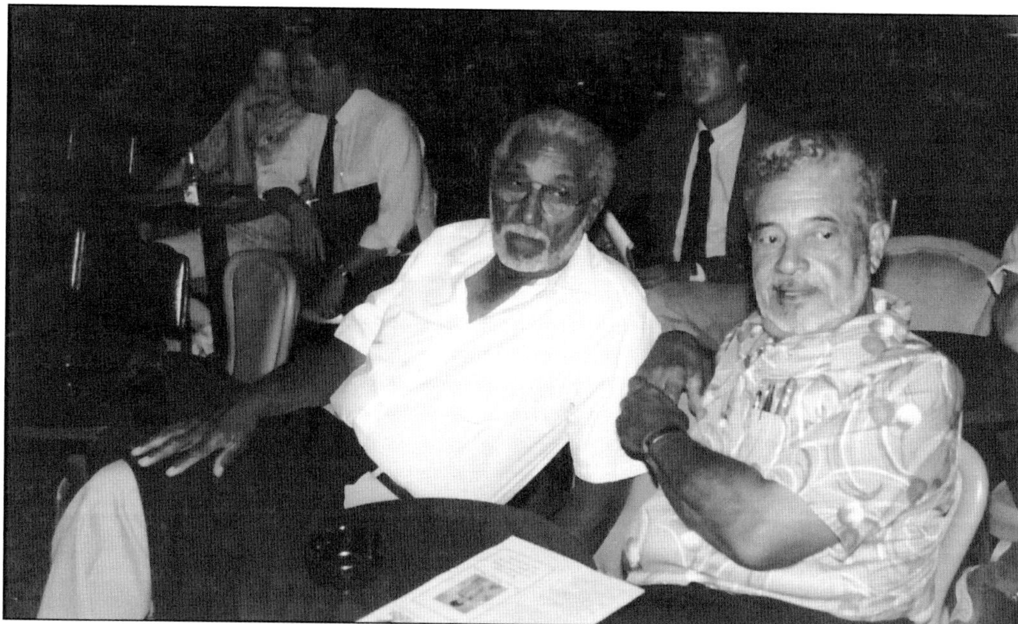

McMillan and Hoggard. This photograph of two Westside icons, Dr. James McMillan and J. David Hoggard, was most likely taken at the Moulin Rouge in the 1990s at one of many civil rights meetings. J. David Hoggard was a stalwart of the NAACP for over half a century, as well as a high-ranking member of the Zion Methodist United Church. He is most remembered for his direction of the Employment Opportunity Board. (Courtesy Erma Jai Walker.)

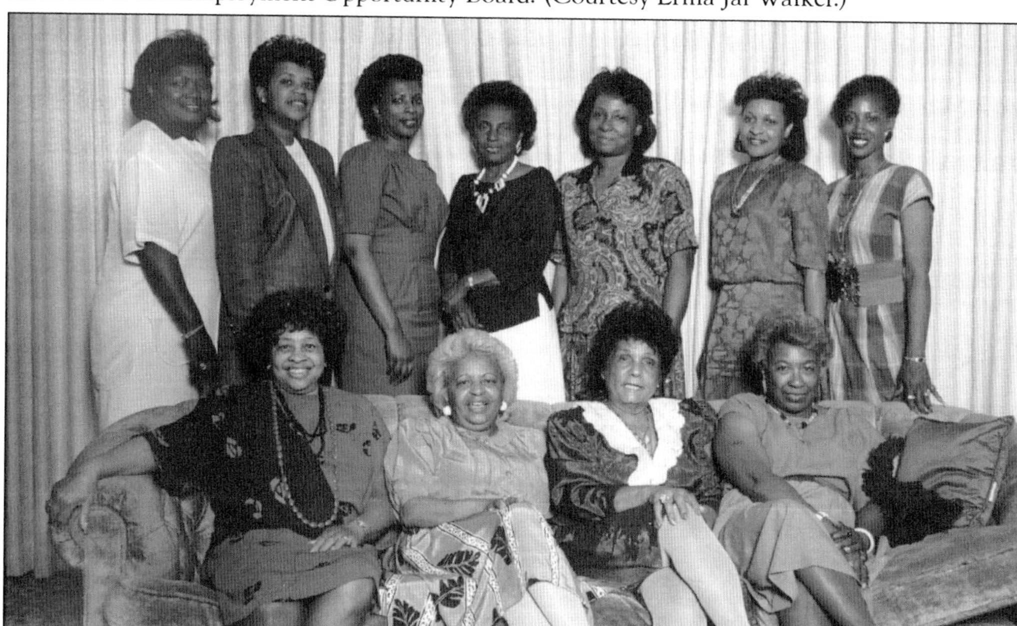

The Woman Who Wore Many Hats. Sarann Knight Preddy (seated second from right) moved to Las Vegas with her father, a contractor with a knack for building concrete-block housing. Her mother later joined them with $7,000. Following in the footsteps of her successful ancestry, Sarann would also make her own indelible mark on West Las Vegas and Nevada in numerous endeavors, all while donning a white hat. (Courtesy Sarann Knight Preddy.)

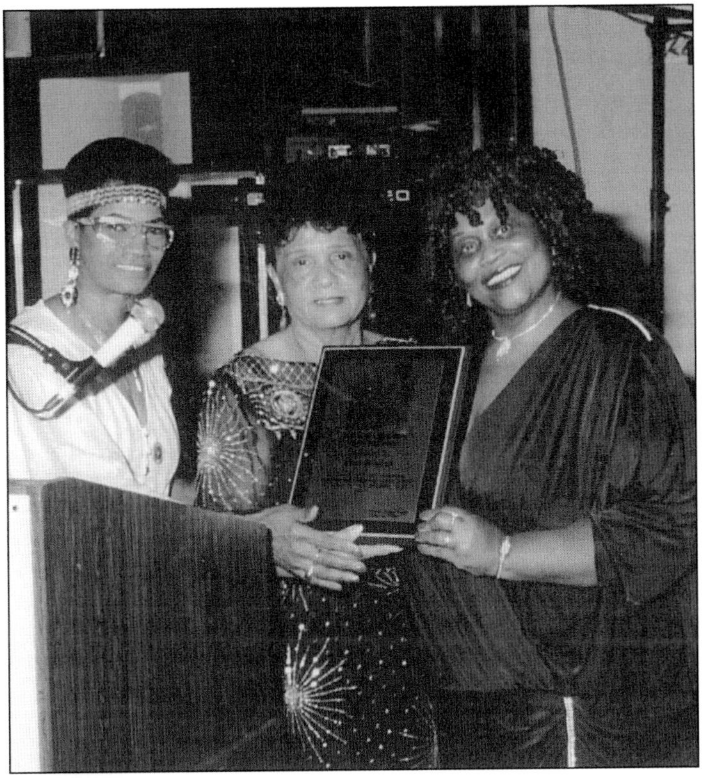

A Queen of Hearts. Though she was a savvy businessperson, as well as the first woman of color in the world to hold a nonrestricted gaming license, Sarann (center) was well known for her generosity, her desire to feed the hungry, and her willingness to loan money to someone down on his or her luck. At right, she bestows an award with Erma Walker (left) unto Ruby Duncan. (Courtesy Erma Jai Walker.)

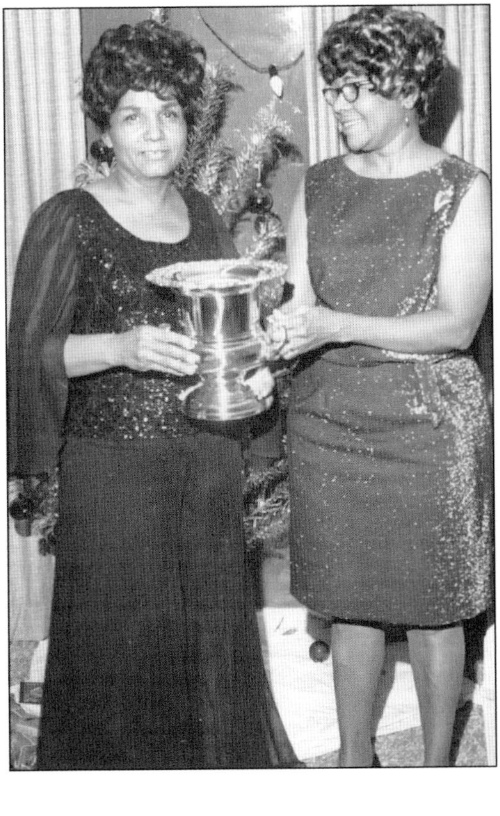

Receiving Awards Galore. After a lifetime of service with various organizations, including the NAACP, running for office, and sitting on numerous boards in the areas of gaming, real estate, and retail, Sarann (left) boasts dozens of certificates, plaques, trophies, and other distinguished reminders of her 90 years of giving to date. (Courtesy Sarann Knight Preddy.)

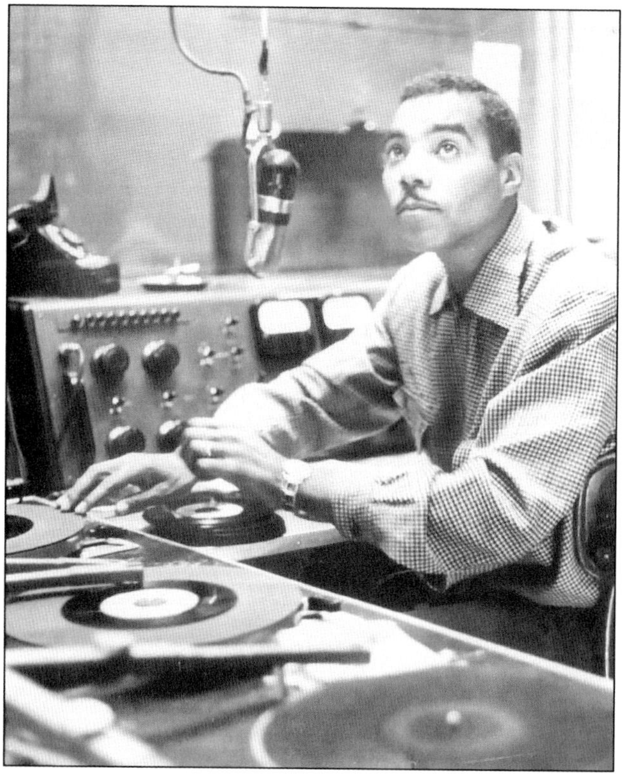

Master of Ceremonies. In 1955, Bob Bailey relocated to Las Vegas to help open the Moulin Rouge as a master of ceremonies and show coproducer. His wife, Anna Bailey, a celebrated dancer, joined the show. Like many others, Bob would involve himself in numerous statewide movements and groups to advance the position of African Americans, especially in minority businesses. (Courtesy Nevada State Museum, Las Vegas.)

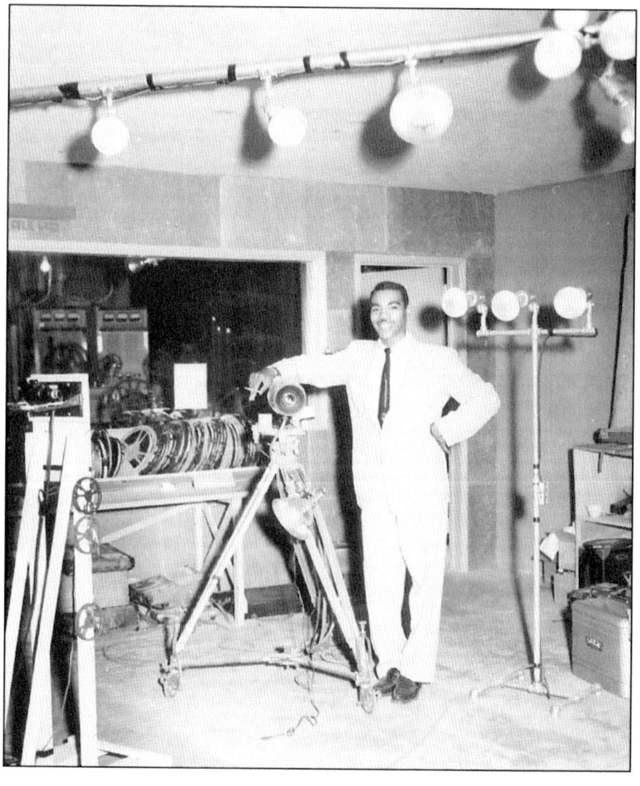

Showman on and off Stage. With his own television show, Bob Bailey broke new ground in Las Vegas as the first black to host a regular television show, *Talk of the Town*. He excelled in his speaking voice and demeanor. (Courtesy Nevada State Museum, Las Vegas.)

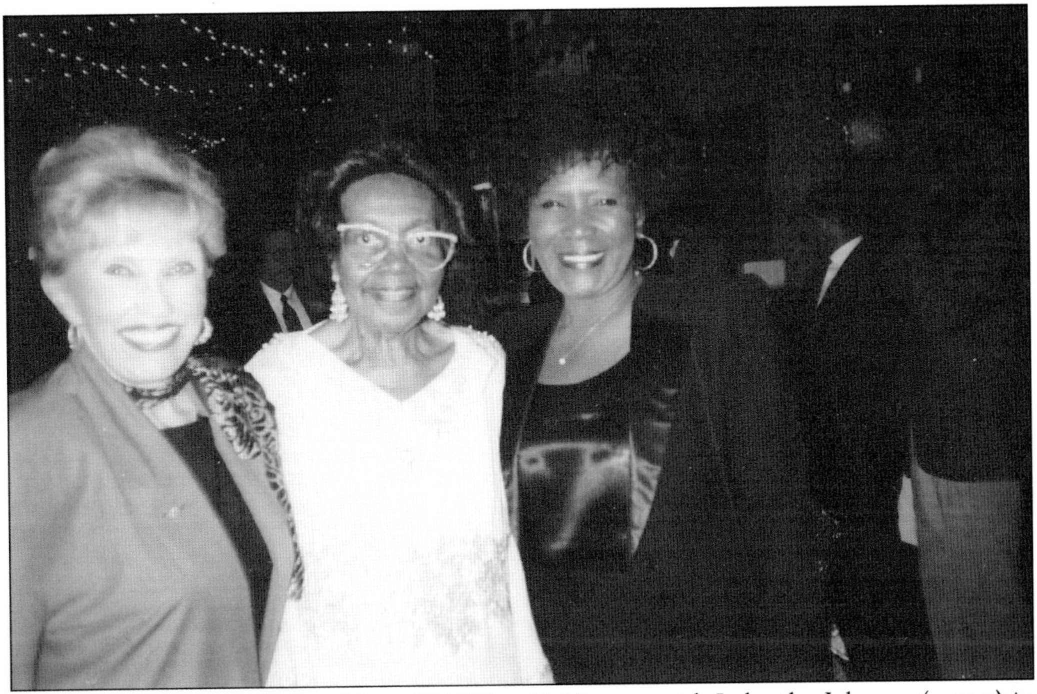

Celebrities Gather. Above, Marie McMillan (left) poses with Lubertha Johnson (center) in a rare later photograph of the civil rights pioneer with Katherine Joseph (right). Joseph, who danced with Josephine Baker in her youth, is a well-known local historian. Below, Dr. James McMillan stands with Marie McMillan, J. David Hoggard, and Lubertha Johnson. Civil rights advocates of today recall people like Lubertha Johnson, who inspired and kept them going. (Both, courtesy of Marie McMillan.)

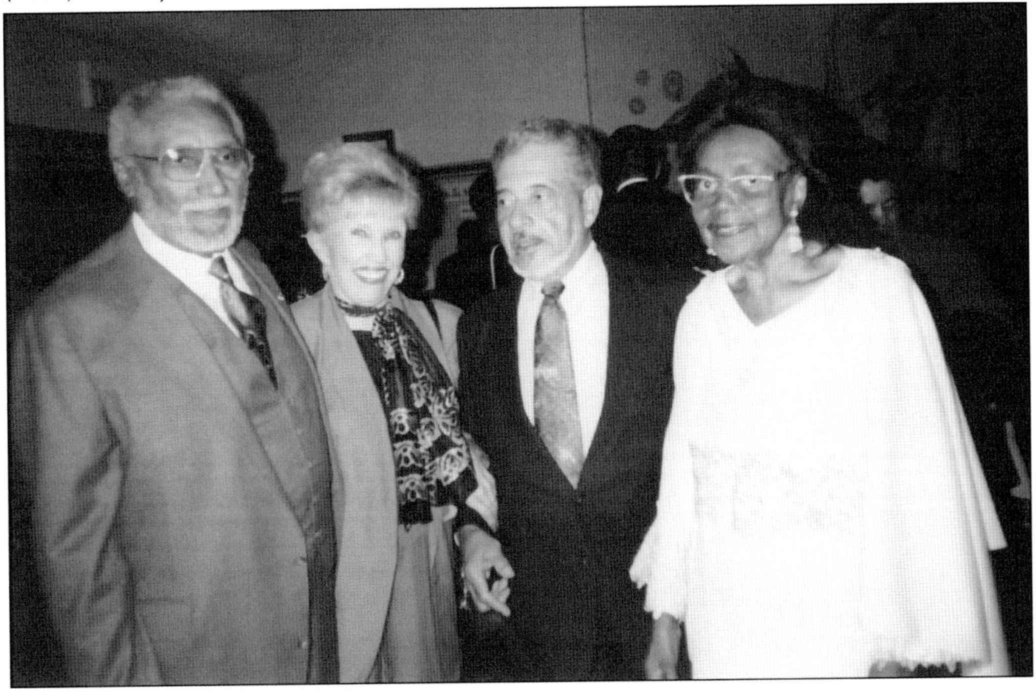

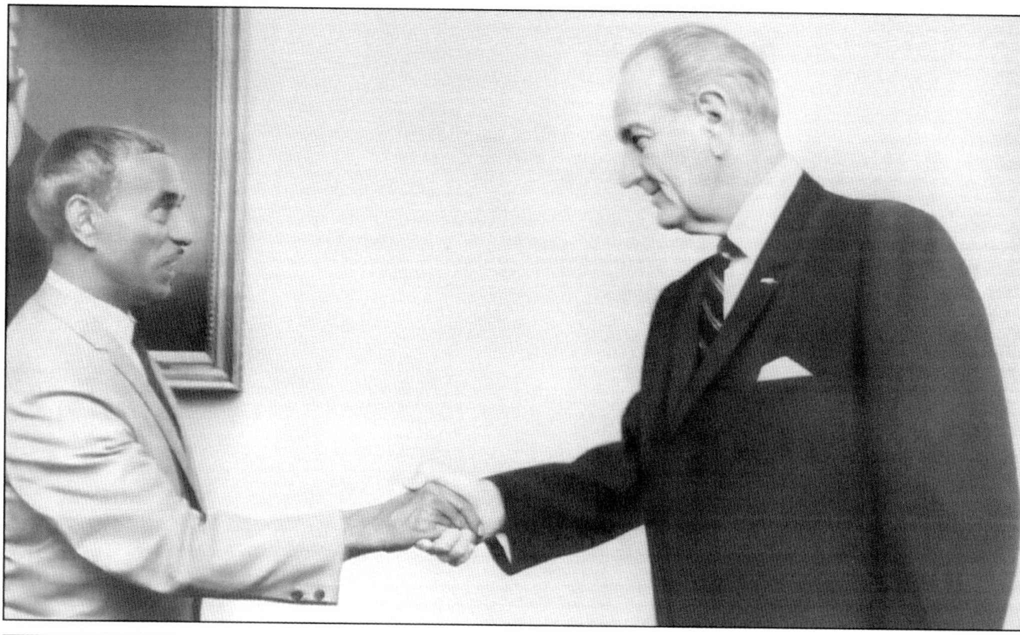

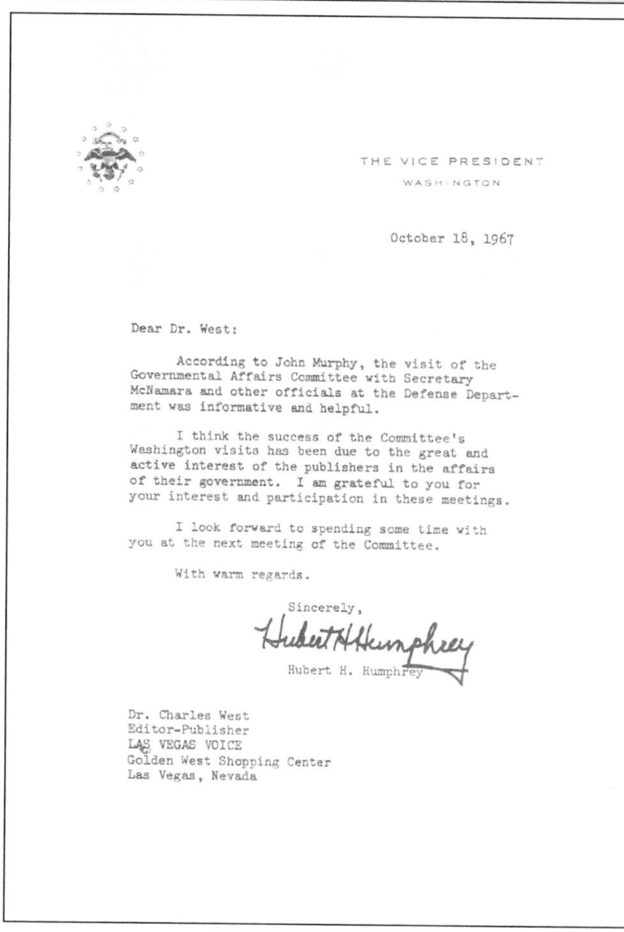

THE VICE PRESIDENT
WASHINGTON

October 18, 1967

Dear Dr. West:

According to John Murphy, the visit of the Governmental Affairs Committee with Secretary McNamara and other officials at the Defense Department was informative and helpful.

I think the success of the Committee's Washington visits has been due to the great and active interest of the publishers in the affairs of their government. I am grateful to you for your interest and participation in these meetings.

I look forward to spending some time with you at the next meeting of the Committee.

With warm regards.

Sincerely,

Hubert H Humphrey

Hubert H. Humphrey

Dr. Charles West
Editor-Publisher
LAS VEGAS VOICE
Golden West Shopping Center
Las Vegas, Nevada

THE ELITE OF THE LEADERS MEETING WITH THE PRESIDENTS. In this famous photograph, Dr. West shakes Pres. Lyndon B. Johnson's hand. Dr. West's correspondence with the White House even extended to other Washington notables who followed Kennedy and Johnson, like Hubert Humphrey, who thanked him in a special letter. (Courtesy West Prep Academy, Las Vegas.)

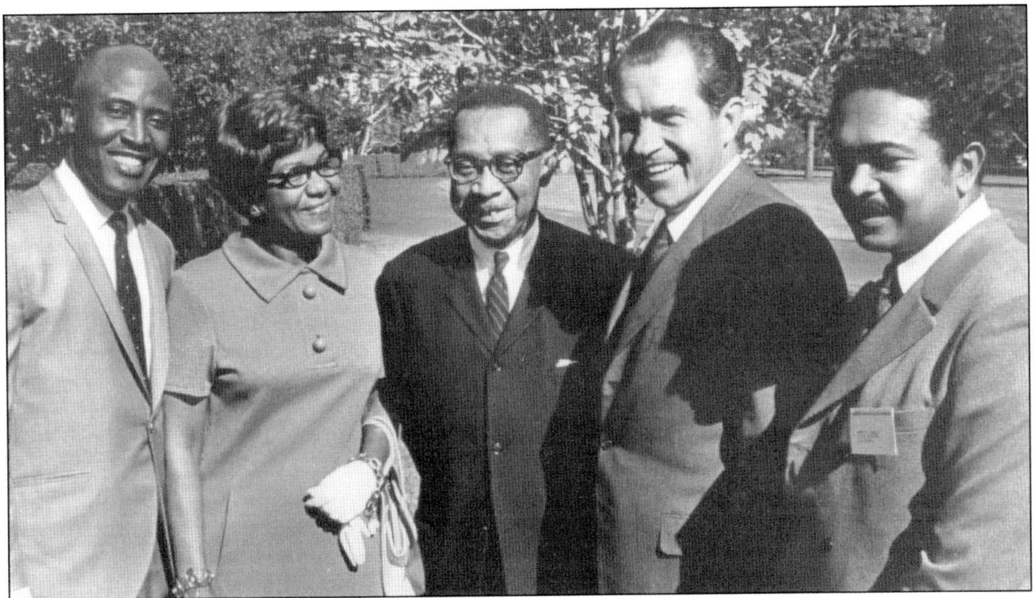

NIXON AND THE WESTSIDE. In the image above, civil rights leader and state legislator Woodrow Wilson (left) enjoys an opportunity to greet Pres. Richard Nixon. Below, Wilson is among several along a greeting line. It seems that the Republicans did not want to be bested in their outreach by the Democrats. Still, there were some strong Republican loyalists among Westside residents. Dr. West began the tradition of reaching out to the highest-ranking leader of America several years earlier.

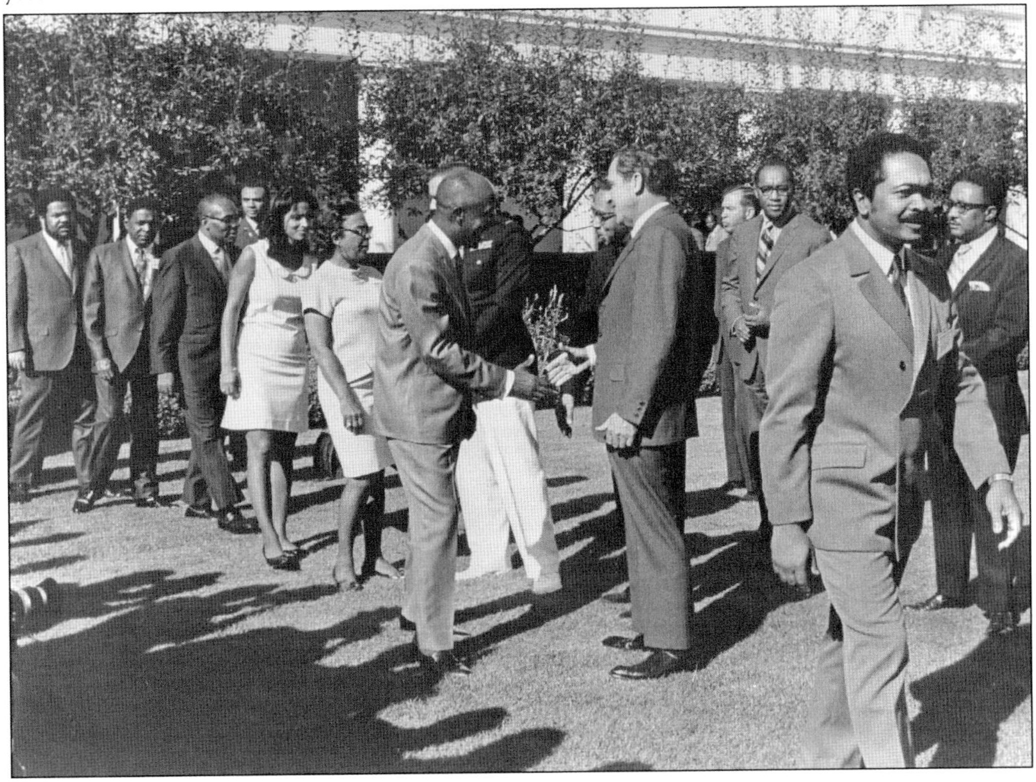

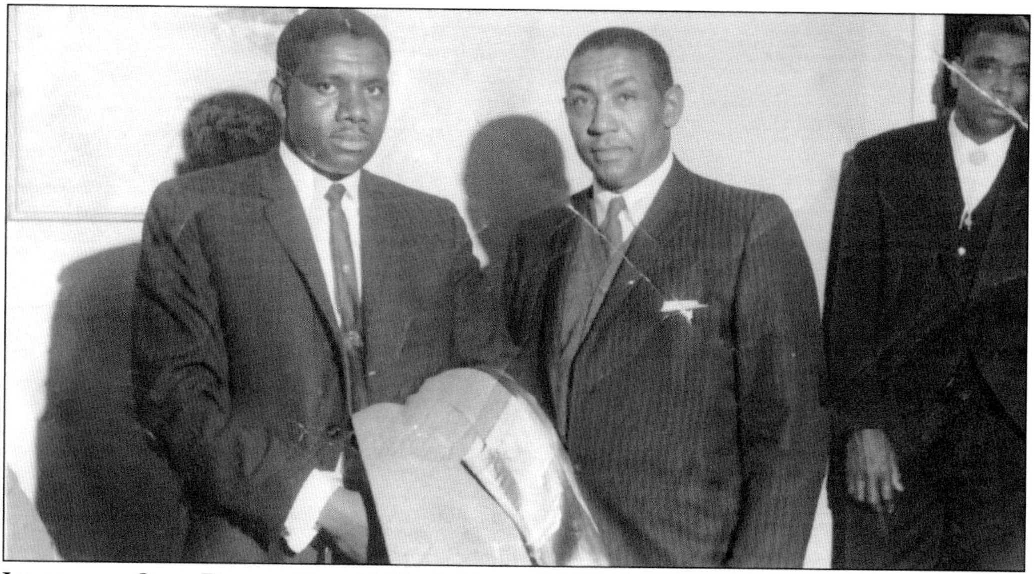

Leaders in Civil Rights. Donald Clark (above, left) came to Las Vegas during a peak period of segregation in 1952 and strove to eliminate racial discrimination for the remainder of his life. He was a major force in forming Operation Independence and the Clark County Community Action Agency, a forerunner to the Equal Opportunity Board. Charles Keller (above, right) was also influential in this area and a familiar face in many enclaves, as was Woodrow Wilson, the state's first black legislator. Below, Keller, Wilson, Clarence Ray, Jim Anderson, and Rev. Willie Davis hold a crucial conversation during a 1957 leadership meeting.

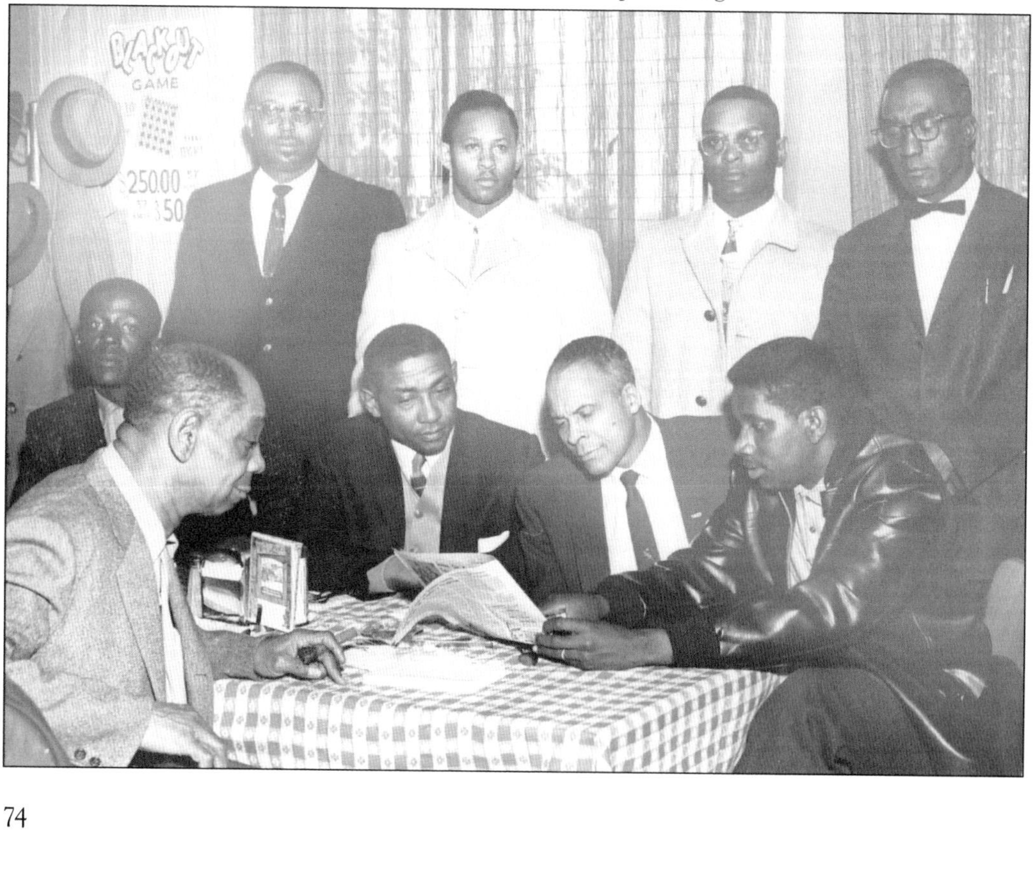

FIRST BLACK DEPUTY CHIEF OF LAS VEGAS METROPOLITAN POLICE. This steadfast person rose from the ranks of patrolman in 1958 to become the first black police sergeant in the department. A Las Vegas native, Larry Bolden raised a family in West Las Vegas, where a police station is named after him. He is remembered for his leadership and groundbreaking role in law enforcement.

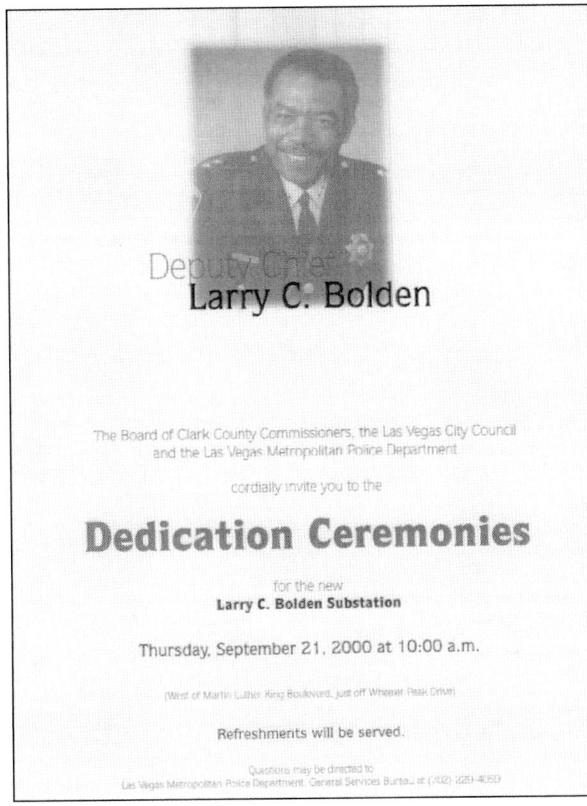
Deputy Chief
Larry C. Bolden

The Board of Clark County Commissioners, the Las Vegas City Council and the Las Vegas Metropolitan Police Department

cordially invite you to the

Dedication Ceremonies

for the new
Larry C. Bolden Substation

Thursday, September 21, 2000 at 10:00 a.m.

(West of Martin Luther King Boulevard, just off Wheeler Peak Drive)

Refreshments will be served.

Questions may be directed to
Las Vegas Metropolitan Police Department, General Services Bureau at (702) [illegible]

FIRST IN FOOD AND HOSPITALITY. Louis A. Conner Sr. was the African American food and beverage director in major casinos. Since 1977, he has owned Seven Seas Restaurant and Lounge in West Las Vegas. He also was instrumental in the Black Chamber of Commerce and other endeavors affecting the community and youth.

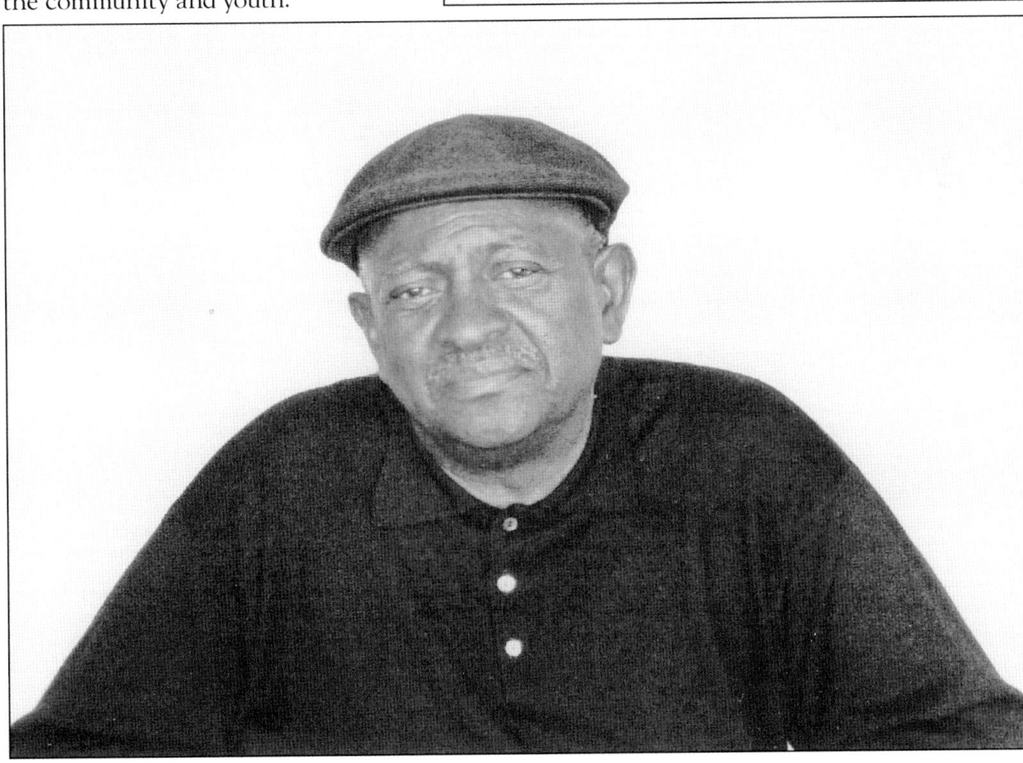

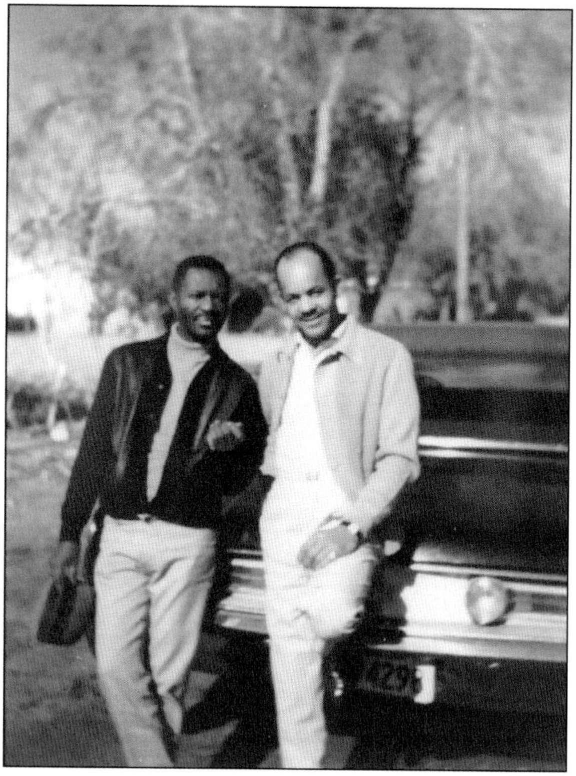

MANY PLAYERS ON THE SCENE. Others played several roles, like Rev. Robert Tolefree (left) and Ernie Marshall (right), editor of a black newspaper, posing informally for the camera at left. Below, a local volunteer poses with the candidate of her choice. It was the perseverance of many who moved the Westside forward. Some of the names have been forgotten, but their deeds will always be remembered.

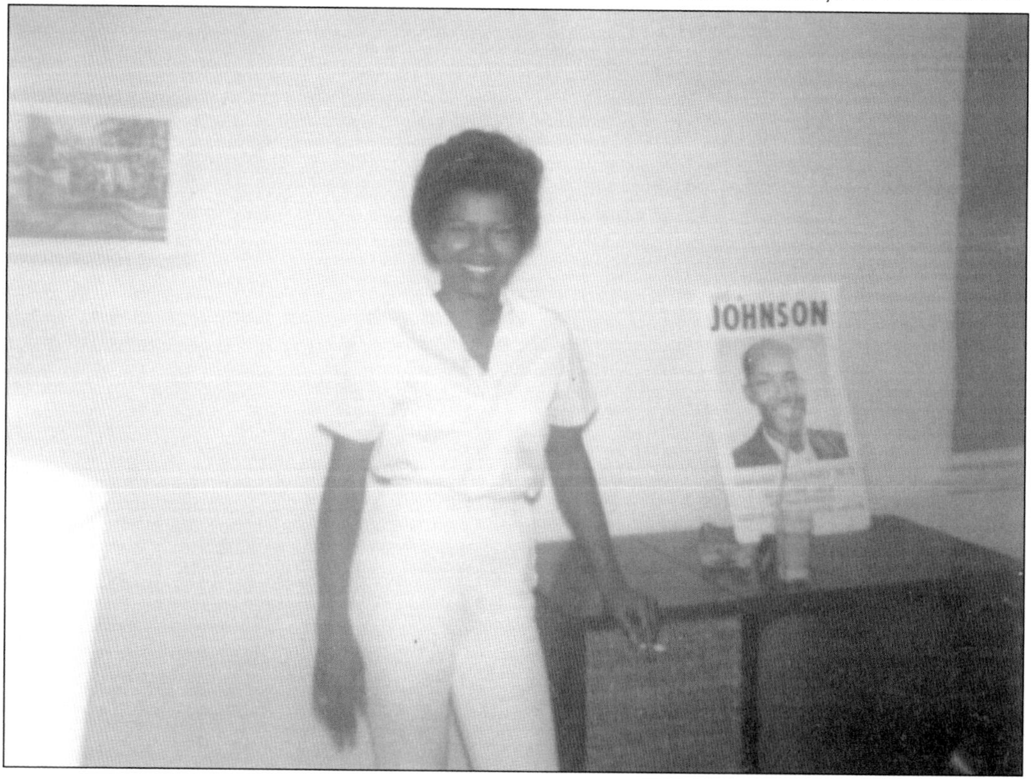

First Fire Chief. David Washington earned the distinction of being the first black fire chief. Persons of color made great inroads in the 1980s, though many were left behind in the glitz of those firsts. Even today, there is an ongoing struggle to ensure equitable education and employment rights.

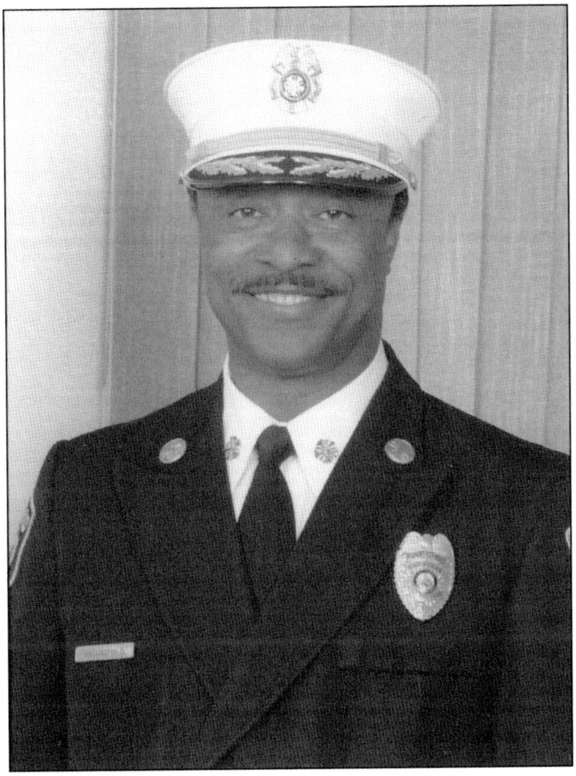

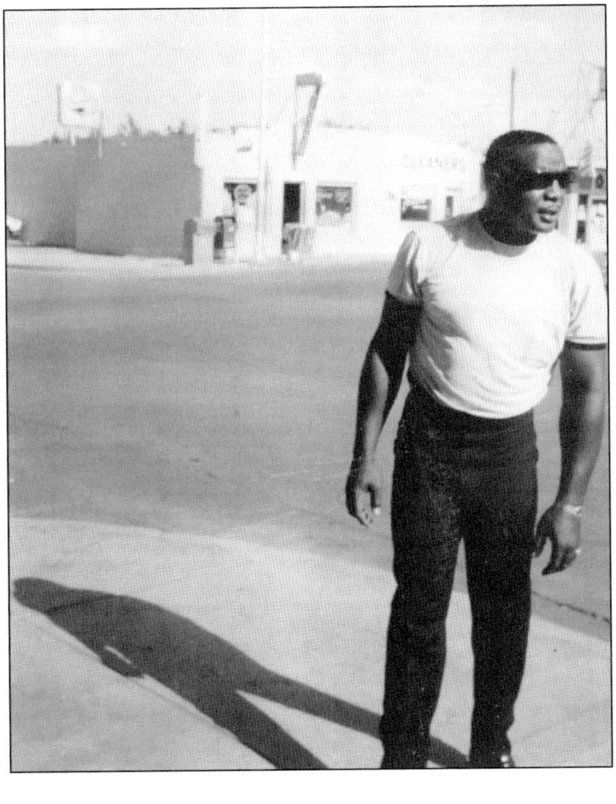

On the Town During the Day. Sonny Liston walks in the Westside, not far from the Town Tavern. Throughout the late 20th century, sports and entertainment celebrities could be spotted at almost any time in many places throughout West Las Vegas. Jackson Street drew many famous people 24 hours a day.

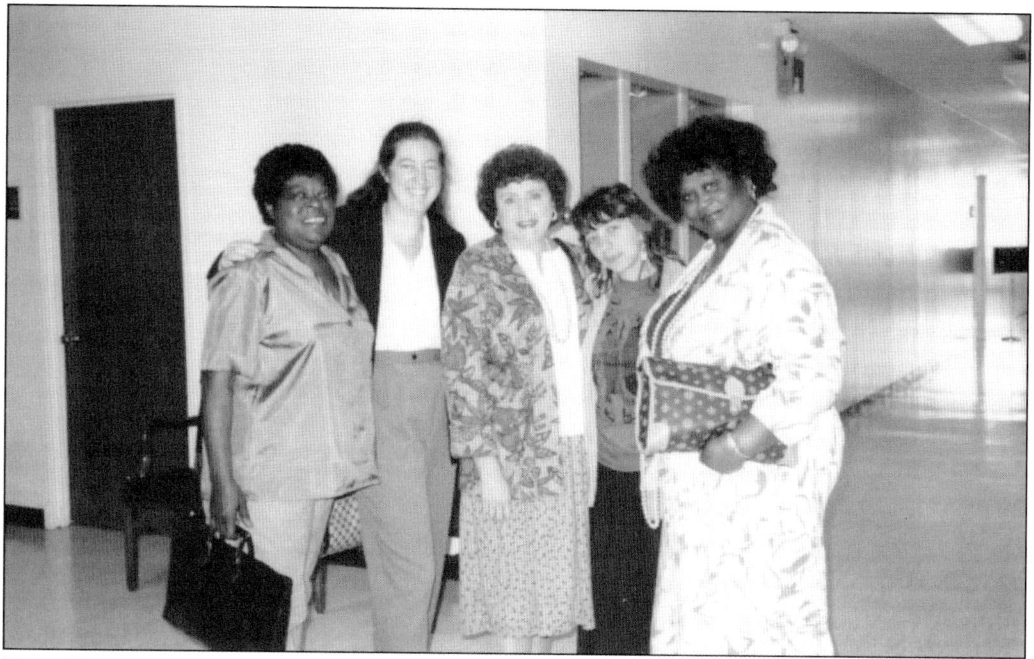

Ruby Duncan, a Gem in Town. From the late 1970s to the present day, Ruby Duncan (right), a self-educated leader for single mothers, has used every resource and contact to encourage self-reliance among welfare moms. Her march on Caesar's Palace was chronicled in a biography that may have misled readers on her salient insistence for sustainable success beyond dependence on government assistance. A woman with a big heart, Ruby enjoyed sharing holiday fare and cheer with other women (below), often unsung heroes of that era. Many Westside leaders would readily admit that it took everyone to succeed in anything. (Both, courtesy West Las Vegas Library.)

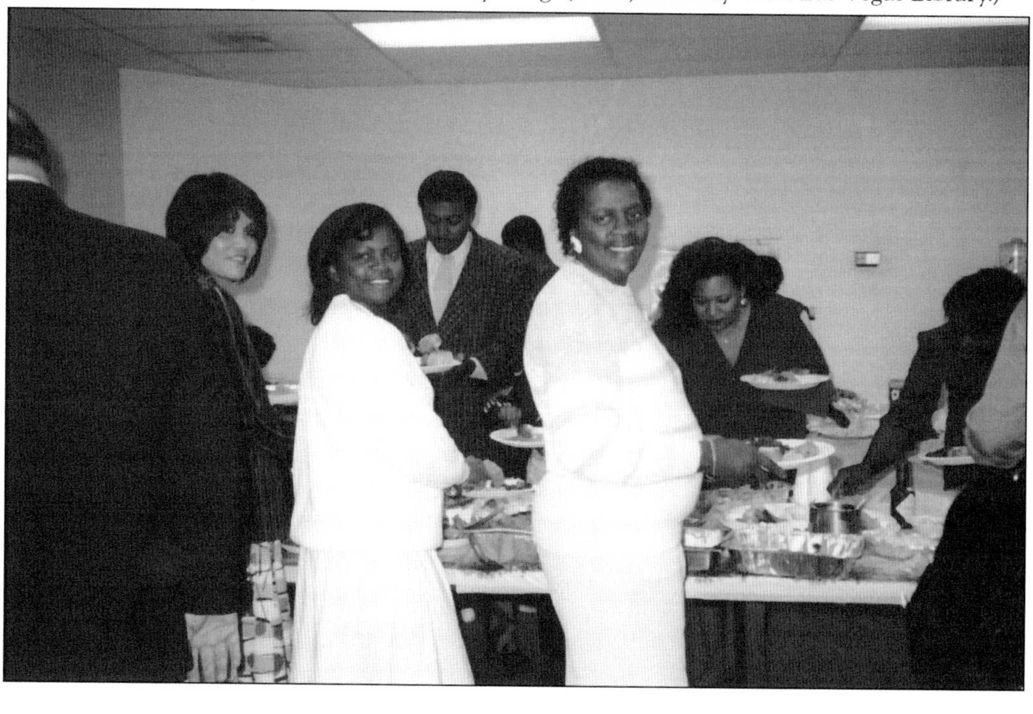

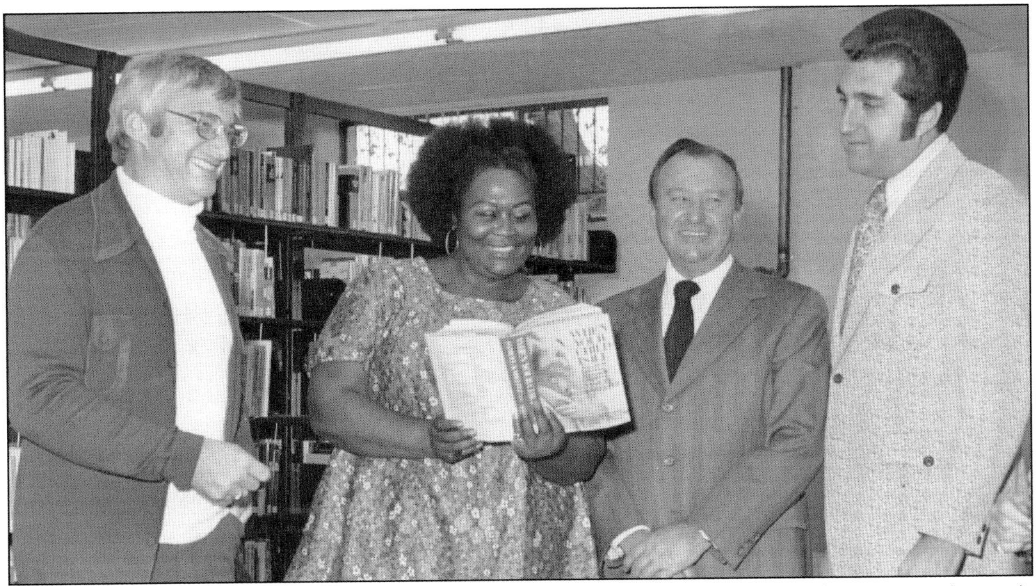

The Opening of the West Las Vegas Library. Sen. Jim Santini (left), Ruby Duncan (center), and Mayor Ron Lurie (right) helped dedicate the complex on Lake Mead Boulevard near J Street in 1989. A theater and performing arts center have been the site of historic meetings, entertainment, displays, and presentations. (Courtesy West Las Vegas Library.)

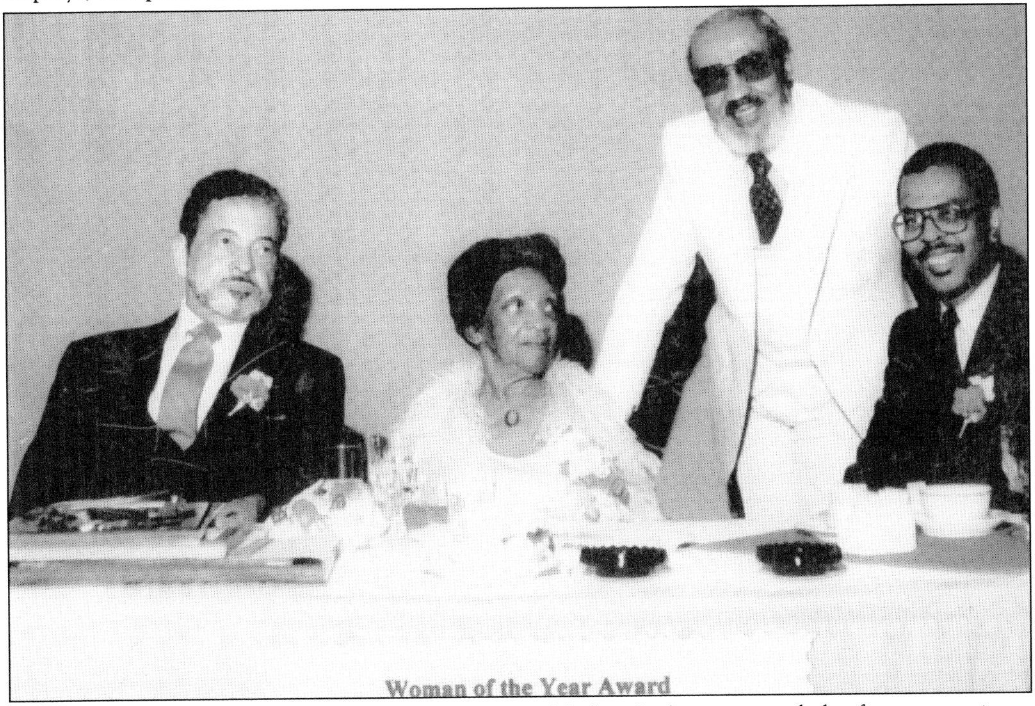

Woman of the Year. Mabel Hoggard, the grand lady of education and the first to receive a teaching contract in Clark County, Nevada, is feted by well-known peers, including her husband, David Hoggard (left), and Dr. Paul Meachum (right). Mabel Hoggard was known as a selfless servant in advancing educational opportunities on the Westside. (Courtesy Mabel Hoggard Elementary School, Las Vegas.)

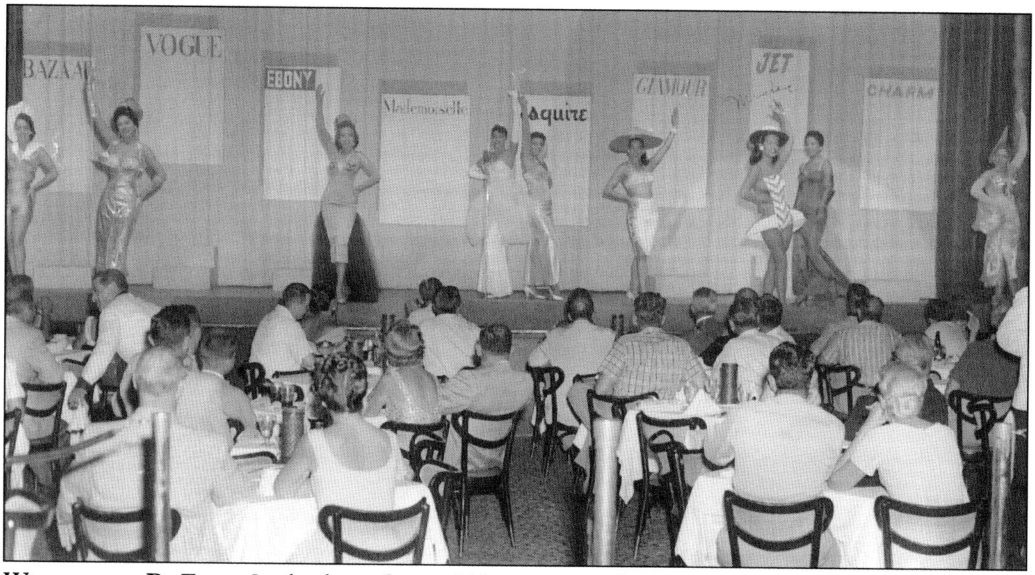

WORKING TO BE FIRST. In the face of incredible injustice, the community came together to better its environment and let the world know of its accomplishments. Even at a time when they could not sit in the Dunes audience, the celebrated African Americans of the Westside proudly paraded their accomplishments in various white and black media. Here, many leading ladies pose beside national publications that featured them. Below, a newspaper touts the persistence of community leaders to fight area blight. Sadly, many such stories were lost in a fire that destroyed many *Review Journal* photographs in the early 1960s. (Both, courtesy Jarmilla McMillan Arnold.)

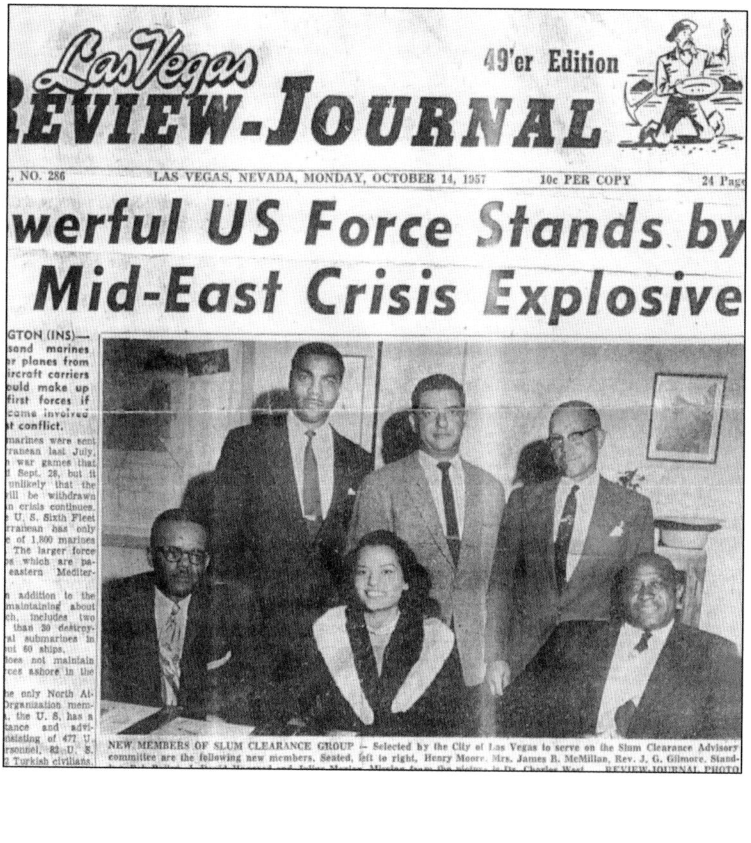

Las Vegas
REVIEW-JOURNAL
49'er Edition

, NO. 286 LAS VEGAS, NEVADA, MONDAY, OCTOBER 14, 1957 10c PER COPY 24 Page

werful US Force Stands by
Mid-East Crisis Explosive

GTON (INS)—
sand marines
r planes from
ircraft carriers
ould make up
first forces if
came involved
t conflict.
marines were sent
ranean last July,
n war games that
l Sept. 28, but it
unlikely that the
ill be withdrawn
n crisis continues.
U. S. Sixth Fleet
rranean has only
e of 1,800 marines
The larger force
s which are pa-
eastern Mediter-

n addition to the
maintaining about
ch, includes two
than 30 destroy-
al submarines in
ut 60 ships.
loes not maintain
rces ashore in the

he only North At-
Organization mem-
, the U. S. has a
tance and advi-
nsisting of 477 U.
rsonnel, 82 U. S.
2 Turkish civilians.

NEW MEMBERS OF SLUM CLEARANCE GROUP — Selected by the City of Las Vegas to serve on the Slum Clearance Advisory committee are the following new members. Seated, left to right, Henry Moore, Mrs. James B. McMillan, Rev. J. G. Gilmore. Stand-

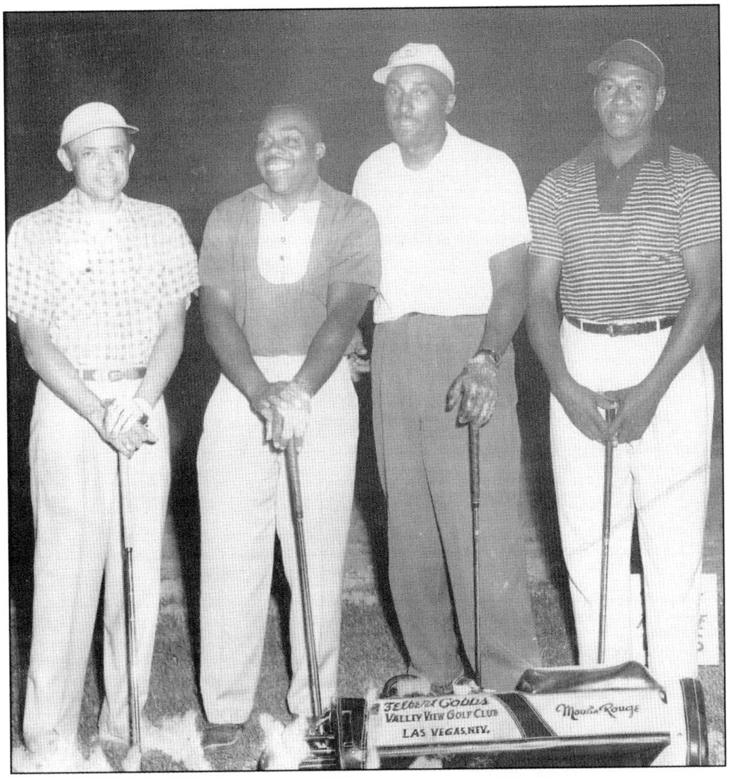

Fun for Everyone. Among the accomplishments of the leaders was the first black golf club, the Valley View Gold Club. From left to right, Oscar Crozier, mediator in the 1960 desegregation announcement; Jimmie Gay, Nevada's first black mortician; Dr. James McMillan; and Mr. Roberts pose for the camera. Business may have been discussed while swinging, but the main objective was to find a good diversion for pent-up energy. Note the Moulin Rouge golf bag, a symbol of prestige and useful advertising. (Courtesy Jarmilla McMillan Arnold.)

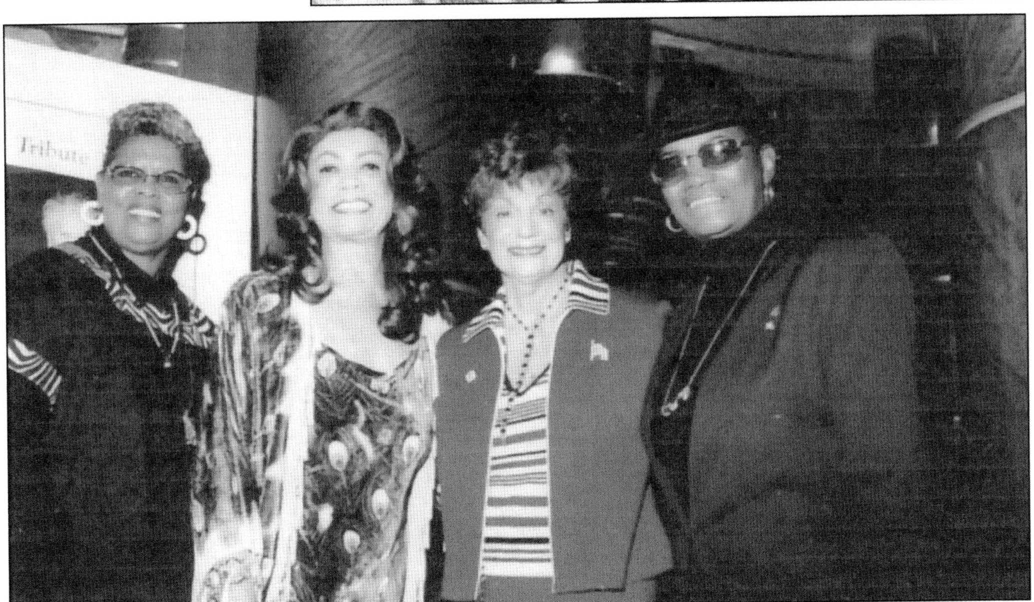

Back to the Future. Regardless of the decade, Washingtonians have traditionally sought a place on the Westside. However, in the present age, women have come to the forefront. Above are, from left to right, Kopoe Brown; Dee Dee Jasmin of Moulin Rouge and screen fame; Congresswoman Shelley Berkley; and Erma Jai Walker, founder and chief executive officer of What About Us?, with tutorial programs focusing on school readiness and preventing drop outs. (Courtesy Erma Jai Walker.)

ACTIVE PALLBEARERS:

DON KING	BRIG. GEN. HARRY WALD
ABE MARGOLIES	MUHAMMAD ALI
FRANK SINATRA	LARRY HOLMES
BEN ROGERS	WILLIAM L. WEINBERGER SR.

HONORARY PALLBEARERS

PENTAGON or MILITARY REPRESENTATIVE	MAYOR TOM BRADLEY
BOB HOPE	FREDDIE SOMMERS
KEN NORTON	AL PATTON
BILLY CONN	WELTON BARNETT
JERSEY JOE WALCOTT	FREDDIE GINYARD
LEONARD REED	BRAD PYE
FLOYD PATTERSON	RAY PLUTO
SUGAR RAY ROBINSON	KEITH KLEVIN
MERELE WOOD	ERNIE BIEN
JOEY CURTIS	WILLIAM WARREN
ASH RESNICK	COL. EDWARD BROWN
HANK GREENSPUN	NICK KIRBAWAY
JACK DEMPSEY	JIM MURRAY
GENE TUNNEY	TOM DISKIN
BILLY ROWE	JIMMIE GAY
CHESTER WASHINGTON	FREDDIE WILSON
LOU NOVA	ED KOCH
IRVING ALFASSO	PAT ARNOLD
MARSHALL MILES	JOHN JOHNSON
MAX SCHMELING	BERRY GORDY
FRANK BANNISTER	JUNIUS GRIFFIN

INTERMENT

ARLINGTON NATIONAL CEMETERY
ARLINGTON, VIRGINIA

THE PALM MORTUARY
LAS VEGAS, NEVADA

Memorial Services
for

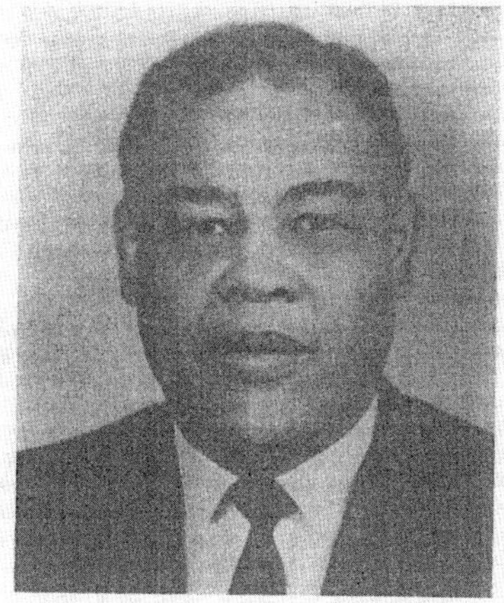

Joe Louis
(Barrow)

May 13, 1914 —*April* 12, 1981

SPORTS PAVILLION

3570 Las Vegas Boulevard South

Las Vegas, Nevada

DR. JESSE JACKSON
Officiant

THE END OF AN ERA. Joe Louis's funeral brought out the Westside. The former heavyweight champion and Moulin Rouge host was much loved in the community. Note the mix of high-level officials and celebrities, along with well-known figures in Las Vegas, including Jimmie Gay as an honorary pallbearer. Jimmie Gay became the first black named to a state office in 1959 when Gov. Grant Sawyer appointed him to the Athletic Commission. (Courtesy Erma Jai Walker.)

Four

Jackson Street Celebrating with Neighbors in the Happening Place

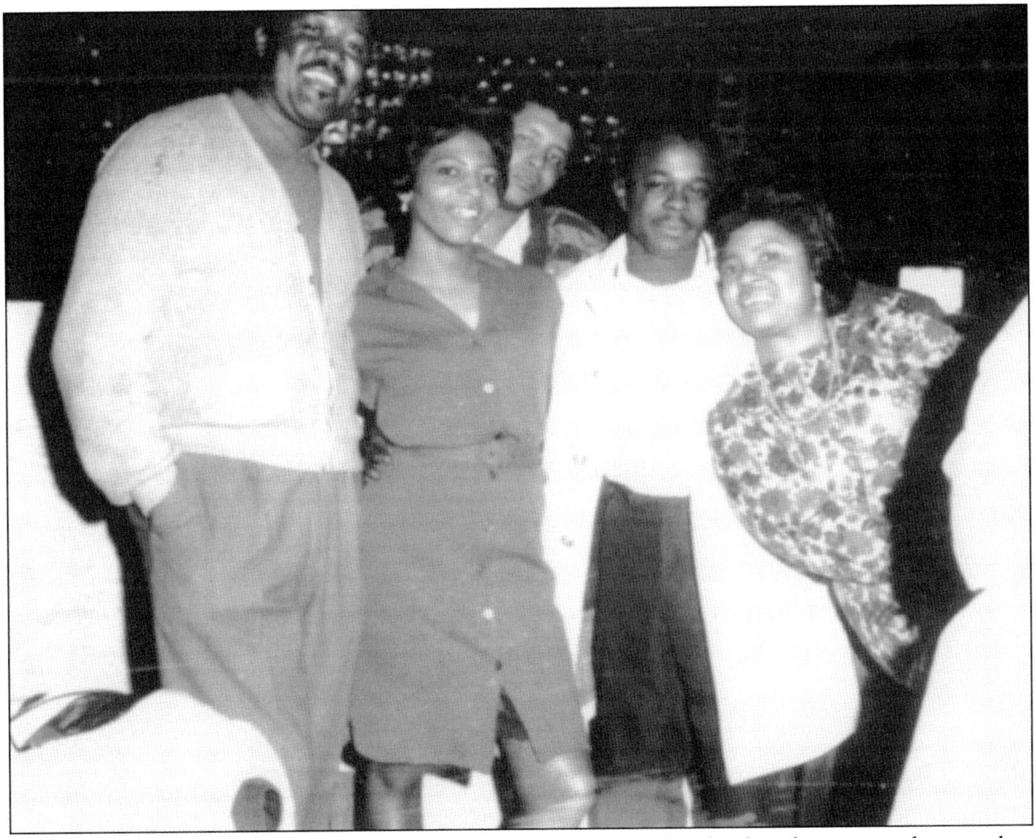

Family Fun on the Town. Edna Mae Williams, right, joins her husband, sister, and son-in-law in a night on the town. Jackson Street was the place to be, and according to Edna, who loved to celebrate with family and friends after many 70-hour work weeks, the Westside was never the same after integration. Members of Edna's family included an uncle who was the first black foreman at the atomic testing site. (Courtesy Edna Mae Williams.)

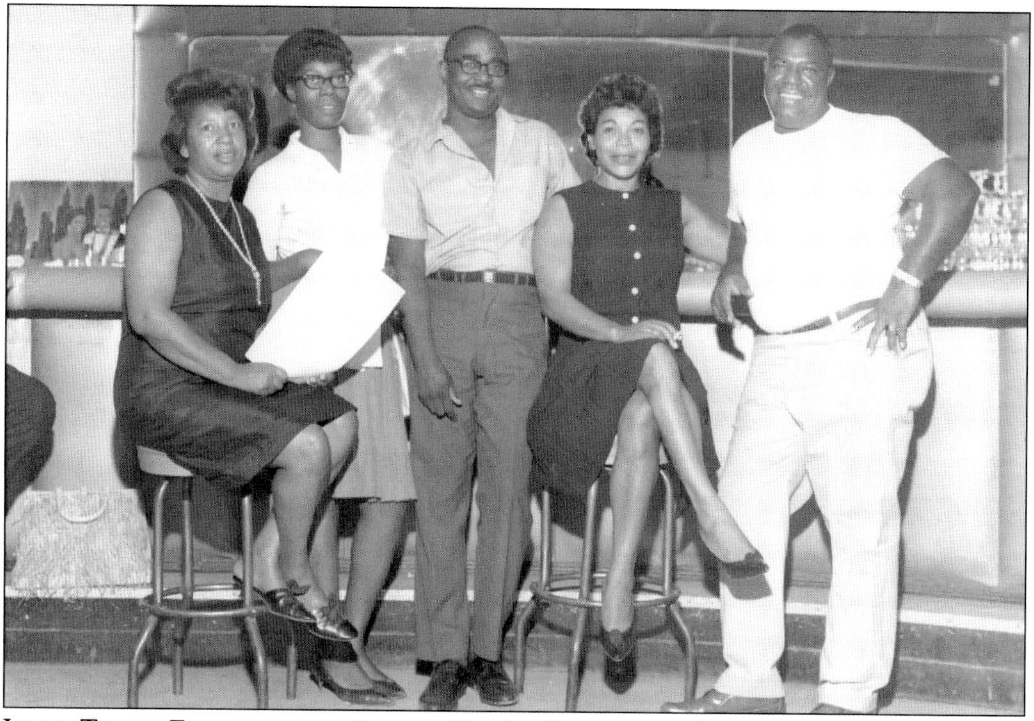

LOCAL TALENT ENTERTAINS THE LOCALS. Despite the presence of megastars, Westside residents truly enjoyed musicians, dancers, and performers and encouraged the local talent. In turn, whether they were a huge draw or a moonlighter in one of the showrooms, entertainers relished playing to the crowds. Through time, some on both sides of the stage have been lost to memory, but their spirits carry forth.

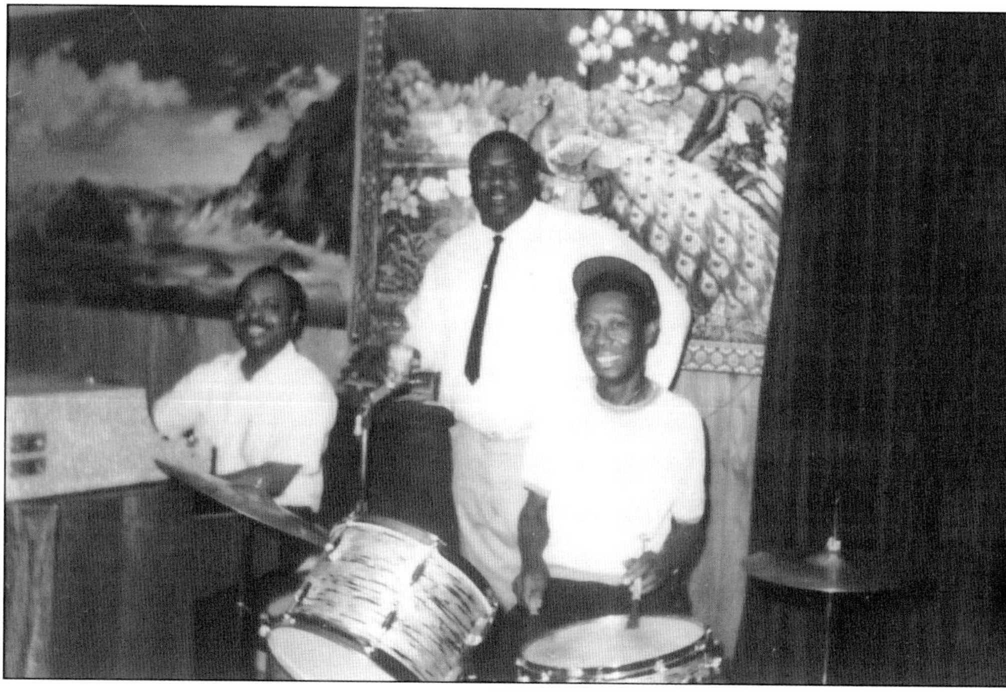

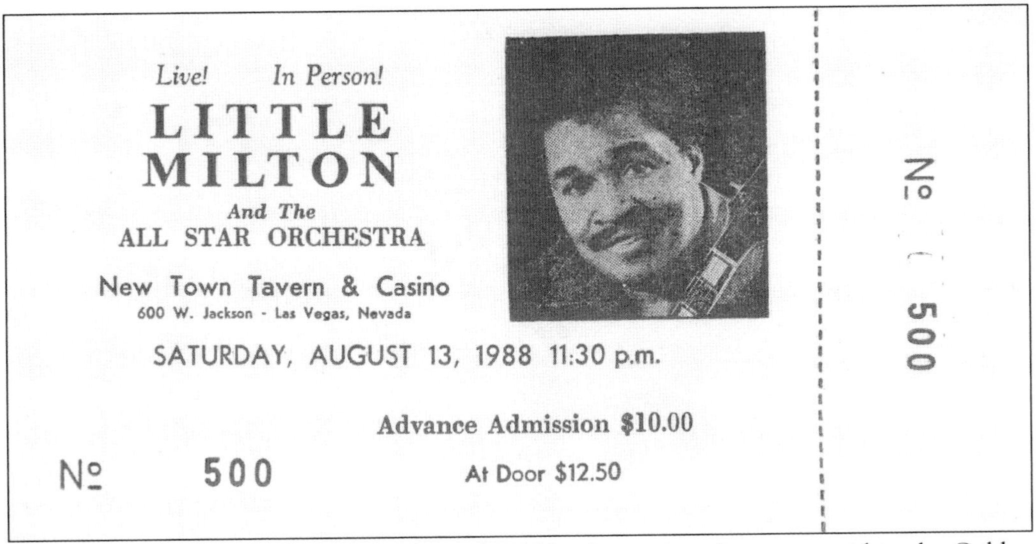

The Town Tavern. Established in the early 1950s, this casino-showroom within the Golden Café restaurant attracted many stars even before the Moulin Rouge. Diverse personalities like Ed Sullivan and Louis Armstrong would drop in. The Starlight Showroom hopped to the beat of such legends as the Milton Brothers, the Ink Spots, and many others. Above is an old ticket for the Little Milton show. Below captures a rare quiet moment, as people were usually shoulder-to-shoulder in the Town Tavern, while the Starlite Room was filled to capacity during its heyday. Many older residents of the Westside boast that Jackson Street establishments were integrated before the Moulin Rouge.

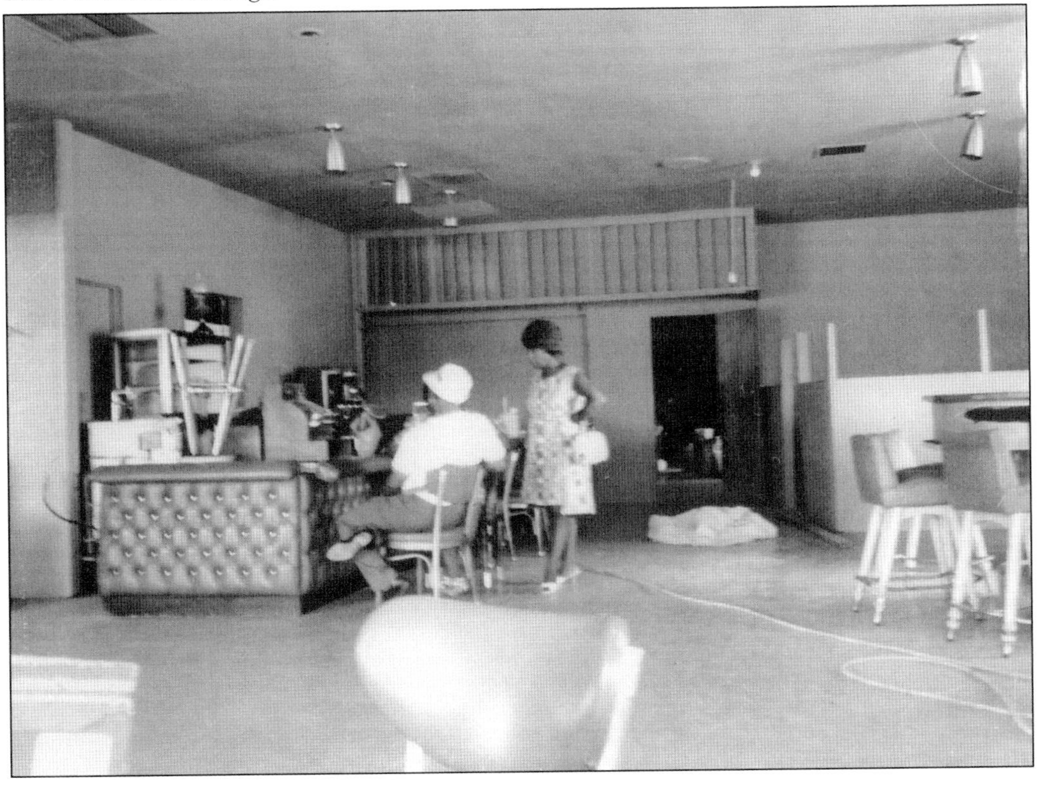

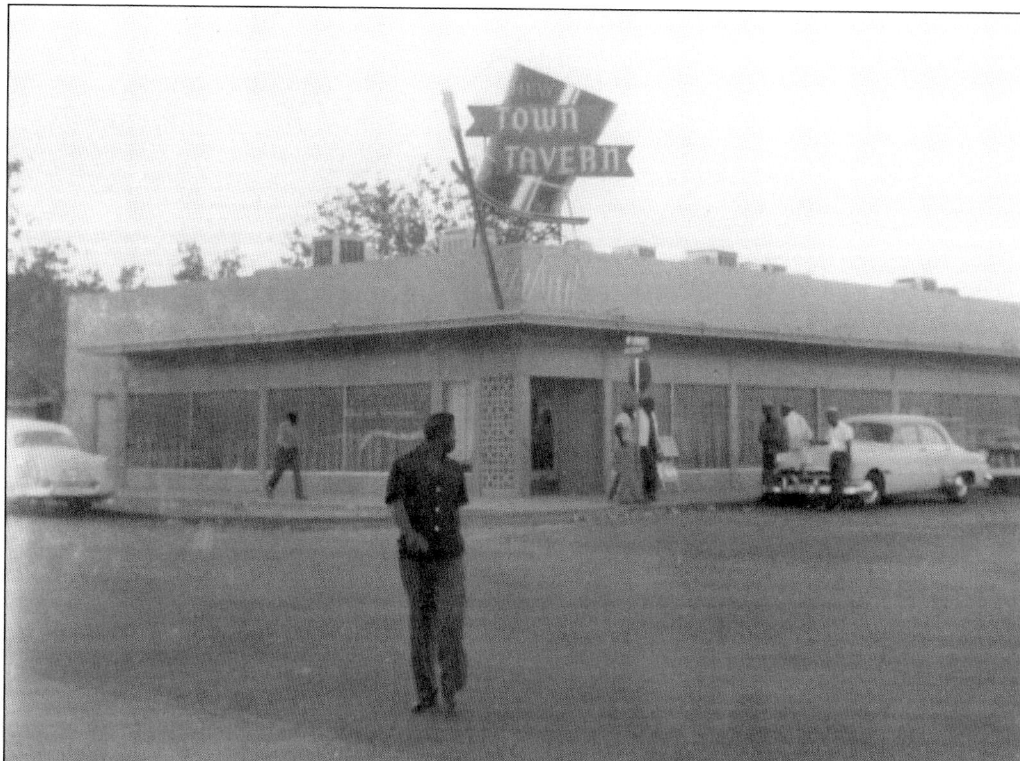

TOP HAT AND TOP ATTRACTION. The New Town Tavern, which once boasted a top hat and top acts through the 1990s, is the last standing casino on Jackson Street but was recently closed for major repairs. Below, note the quirky Louisiana Club chip that depicts a pelican. To the right is a $5 Town Tavern chip. (Below, courtesy James Paganilia.)

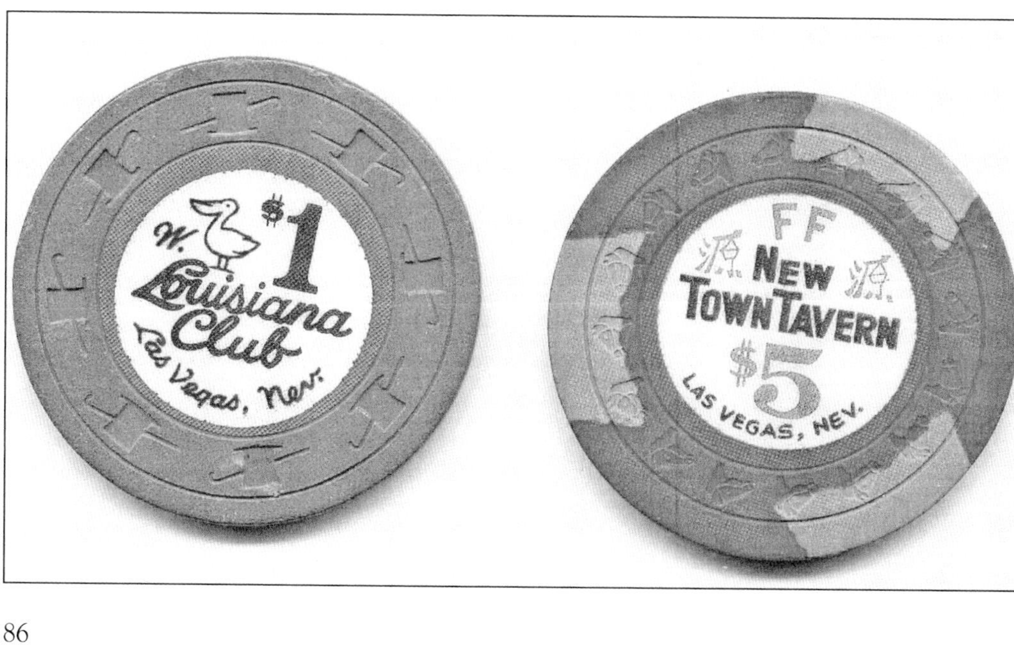

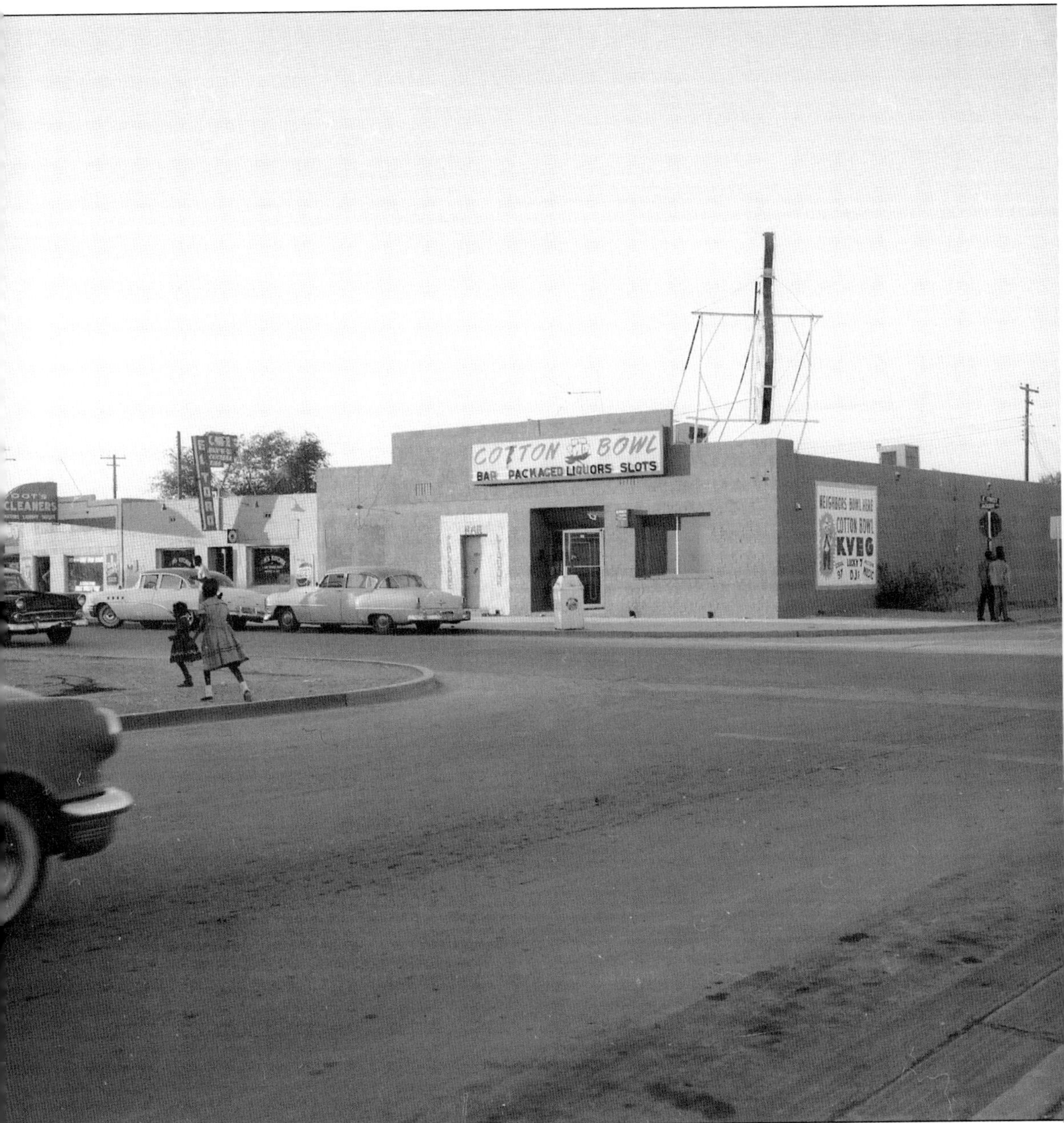

COTTON CLUB BOWL. This popular site was nestled next to Dot's Cleaners and the popular Mom's Kitchen. Although some say the club was named after its famous predecessor in Harlem, it was not considered fancy. Most Westside clubs were little more than oversized rooms with slots, craps tables, a dancing floor, and maybe a stage or jukebox. Still, personalities like Sammy Davis Jr. would take over the dice and provide everyone with lifelong memories. Louis Armstrong was known to drop by and entertain guests with his horn until 4:00 a.m. (Courtesy Nevada State Museum, Las Vegas.)

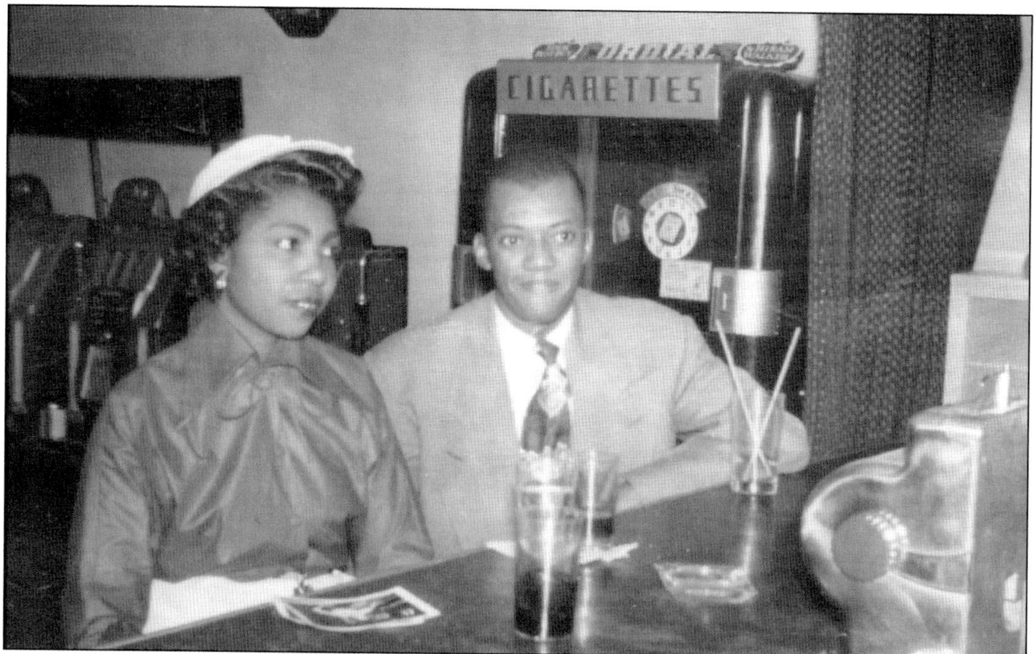

DRESSED UP WITH PLACES TO GO. A Saturday night at the Cotton Club or another fun spot always meant fine attire. Edna Mae Williams claims to still have boxes of gloves to match her evening dresses and remains aghast at the way people dress for evening outings. In the photograph above, she sits with a friend at the Cotton Club bar. Note the old-style cigarette machine in the background. Below, she and a couple of friends, recalled only as Baby and Christ, enjoy a night on the town. Partiers frequently mingled in couples and groups. (Both, courtesy Edna Mae Williams.)

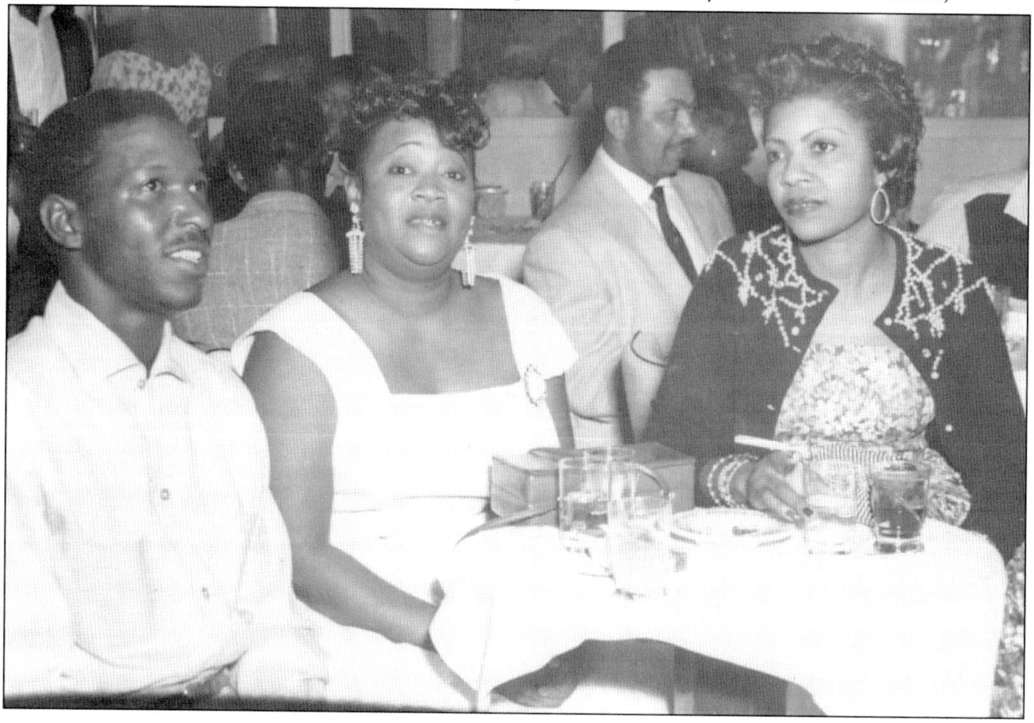

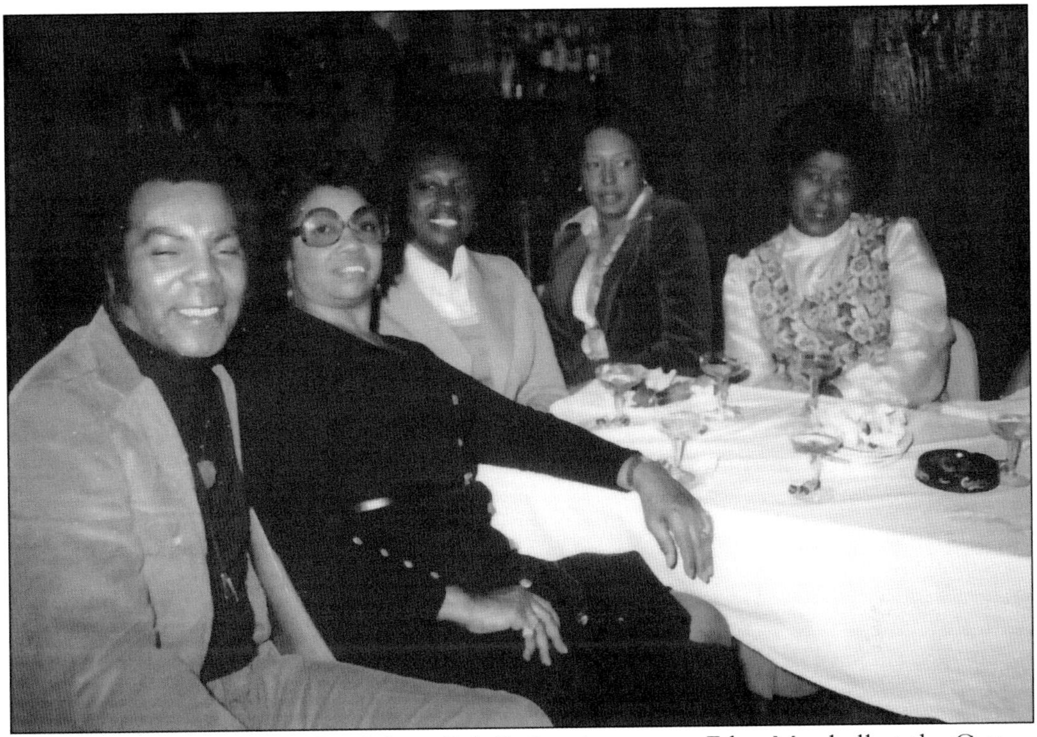

Never Know Who You Will Meet. Bob Bailey sits next to Edna Marshall at the Cotton Club. Jackson Street hopped during the 1950s, and personalities like Bob Bailey were often on the scene with many local revelers. Though the Moulin Rouge would be designated as the first interracial casino-hotel, as seen in the image below, Jackson Street was always open to whites. Above, a trio of unidentified night clubbers enjoys the Cotton Club's fare. (Both, courtesy Edna Mae Williams.)

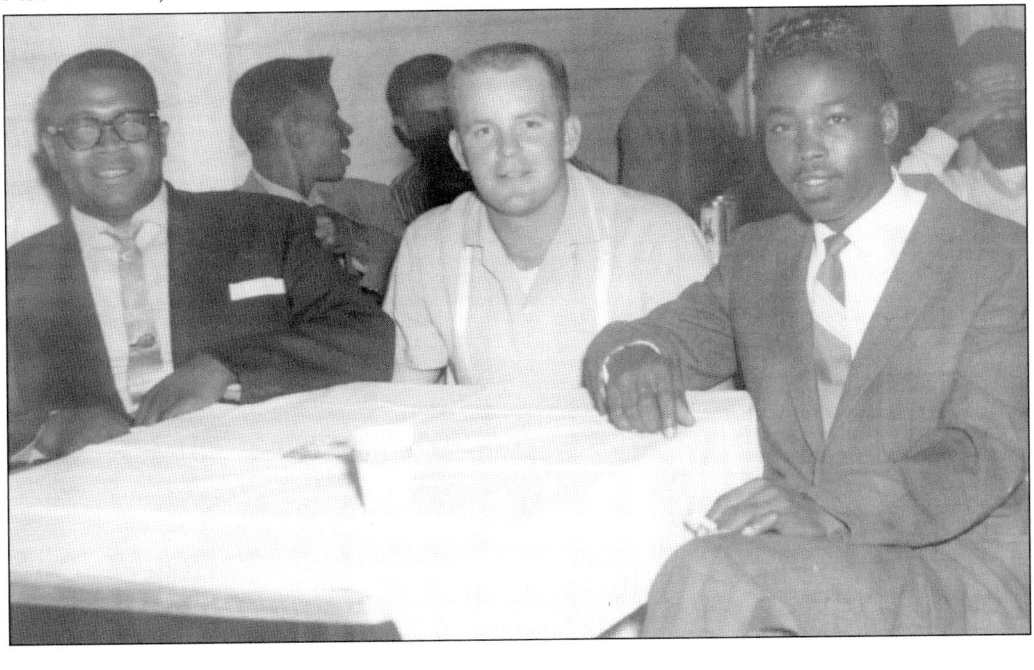

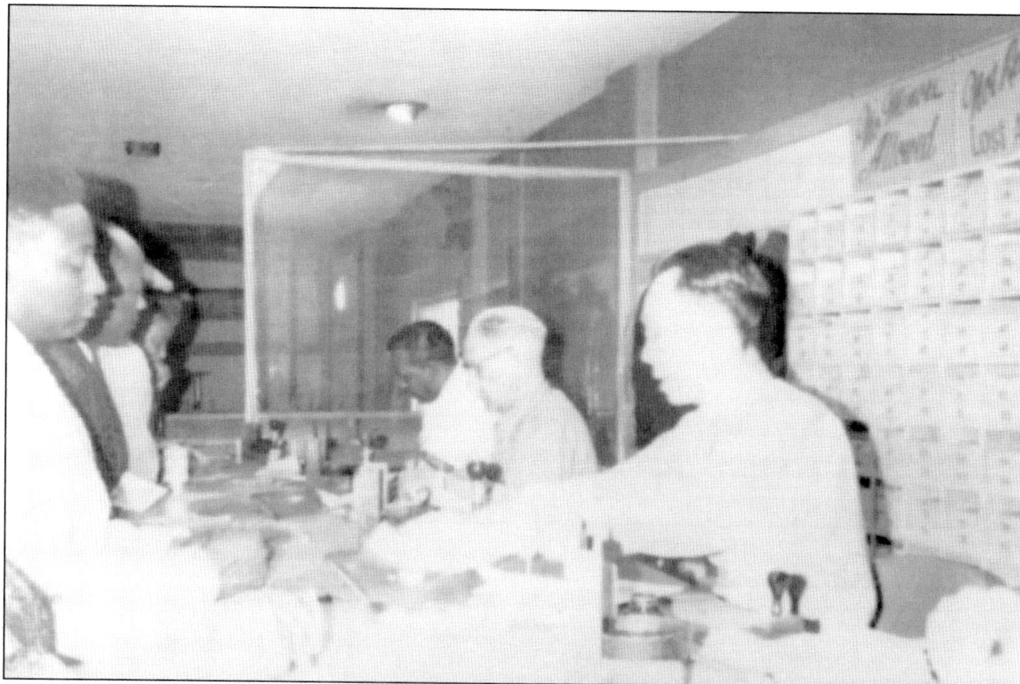

Celebrating Special Occasions. Frequently, clubs like the El Rio offered a great environment to celebrate all types of events, including birthdays. Today, many veteran Westsiders lament the fact that desegregation broke up the harmony and buzz of lively business there.

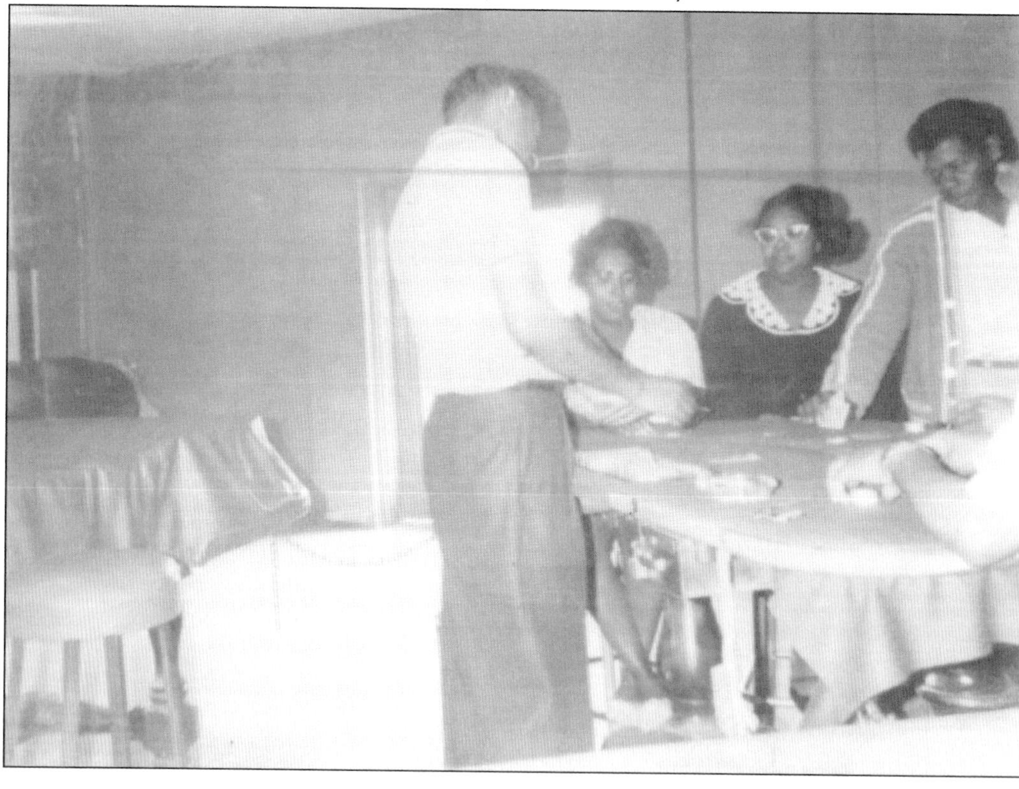

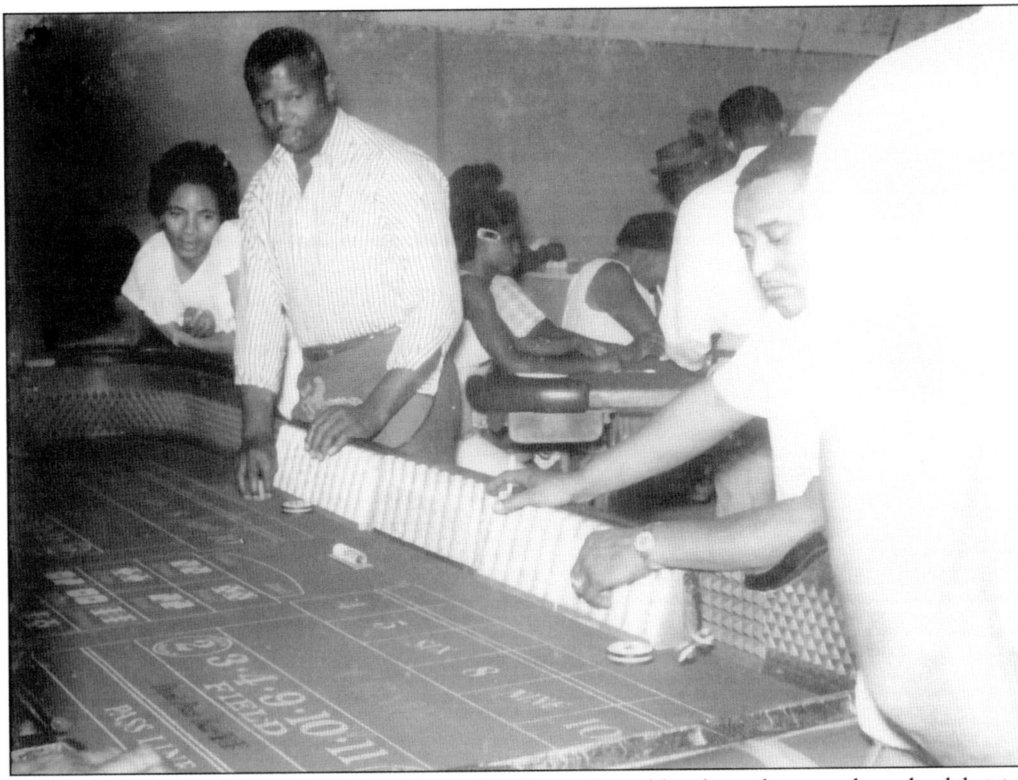

At the Tables. Whether at the El Rio or elsewhere, the tables drew the crowds and celebrities. Former Cab Calloway dancer Roxie Young remembers watching the great Nat King Cole roll craps "across the railroad tracks" and other fun-filled nights in the Westside.

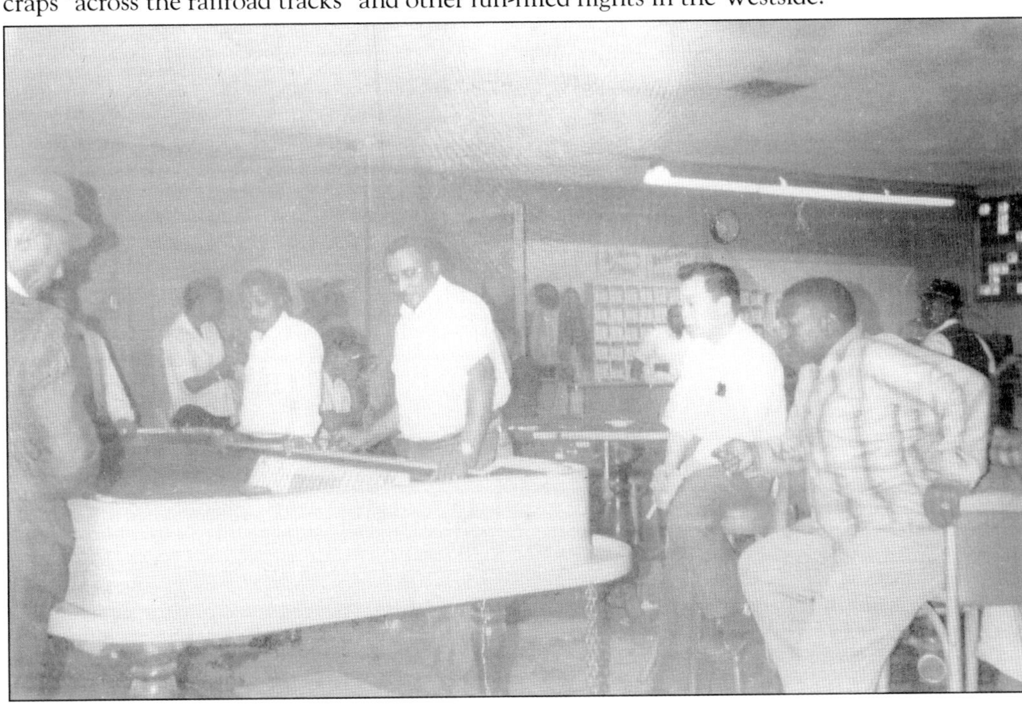

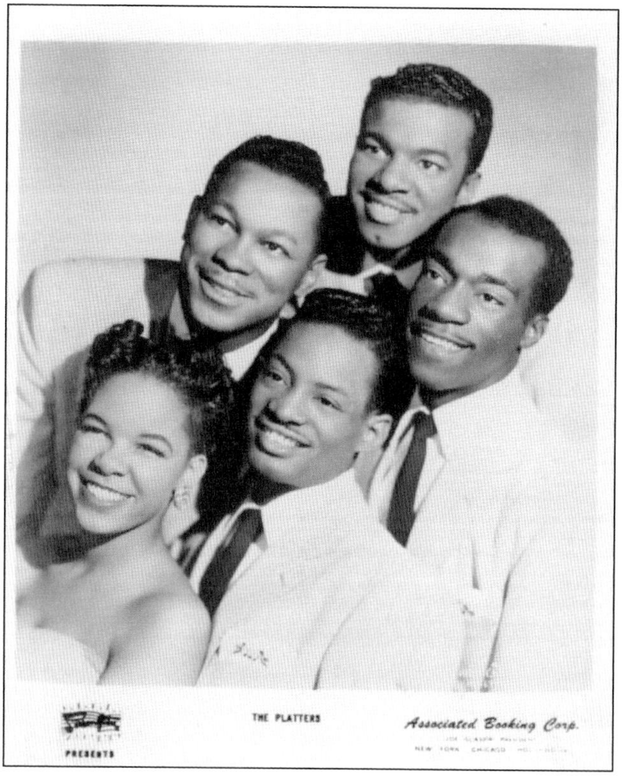

The Platters Making Great Music. The Platters could be heard at many spots other than the Moulin Rouge during the 1950s. Many residents love to recall the time they sat with group members and how the musical greats loved to be in with the crowds. Other popular groups included the Four Tunes and the Mills Brothers. (Both, courtesy Edna Mae Williams.)

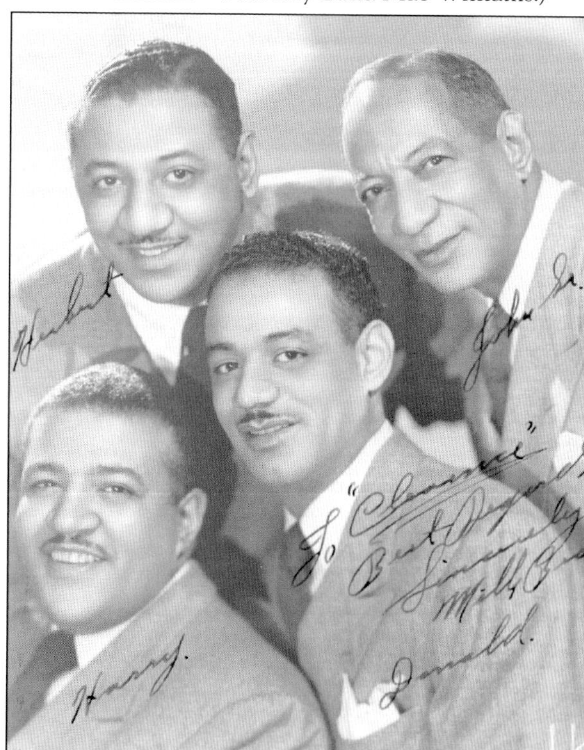

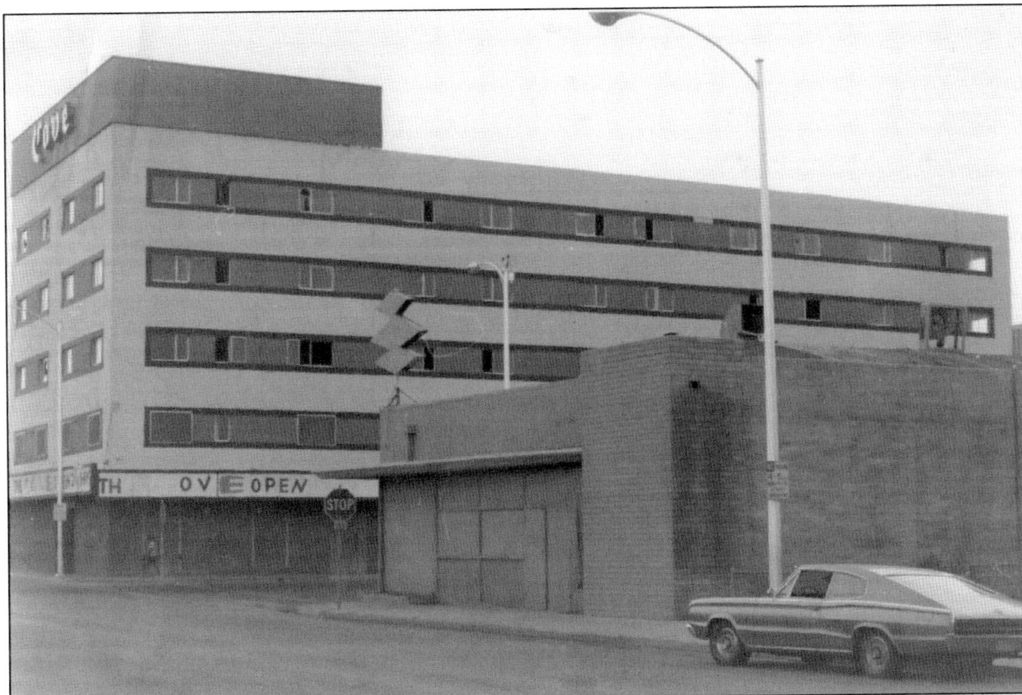

The Cove and Carver House Exteriors. Today, it is difficult to believe that Jackson Street boasted this multistory hotel, first operated as the Carver Hotel. However, due to increased crime including drug trafficking, the mostly vacated building was deemed a safety hazard, even after some, like Ruby Duncan, moved to convert it to a resource center. Though demolished, the memories linger for those who want to rebuild the legend in a proposed multiblock complex.

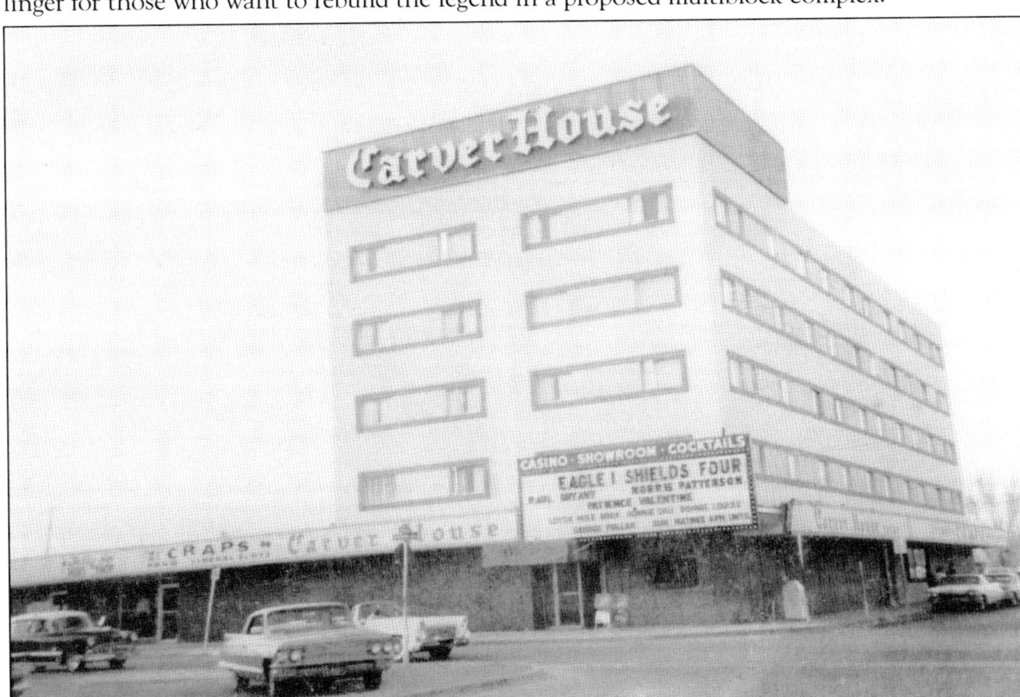

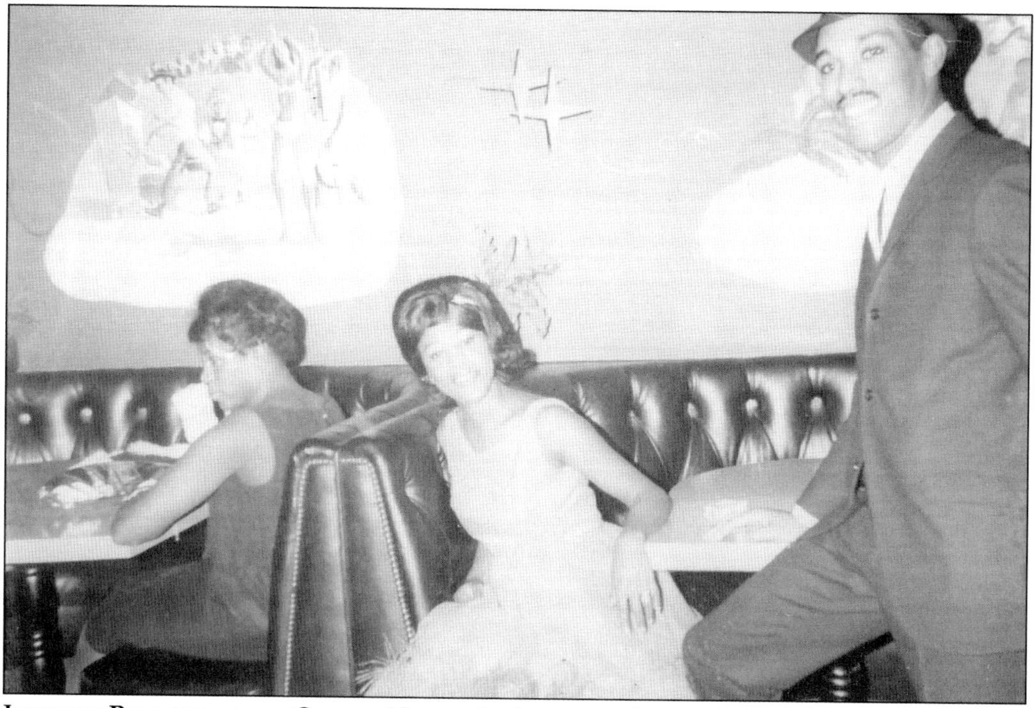

Interior Rocking in the Carver House. In the image above, a beautiful young couple poses for the camera during a night on the town. They appear ready to jump up and dance to the tunes of an equally youthful trio of musicians. Those on the Westside remember nights when the sidewalks were so crowded, people had to walk on the streets in between the various clubs. (Both, courtesy Nevada State Museum, Las Vegas.)

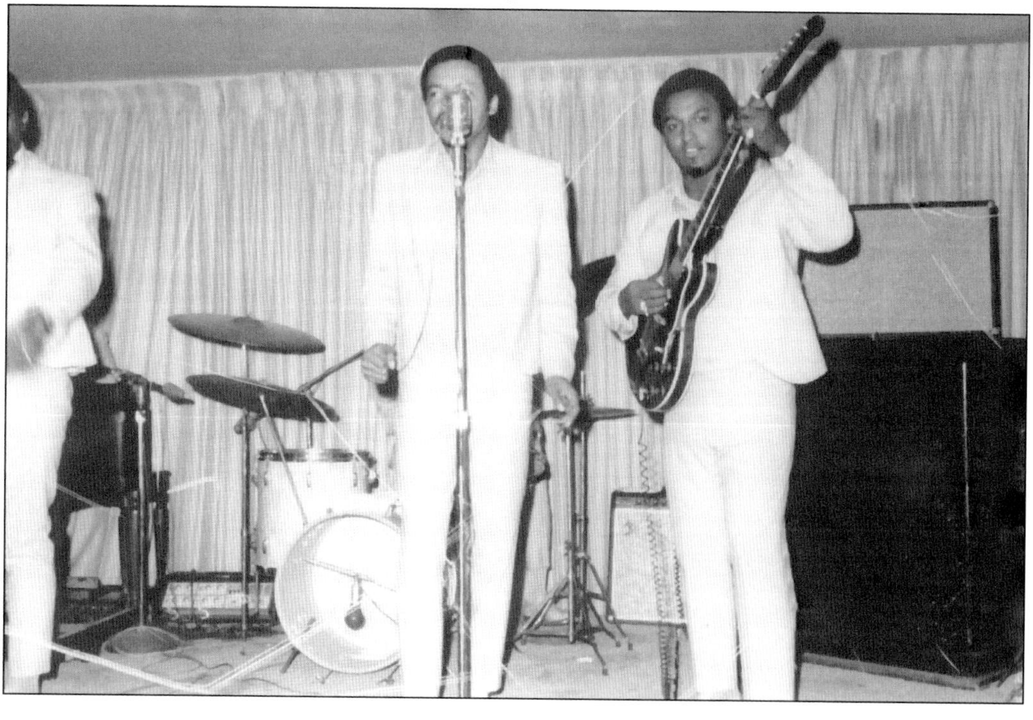

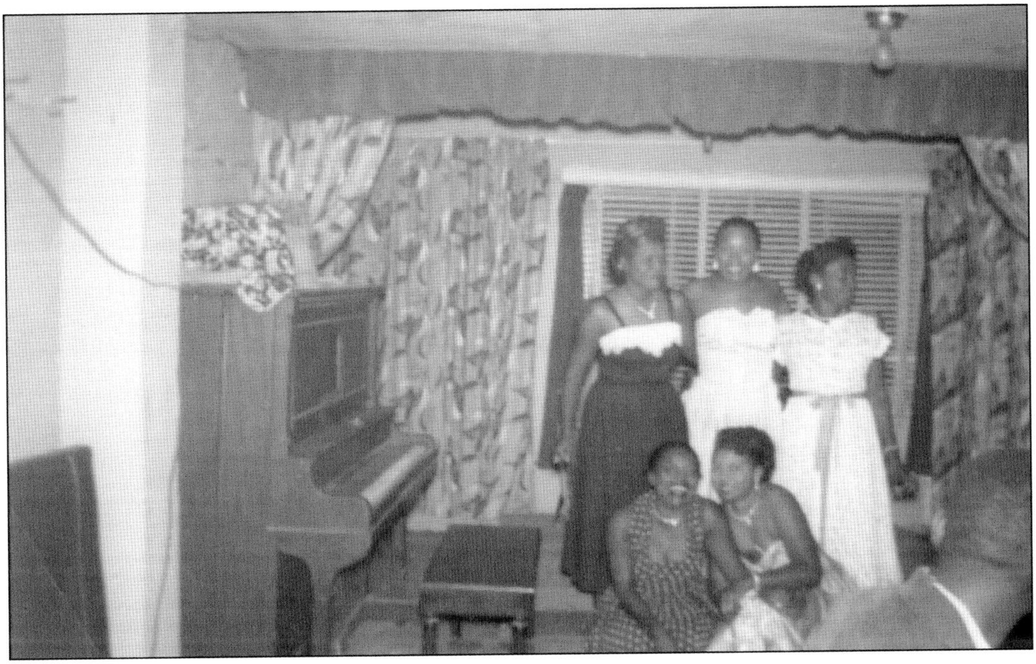

The Elks Club, an at-Home Atmosphere. Many congregated at this site for its warm environment and impromptu shows with big names like Pearl Bailey and Nat King Cole. Because of Jackson Street's central location, most of the clubs were in walking distance for residents. (Both, courtesy Edna Mae Williams.)

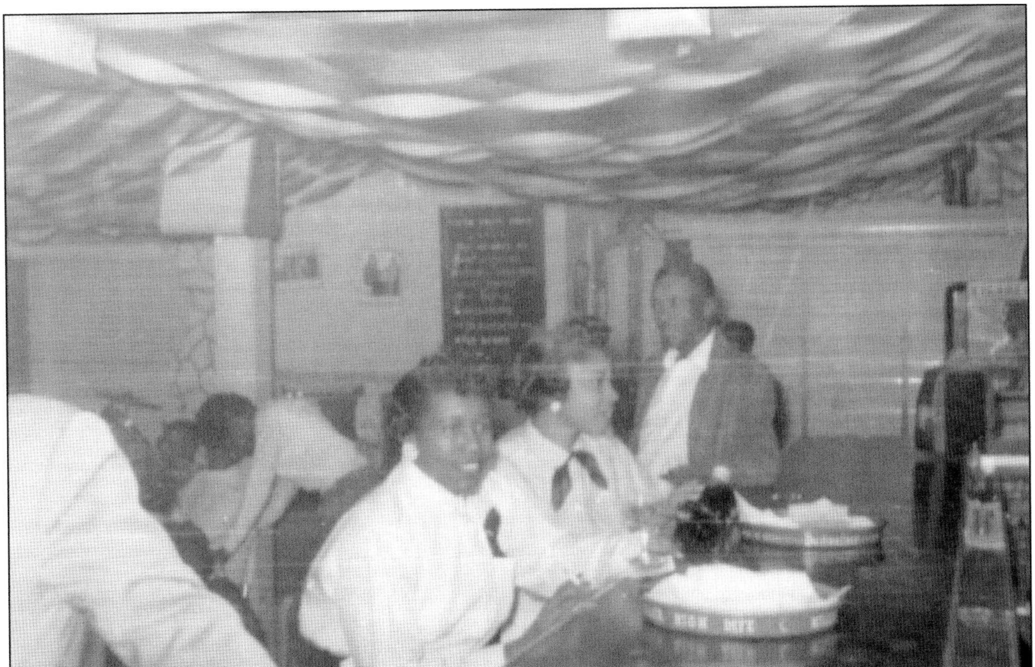

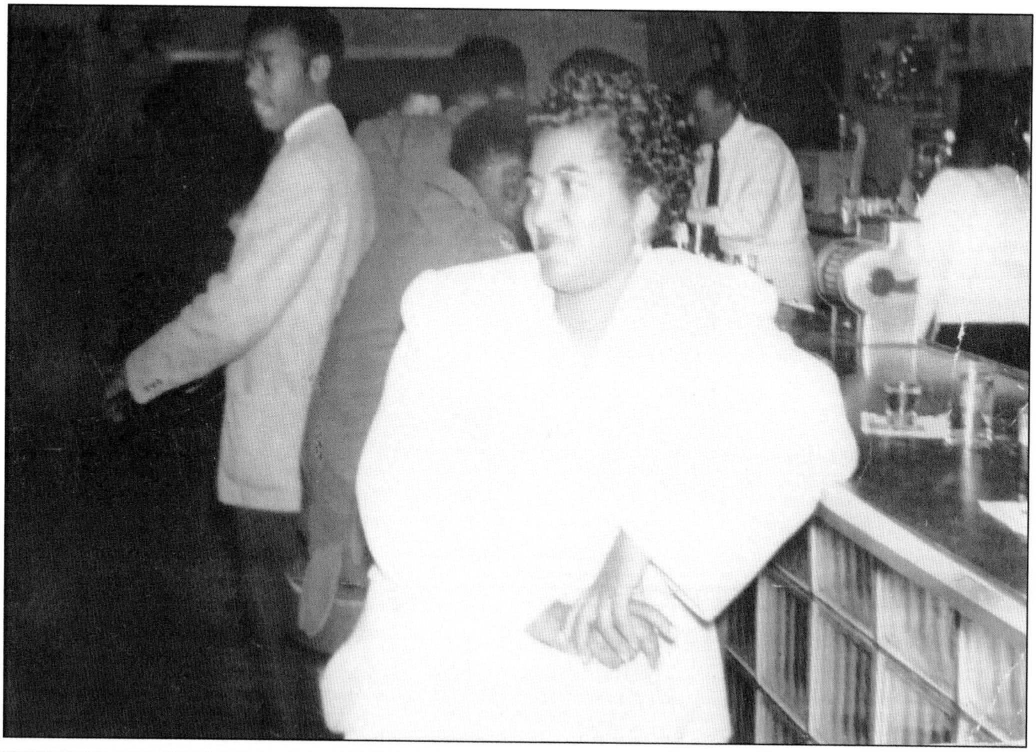

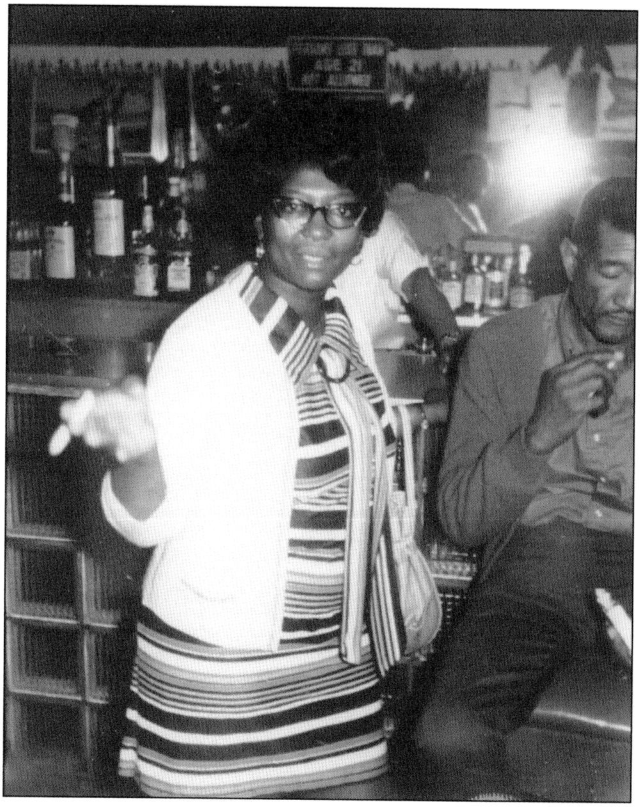

SMILING PATRONS. Since everyone knew just about everyone else, sitting solo at a bar was likely a short period of solitude. Here, an unidentified woman seems to be waiting for her friends to come join her for an evening of song, gaming, socializing, and relaxing.

THE BROWN DERBY. Mixed memories remain of this establishment, as some locals imply that it was a far cry from the Hollywood version. Still, one local patron identified as only Woneta enjoys her evening in the photograph above.

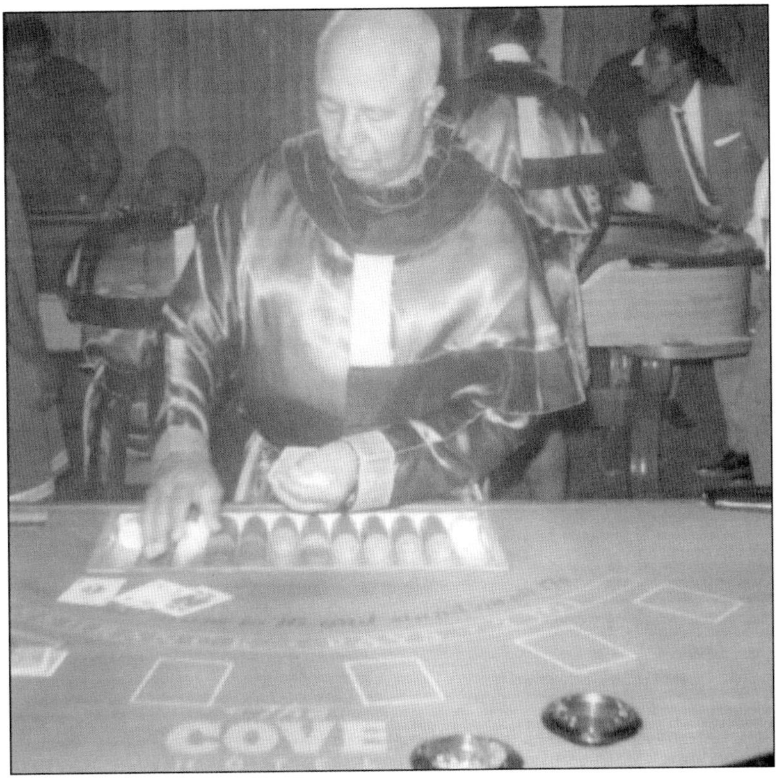

Clarence Ray Dealing Cards at the Cove. Many local celebrities crossed over numerous business, civic, and entertainment domains. Clarence Ray was known in several circles but primarily in gaming.

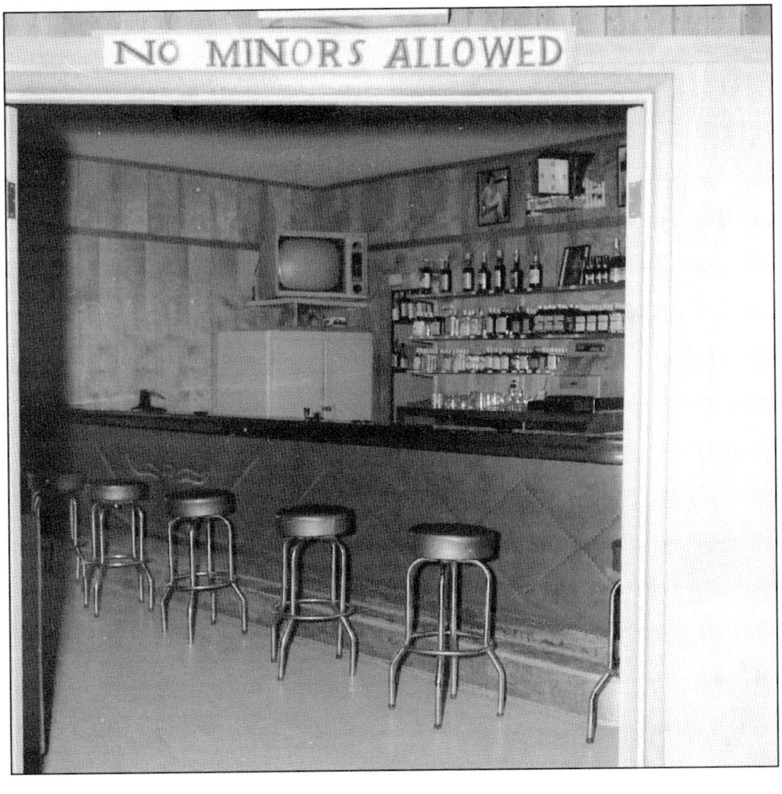

No Minors Allowed. Pictures tell the story throughout Jackson Street. "No minors" signs were prominently displayed, and local residents recall that nightlife was an adult affair. Here a sign is boldly placed at the entrance to the Cotton Club.

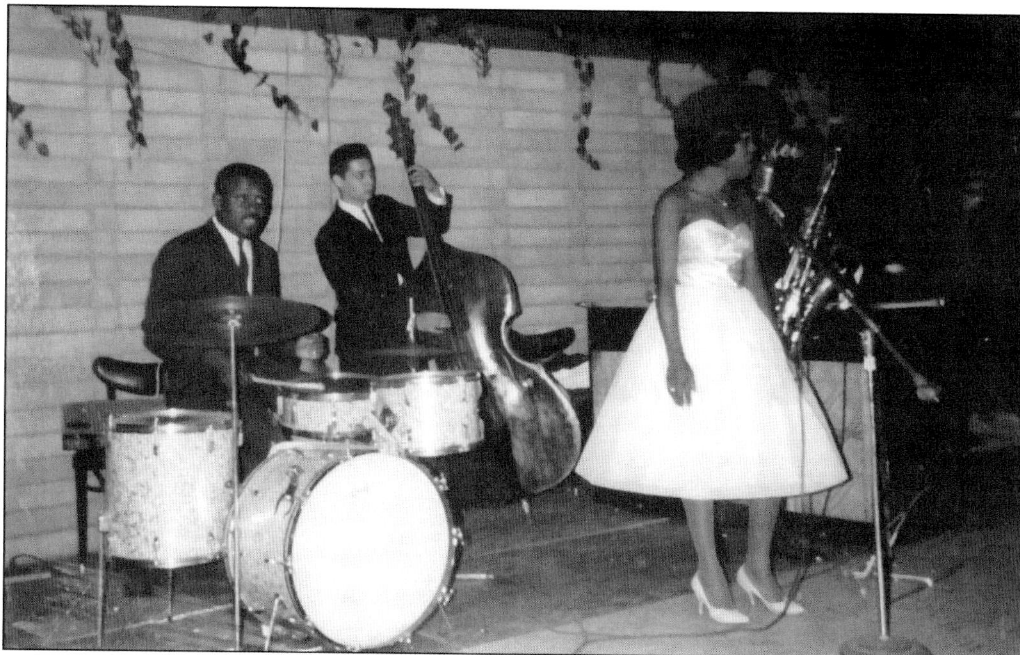

Local Legend the "Eagle Eye Shields" Band. Local talent often brought down the house. Calvin Shields, drummer of the All Star Band, played at the Carver House at D and Jackson Streets. He went on to become music director for Della Reese and Redd Foxx and was a member of the Valley View Golf Club. (Courtesy Nevada State Museum, Las Vegas.)

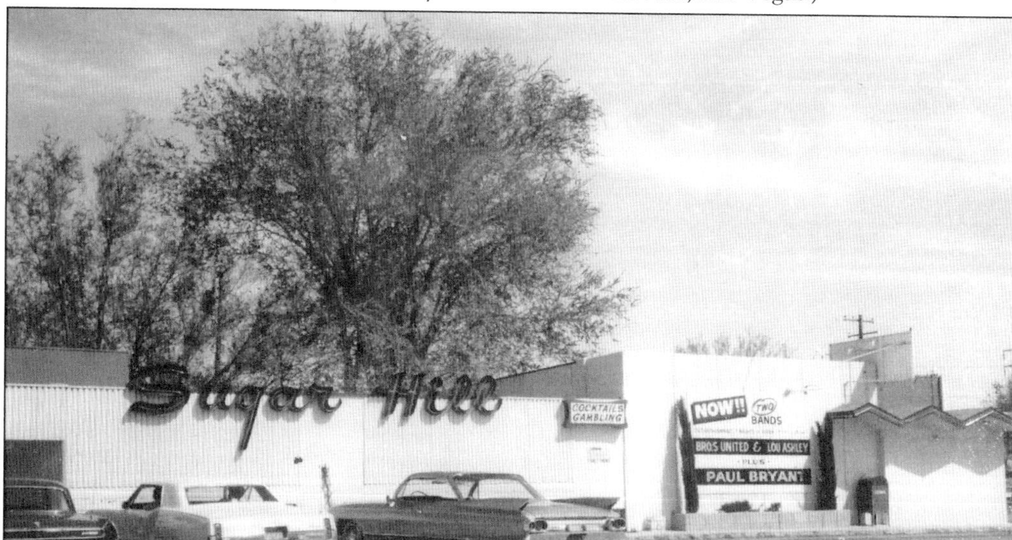

Sugar Hill Sparkles in the Daylight. Photographs primarily capture interior scenes of nightlife and daytime images of the buildings' exteriors. Here, the popular Sugar Hill, a bit away from the Jackson Strip action, boasts two clubs for entertainment, along with cocktails and gambling.

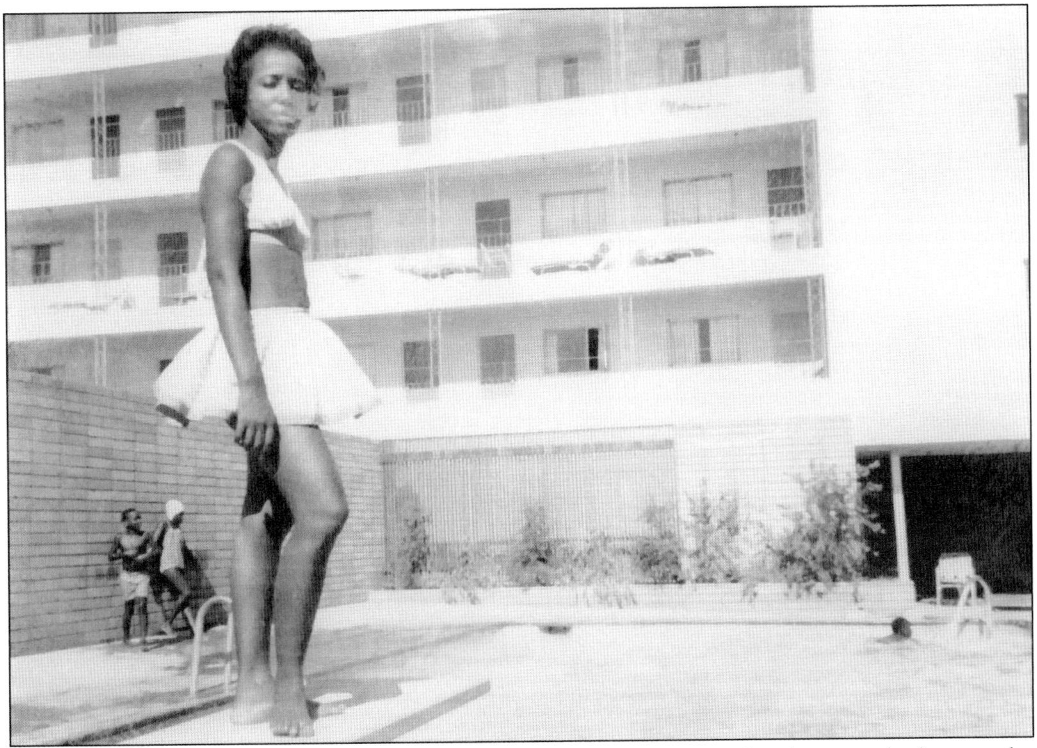

POOL AND POOLS. Jackson Street was alive during the day, as seen in the photograph above at the Carver House pool, or at Big Jim's Pool Hall, seen below. Edna Mae Williams and her husband owned a popular pool hall at H Street and Owens Avenue. With a strong job history of bartending and waitressing, both ably handled the heavy demands of both a day and evening hot spot. (Above, courtesy Nevada State Museum, Las Vegas; below, courtesy Edna Mae Williams.)

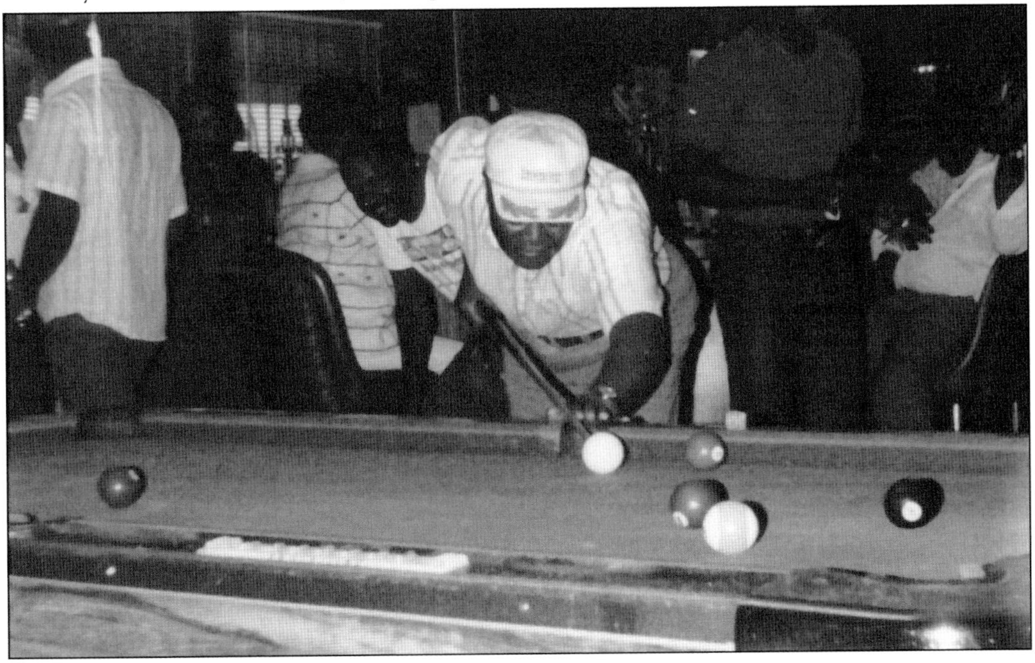

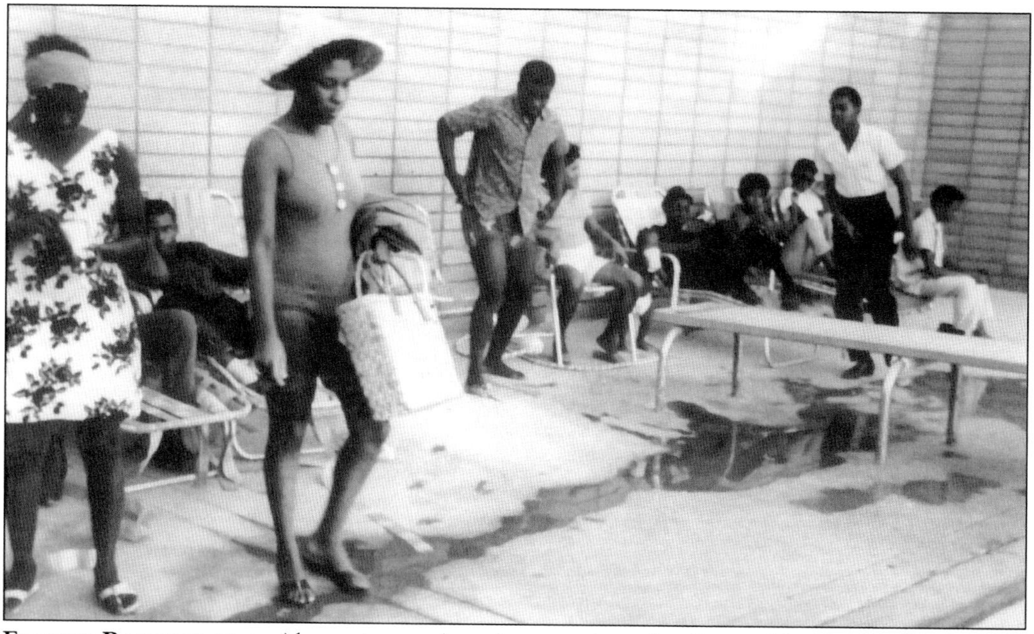

Families Poolside, too. Above, in another photograph at the Carver Hotel, crowds enjoy the pool. On the Westside, hotel patrons of all races were welcome. African Americans did not have to be concerned about the establishment burning their used sheets after a stay, as was the case at some top-notch Strip hotels after they gave into pressure and allowed a famous black star to spend the night.

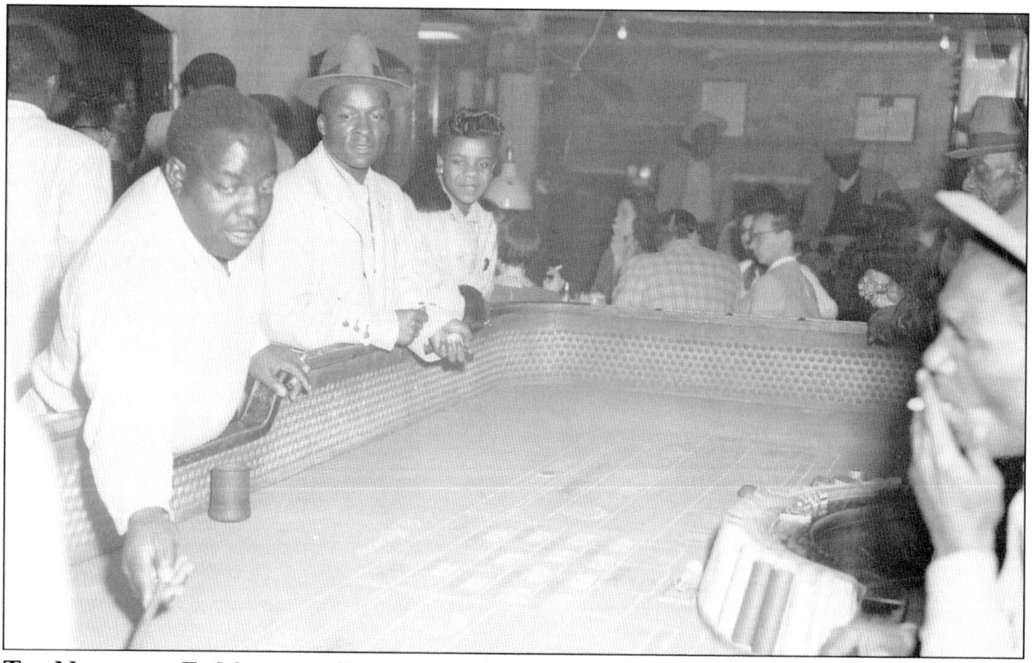

The Night the El Moracco Closed. One by one, the establishments dwindled in patrons as the locals left to enjoy the Strip and Downtown, a once-forbidden area before 1960. Yet, even as they ventured into these clubs, it took a few decades for many of the smaller casinos, particularly the ones Downtown, to catch up with desegregation.

Five

The Moulin Rouge Reflecting the Best and Worst of Times

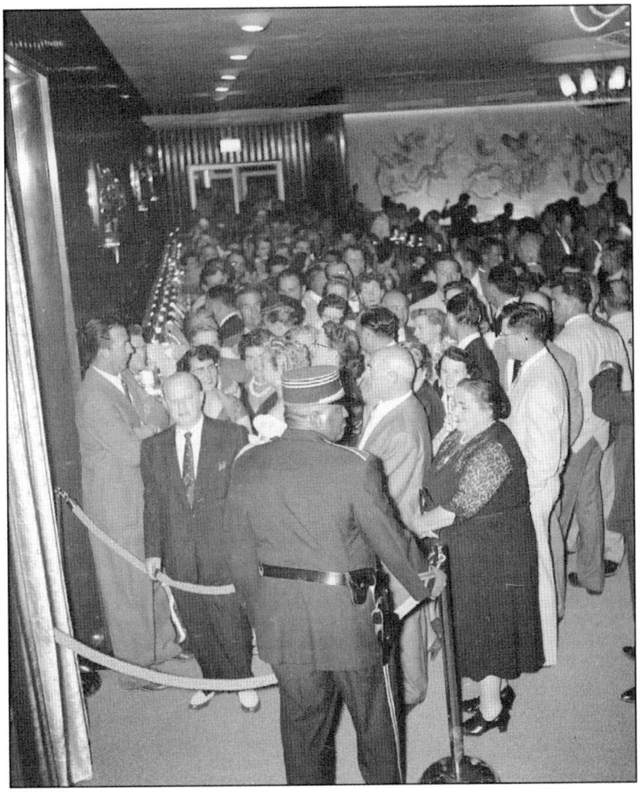

Opening Night of the Moulin Rouge. Hundreds arrived to celebrate the fruits of the first integrated hotel-casino in the country. The grand opening featured top talent, including Stump and Stumpy, Gregory Hines, Dinah Washington, the Platters, jazz great Benny Carter, Lionel Hampton, Les Brown, and the Penguins, and garnered the attention of *Life* magazine, which gave it cover attention in June 1955. Reportedly, the regular 2:30 a.m. show vacated the Strip. The $6.9-million complex would become a global icon for its star power, unique clientele, food fare, and as a center for civil rights. Its indelible spirit has endured for nearly six decades though fire, lightning, numerous ownerships, and controversy, especially its closing after only five months of operation. (Courtesy Nevada State Museum, Las Vegas.)

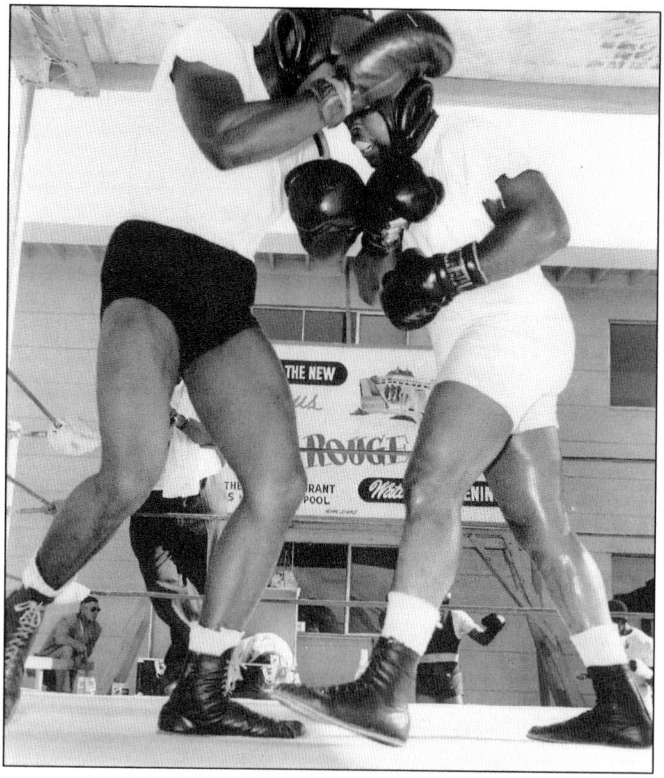

ARCHIE MOORE FIGHTING AT THE MOULIN ROUGE. Light heavyweight champion Archie Moore lived at the Moulin Rouge while preparing for his fight with Nino Valdez on May 2, 1955, at Cashman Field. Pictured at left, he spars with an unidentified partner during the previous month. The Moulin Rouge would be a mecca for sports champions as well as other celebrities in 1955 and later, especially in the 1980s and 1990s. (Courtesy Nevada State Museum, Las Vegas.)

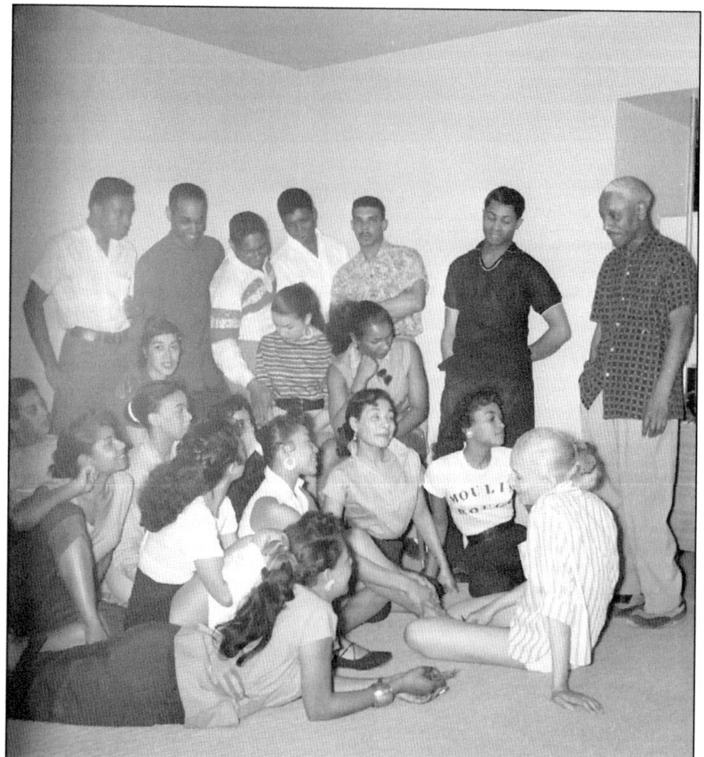

EXPRESSIVE ENTERTAINMENT DIRECTOR. Clarence Robinson, the first African American choreographer hired by the Cotton Club in New York, produced the famous *Cotton Club Revues* and the *Blackbird Varieties.* He is seen here meeting with Moulin Rouge dancers to cover the upcoming grand opening of the Moulin Rouge. (Courtesy Nevada State Museum, Las Vegas.)

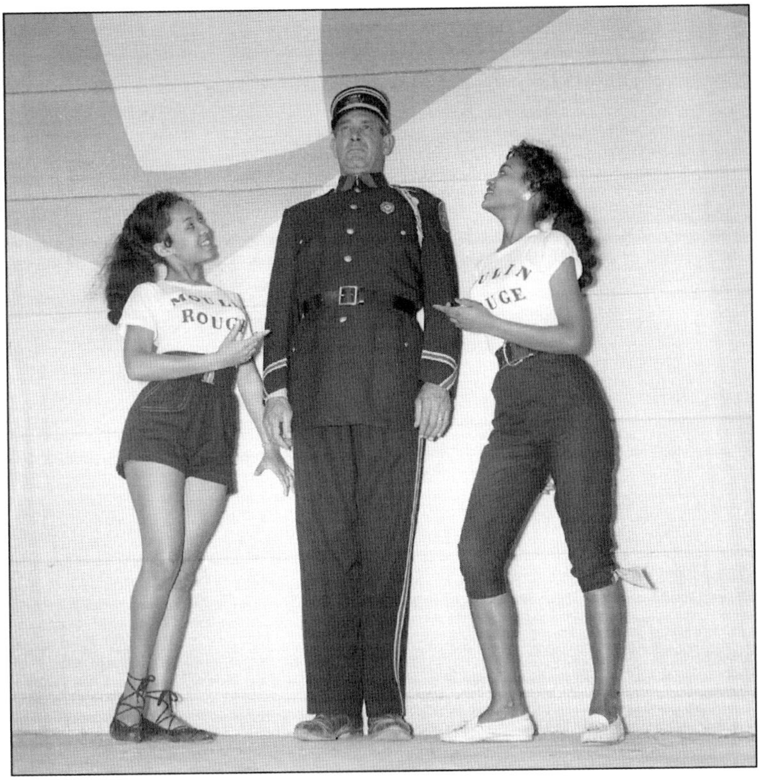

FRENCH ACCENTS. The Moulin Rouge security uniforms were exact replicas of the French gendarmes' uniforms. Chief of security Merle Longnecker remains poised in the presence of dancers Mary Louise Randolph (left) and Theodora Dolcina Boyd (right). Below, the gendarmes seem to pass inspection of the choreographer and dancers alike. (Both, Courtesy Nevada State Museum, Las Vegas.)

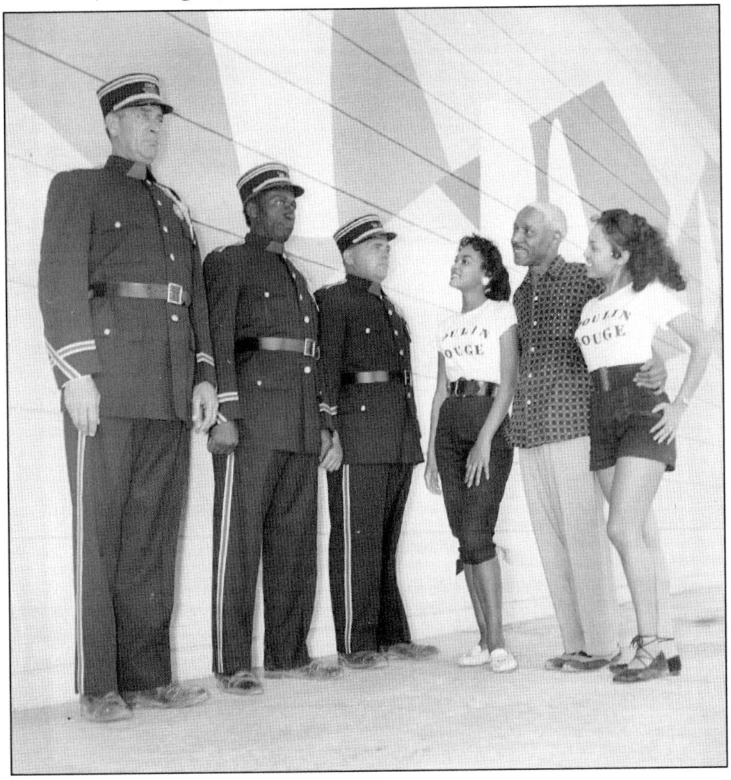

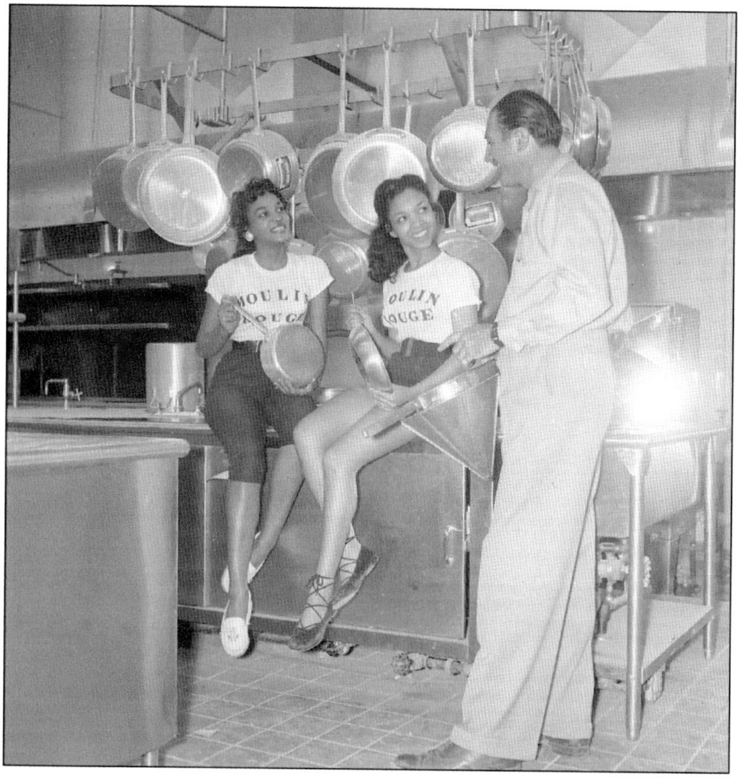

SIZZLING IN THE MOULIN ROUGE KITCHEN. Head chef Dave Nussbaum appears to like what is cooking in his famous kitchen as dancers Theodora Dolcina Boyd and Mary Louise Randolph strike an attractive pose. Celebrated photographer Jay Florian Mitchell captured very unique perspectives of the innovative hotel-casino in its heyday. (Courtesy Nevada State Museum, Las Vegas.)

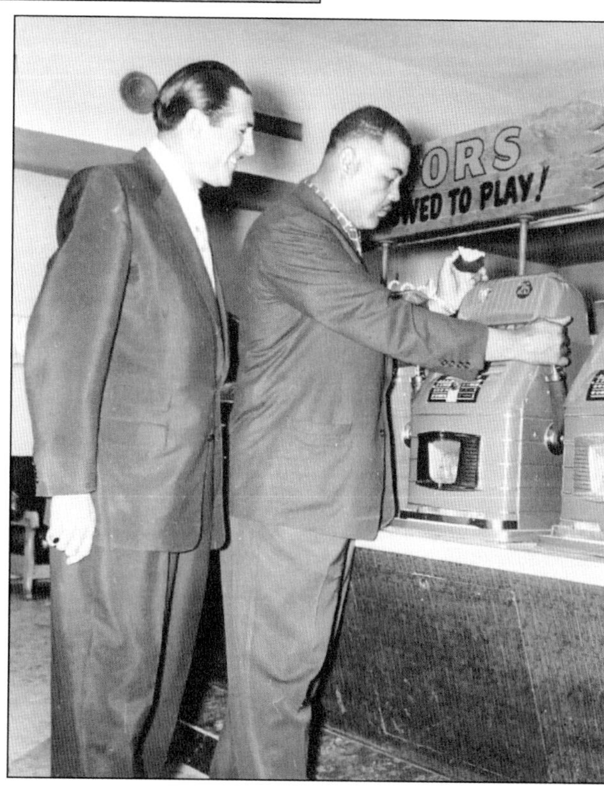

AT THE SLOTS. Head chef Dave Nussbaum takes a break from kitchen duty with Joe Louis to try his luck at the slots. (Courtesy Nevada State Museum, Las Vegas.)

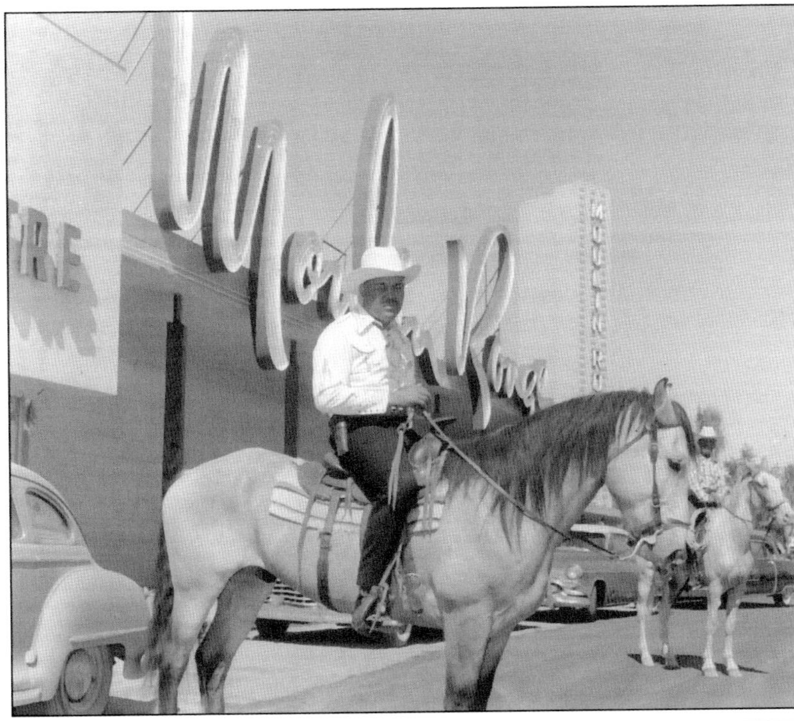

A Champion on Horseback. Joe Louis was the official host of the Moulin Rouge, and a rumor was deliberately circulated that he was part owner of the famous casino, but that was never verified. Some believed that having people think he was invested would be more appealing to black patrons and performers. (Courtesy Nevada State Museum, Las Vegas.)

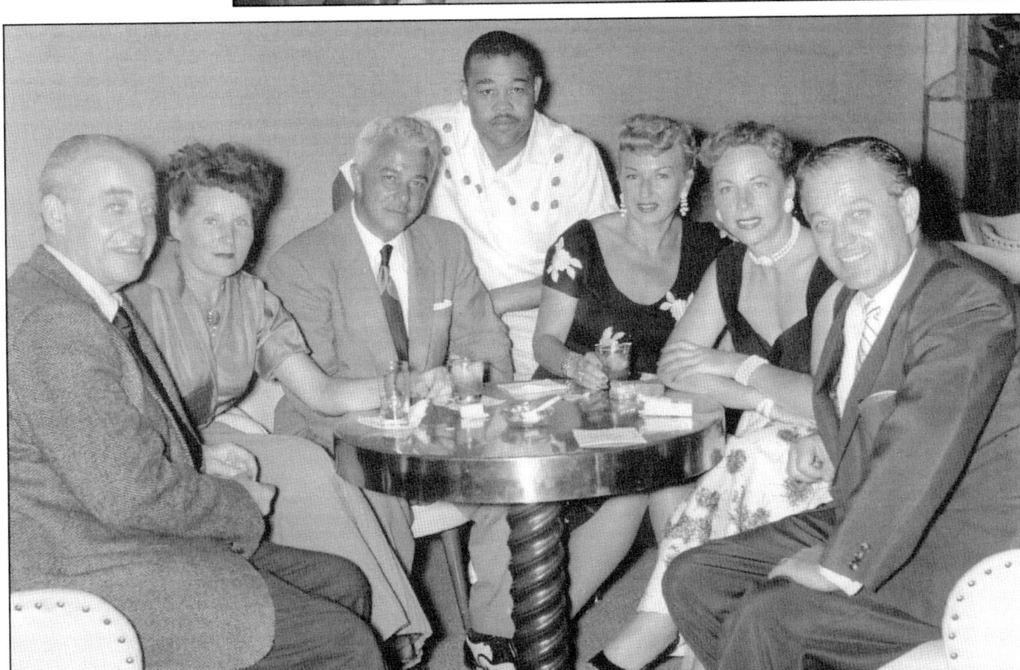

Joe Louis Taking Center Stage. There was no doubt that one of the attractions for guests was former heavyweight champion boxer Joe Lewis, who toured the country for months as a goodwill ambassador for the hotel. (Courtesy Nevada State Museum, Las Vegas.)

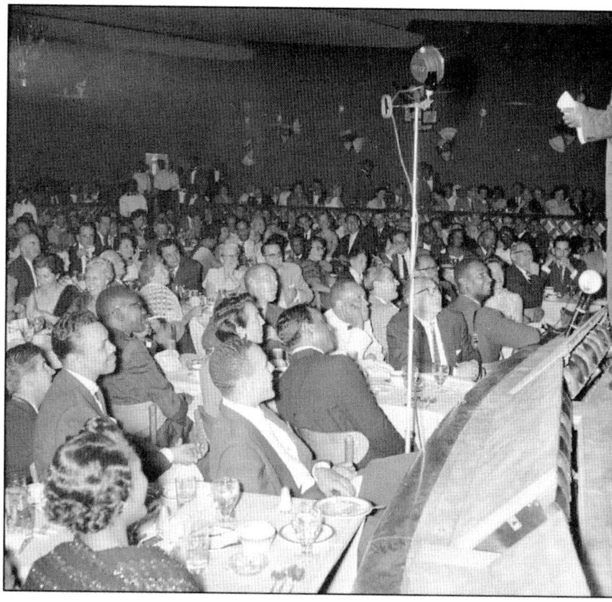

HAPPY CROWDS. According to one source, limos would line up on the Strip to bring eager patrons to the phenomenal 2:30 a.m. show at the Moulin Rouge. Among the people that could be seen there were Harry Belafonte, Louis Armstrong, Lena Horne, Lionel Hampton, Frank Sinatra, Sammy Davis Jr., Joey Bishop, Tallulah Bankhead, Donald O'Conner, the Mills Brothers, Gregory Peck, Dorothy Lamour, Bob Hope, Jerry Lewis, George and Gracie Allen, and Milton Berle. (Courtesy Nevada State Museum, Las Vegas.)

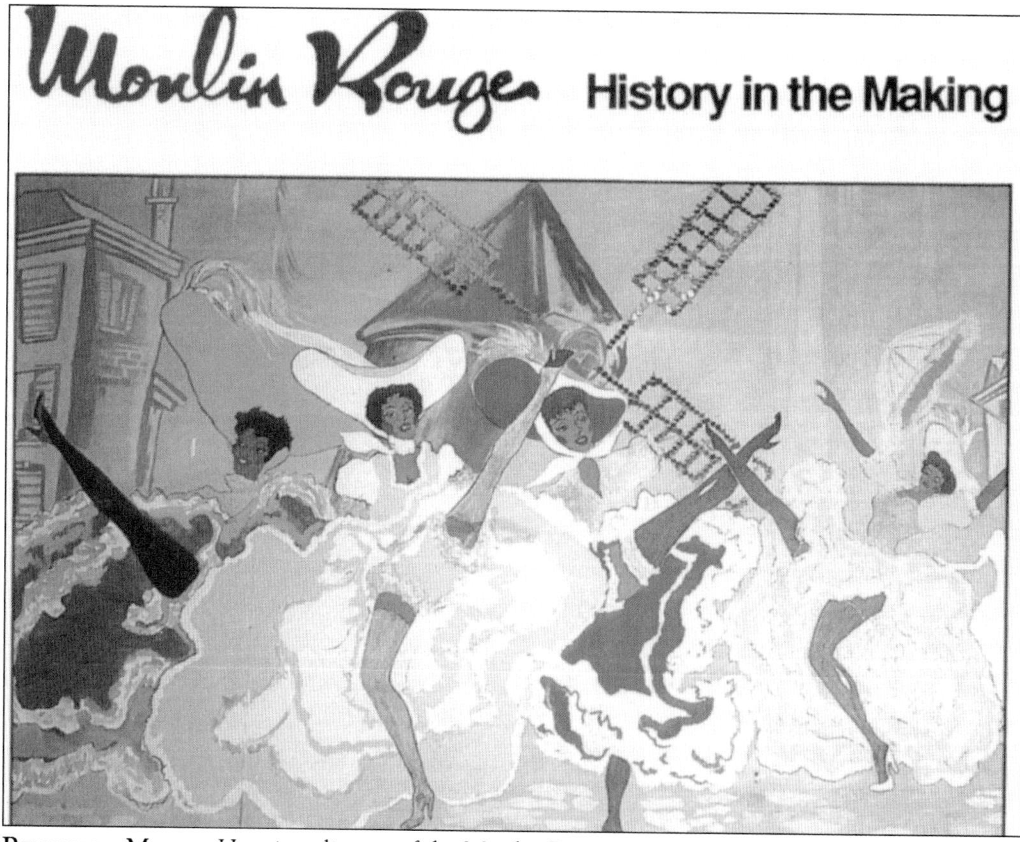

RENOWNED MURAL. Here is a glimpse of the Moulin Rouge's signature mural. The cancan dancers were supposedly painted black to more accurately depict the casino's actual dancers and showgirls. The image has been replicated numerous times in different mediums. Unfortunately, the original mural art, along with other artifacts, was destroyed in the last and most devastating fire of 2009.

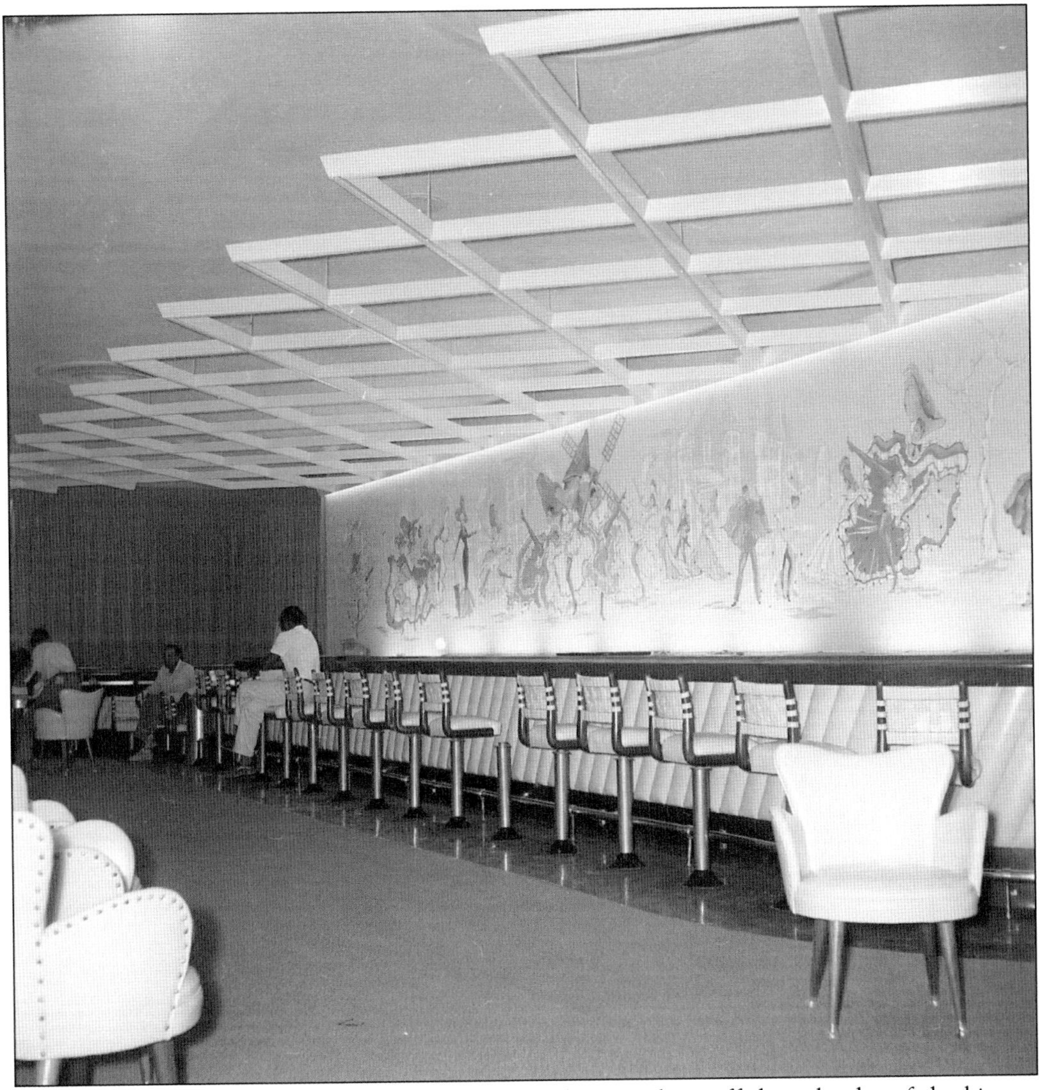

The Full Expanse of the Mural. The spectacular mural set off the splendor of the biggest showroom in all of Las Vegas at the time. Despite its popularity, the Moulin Rouge doors were locked in less than six months. Some assert that there was jealousy on the Strip. Others wondered if money was skimmed, leading to financial ruin. However, a few claim that the Moulin Rouge was too far from the Strip to survive in a recessionary era that would have required at least 70-percent room occupancy in its adjacent hotel. (*Life* magazine, 1955.)

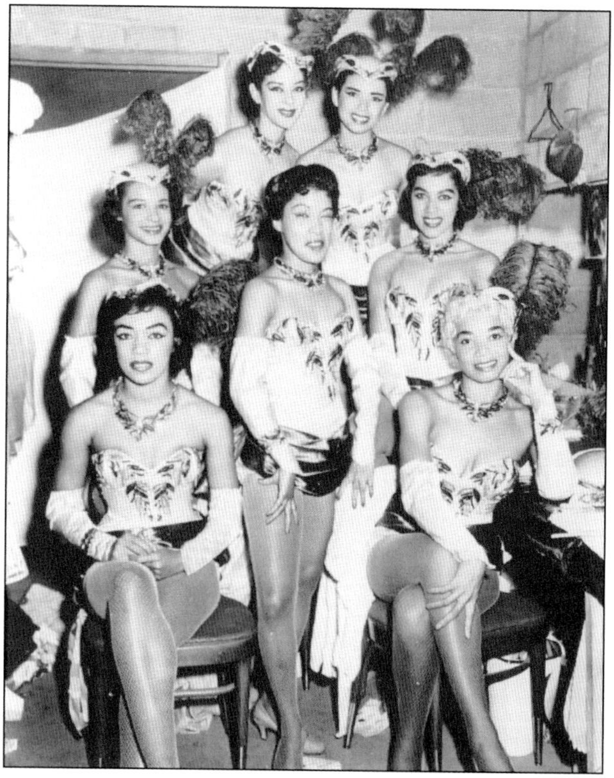

Showgirls Taking the Stage. There were dancers and showgirls galore, many of them striking an iconic pose above. Every night and early morning, their performances left a stunned audience clamoring for more. In between shows, some of the best cuisine in Las Vegas was served with grandeur, and the gaming went wild. Below, dancers mingle with Lionel Hampton, one of the favorite stars at the Moulin Rouge. (Both, courtesy Nevada State Museum, Las Vegas.)

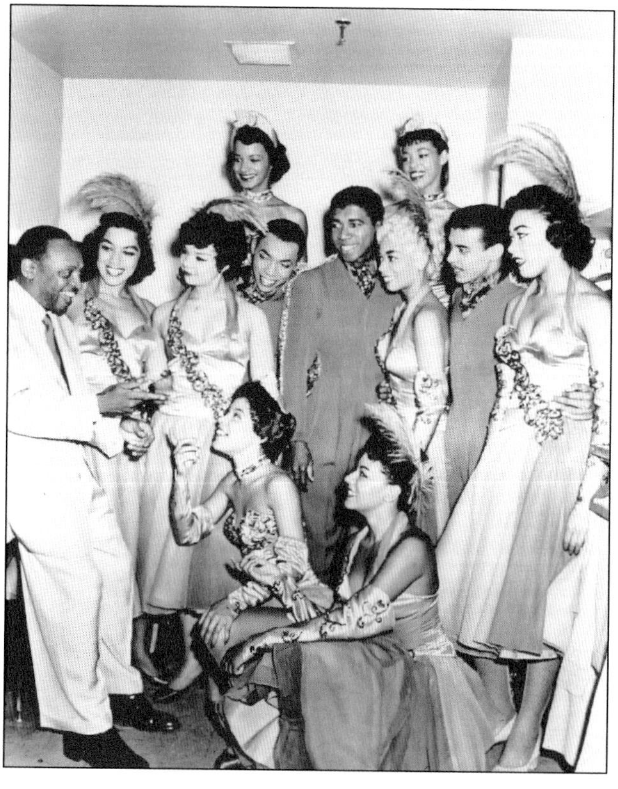

MIXING BARTENDING WITH MUSIC. Theodore Toney was a waiter and dancer at the original Moulin Rouge in 1955 and later worked for Saran Knight Preddy as a waiter. In between, he styled his own music, not unlike many on the Westside who aspired to more creative endeavors.

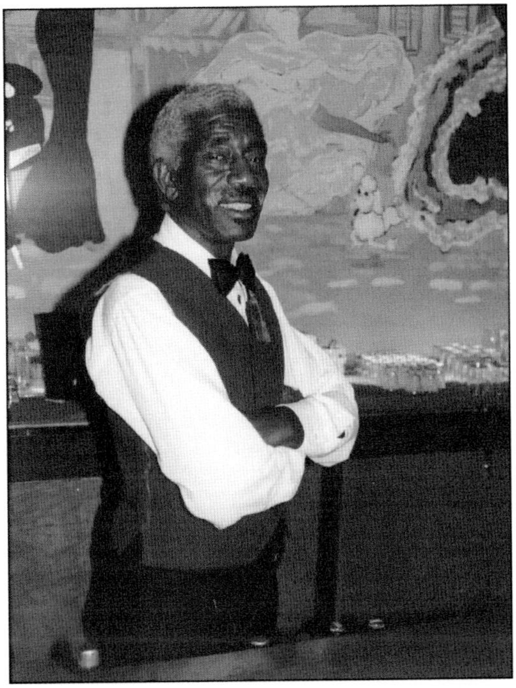

BATHING BEAUTY BY THE POOL. The Moulin Rouge's pool was as large as any on the Strip and drew both regular hotel guests and dancers, like the beautiful woman seen here on the diving board.

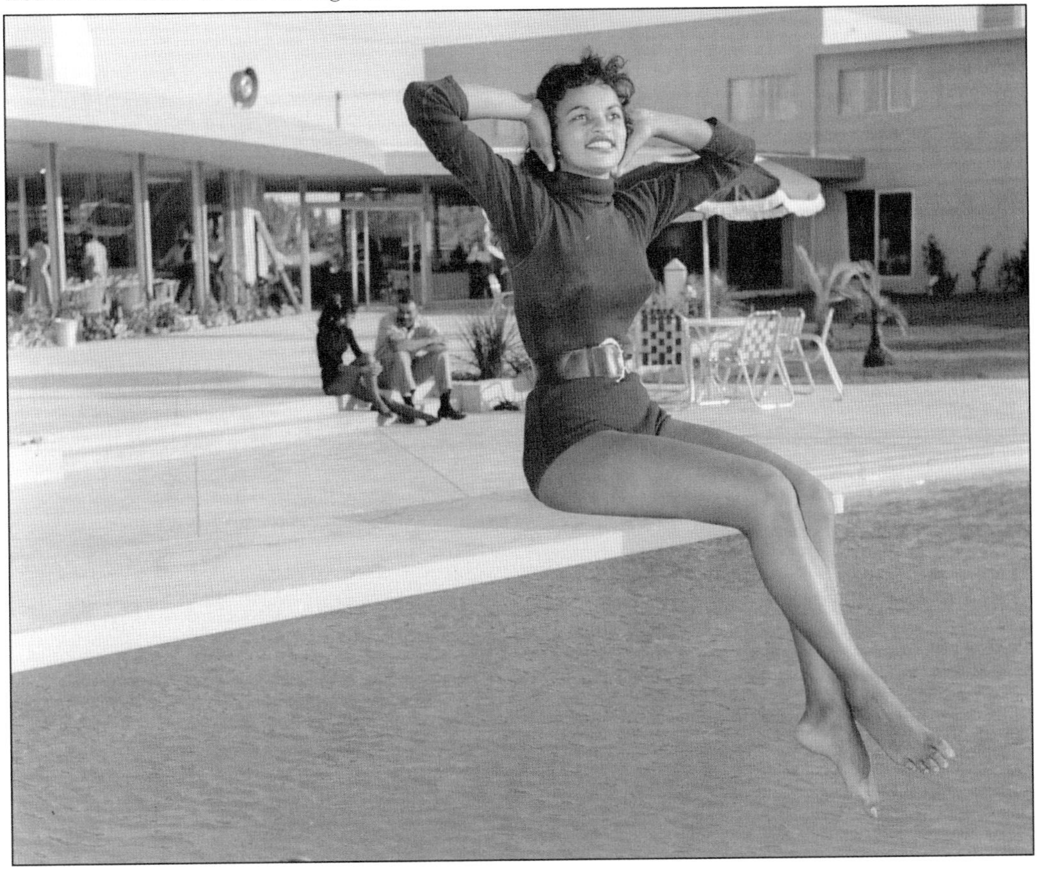

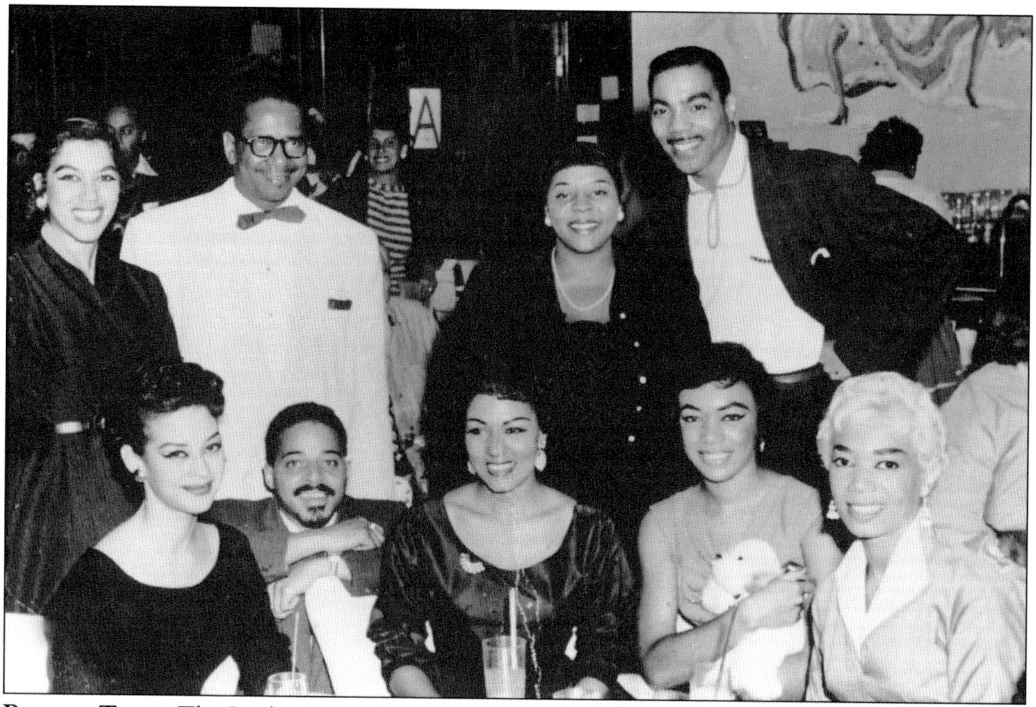

Best of Times. The Lucky Pierre Bar was a great place for performers to relax after the show. Dee Dee Jasmin (bottom right), a noted Moulin Rouge dancer, later moved to movie roles. Anna Bailey, a dancer, and Bob Bailey, master of ceremonies, are left and right in the back row. (Courtesy Nevada State Museum, Las Vegas)

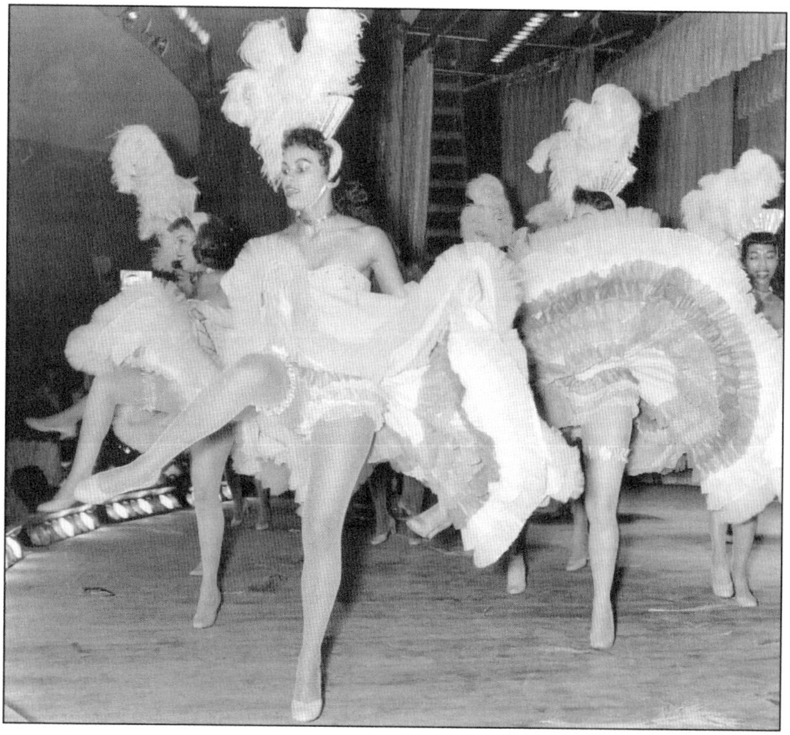

Kicking Up a Storm and Bringing on the Sunshine. The number-one dancing draw was the famous "Tropi-Can-Can" number, although the watusi appeared in *Life* magazine. Clarence Robinson, who directed the dancers, had also worked on the movie *Stormy Weather.* (Courtesy Nevada State Museum, Las Vegas.)

Stump and Stumpy. James "Stump" Cross (right) and Harold "Stumpy" Cromer (left) performed regularly and were the rage, according to the late Maurice Hines. In addition to their zany comedic act, they were considered brilliant dancers, and it was said that they greatly influenced the team of Dean Martin and Jerry Lewis. Cromer (at right below) later held a job as an emcee for rock-and-roll shows and revived his career somewhat, but Cross's life took a downward spiral. In the photograph below, they sit with Rosita Davis, rocking in laughter. (Both, courtesy Nevada State Museum, Las Vegas.)

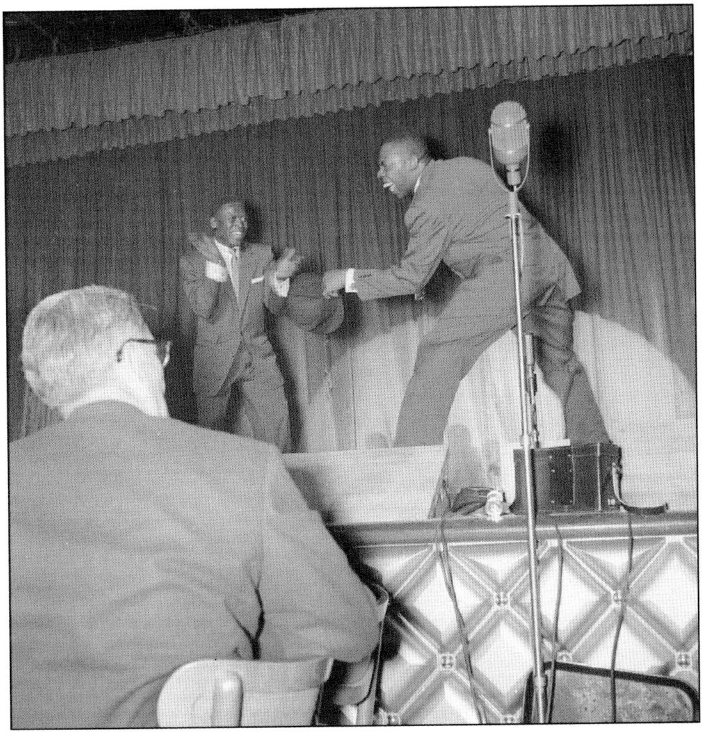

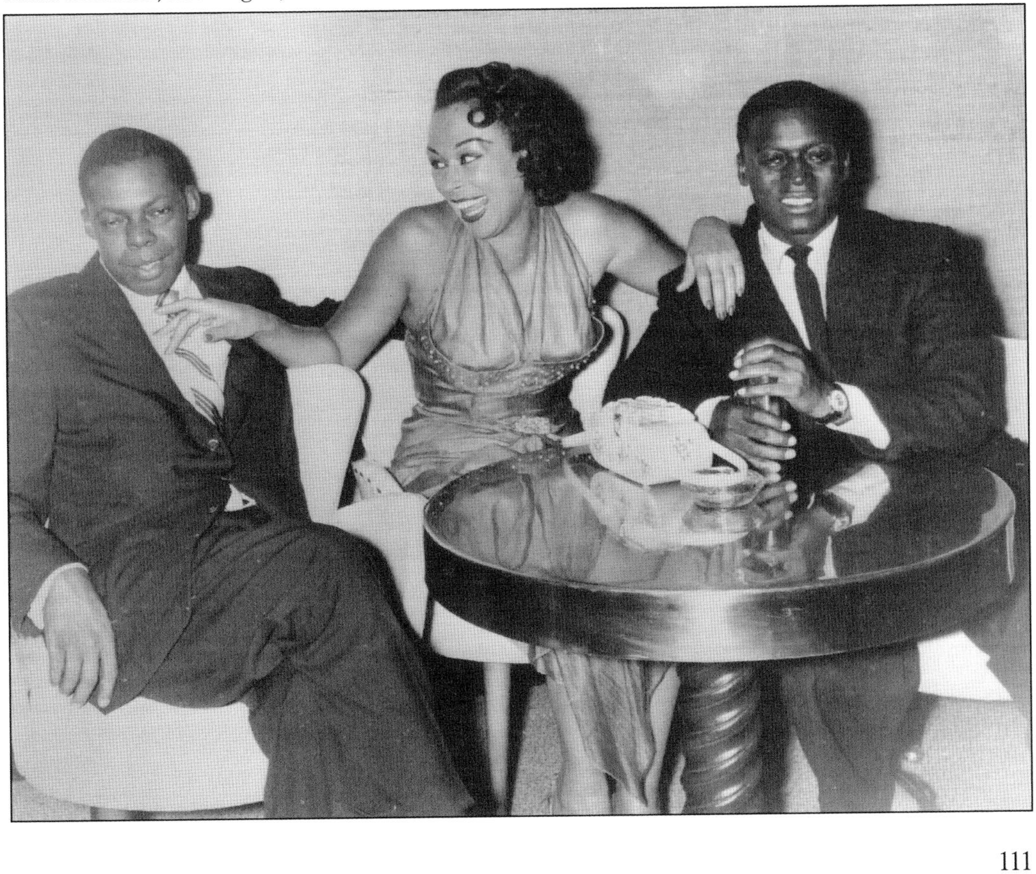

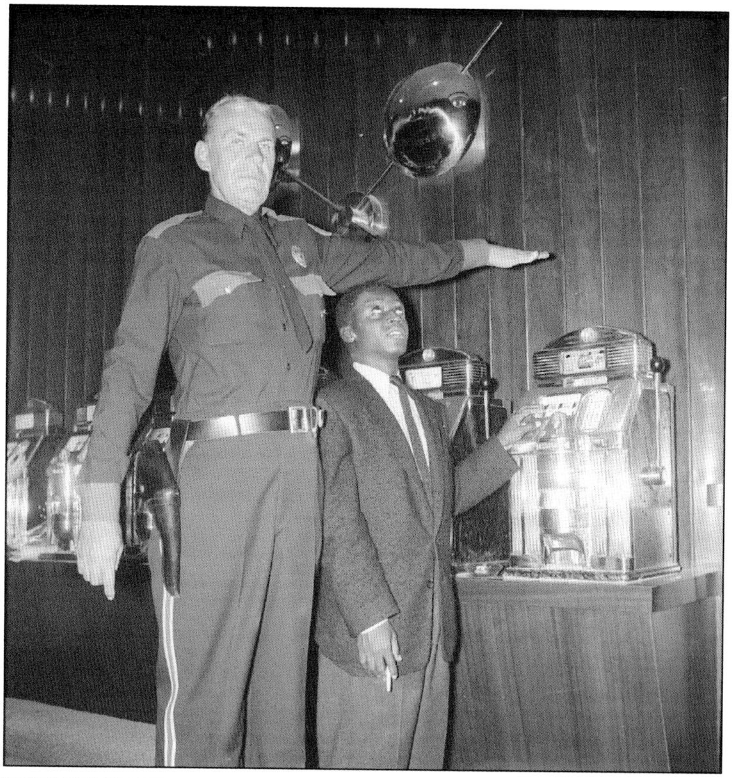

Head and Shoulders above Stumpy. Security guard Merle Longnecker clowns around with Harold Cromer for famed photographer Jay Florian Mitchell. (Courtesy Nevada State Museum, Las Vegas.)

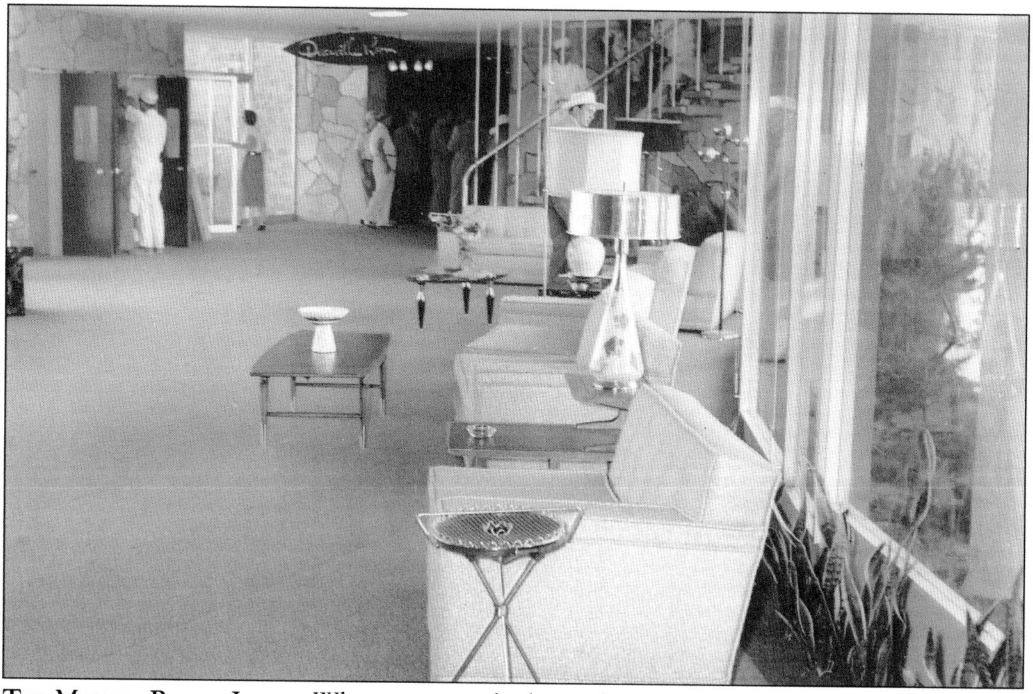

The Moulin Rouge Lobby. When everyone had gone home, sometimes near dawn, the lobby could be eerily silent. Still, its graceful 1950s look made the hotel memorable to those who visited. (Courtesy Nevada State Museum, Las Vegas.)

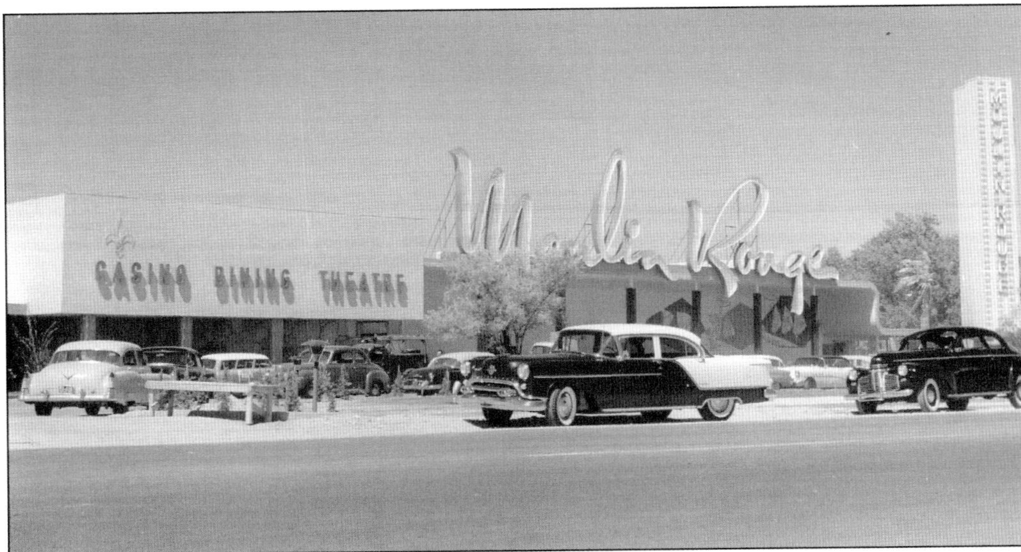

SOON TO BE JUST A PHOTOGRAPHIC MEMORY. No hotel or casino will ever match the unique Moulin Rouge. This exterior shot is one of the more endearing ones of the internationally famous site; its history is indelibly marked on the minds of even the current generation. (Courtesy Nevada State Museum, Las Vegas.)

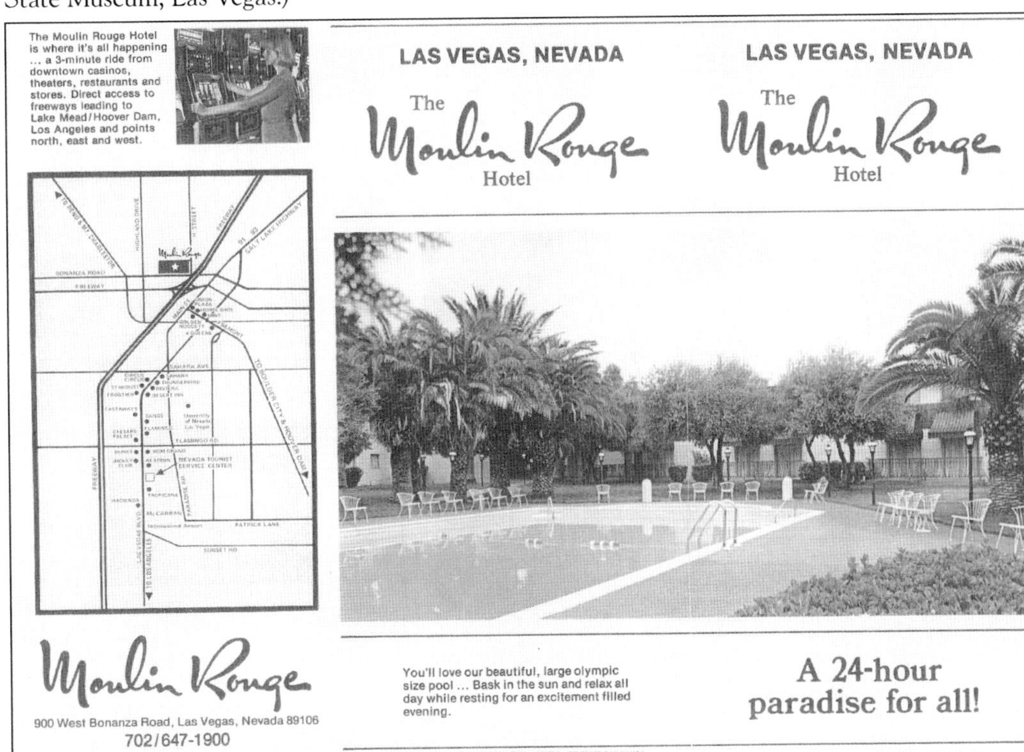

SKIPPING A GENERATION. Though some only recall the short life of the original Moulin Rouge from May 1955 until October 1955, many remain unaware of the tremendous effort and success that Sarann Knight Preddy brought to the Moulin Rouge during the 1980s and 1990s. This 1980 postcard shows the revived Moulin Rouge's pool area.

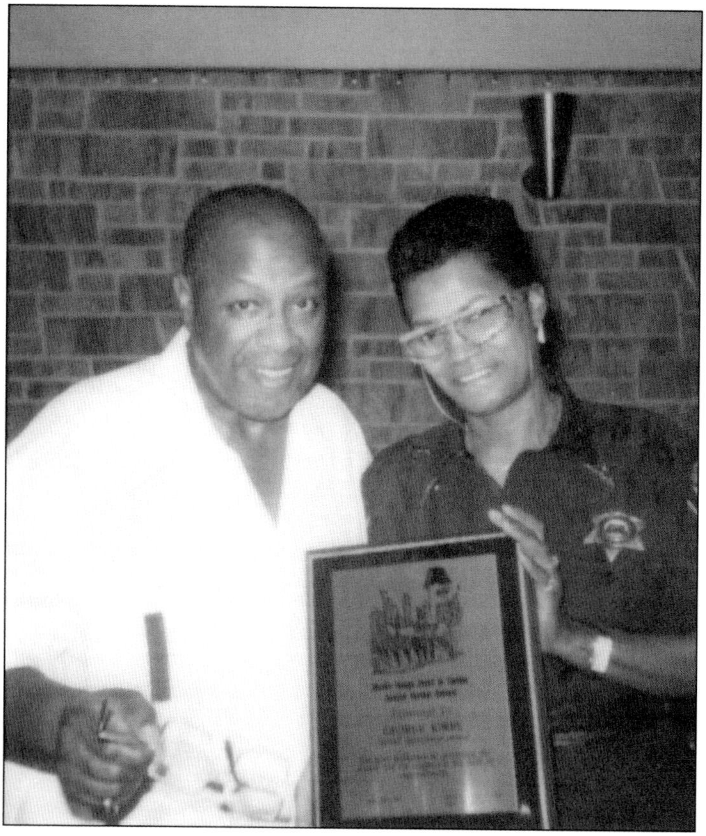

A Birthday Celebration. Erma Jai Walker, who worked with Sarann for over two decades, enlivened the scene with special events like the Gemini Party. In the photograph at left, she is giving George Kirby his birthday plaque. Below is the invitation to the birthday bash for Erma, also known as "Lottie Dottie." Note the many well-known Geminis on the list. (Both, courtesy Erma Jai Walker.)

GEMINI

(May 21 - June 20)

MAY

May 23	Al Anderson
May 25	Earl White Sr.
May 28	Darwin Johnson

JUNE

June 2	Tony Alexander, Chicago
	Leslie Jackson
	Glynn Walker Jr.
	Eddie Jordan
June 3	Debra Reeves
	Bobby Baxter
	Cassandra Cotton
June 4	Carlos Mayes
	Erma Jai Walker
June 5	Darrell Griffin
	Earl White Jr.
	Jearl White
June 7	Soul Joe Miller
	Ruby Duncan
June 8	George Kirby
June 9	Anita Earl
	Sharon Hunter
June 13	Leroy Wilson, Sr.
	Opie Randle, Chicago
	Joseph Madlock Jr., Birm. AL
June 14	Betty McCullen
	Clarence McKinng
June 15	Richard Walker
June 17	Hattie Chiles
June 19	Natasha Emerson
June 21	Luther Walker
June 23	Christine Hunter

You are cordially invited to attend
a Gala Gemini Birthday party
honoring

Erma Jai Walker

(Lottie Dottie)

of Chicago, Illinois
& All Gemini
at the

Moulin Rouge Hotel & Casino
900 West Bonanza Road
Las Vegas, Nevada 89106

Saturday, June 13, 1992 — 9:00 p.m.

Entertainment

Showroom	Guest Soloist	D.J.'s
Total Class Band	Larry Cooks	D.C. Rider
Diamond in the Rough		Antonio

Special Guest
Ghino B.

Deauville Room — Larry (Chi) Evelyn D.J.

Free Food — *(Champagne 10 to 11 p.m.)*

RSVP 702-648-5040
Valet Parking & Security

Six

Spiritual Presence
Moving with the Churches on Every Block

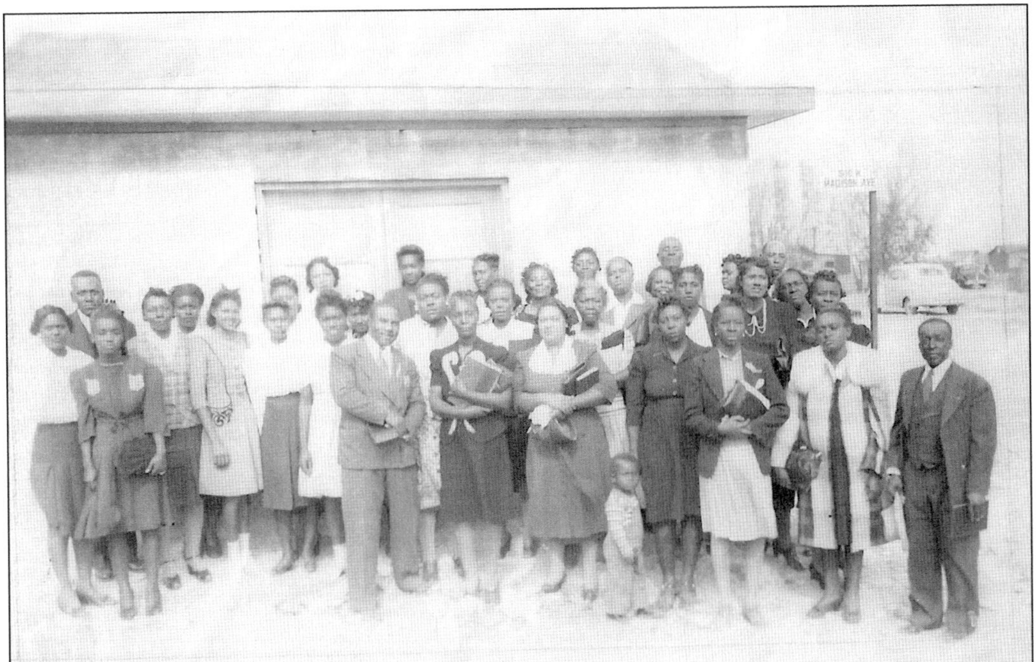

Second Baptist Church, the First for Many. Since the 1940s, the Second Baptist Church was the foremost spiritual and human rights center for the Westside. Although dozens, if not hundreds, of churches and storefronts would fill blocks to the very expanses of West Las Vegas, this church would remain the core of religious movement. This picture depicts the older church during the 1940s. (Courtesy Arby Hambric.)

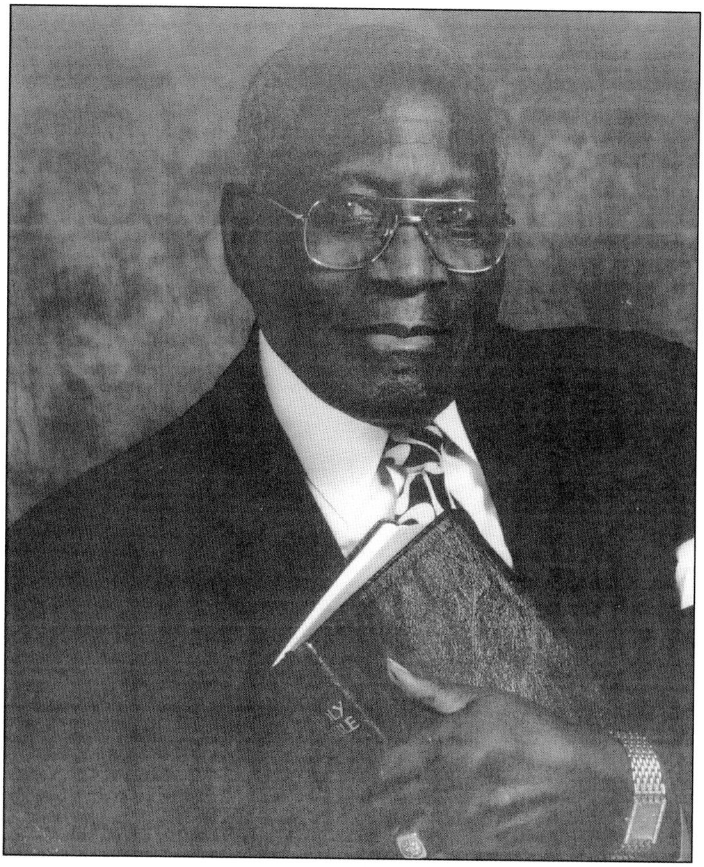

THE REVERENDS. Many popular figures in West Las Vegas were ministers who also led their flocks towards social justice. In fact, it was a rare pastor or reverend who was not involved in almost every aspect of the Westside community life. Pictured here, in a familiar pose with his bible, Dr. Jesse Scott was among those most well known, as was his predecessor, Reverend Davis. Others include Dr. S.S. Rogers and Rev. Marion Bennett, both often a visible presence for peace. Below is a picture of a civil rights meeting at the Pentecostal temple, likely taken during the 1960s.

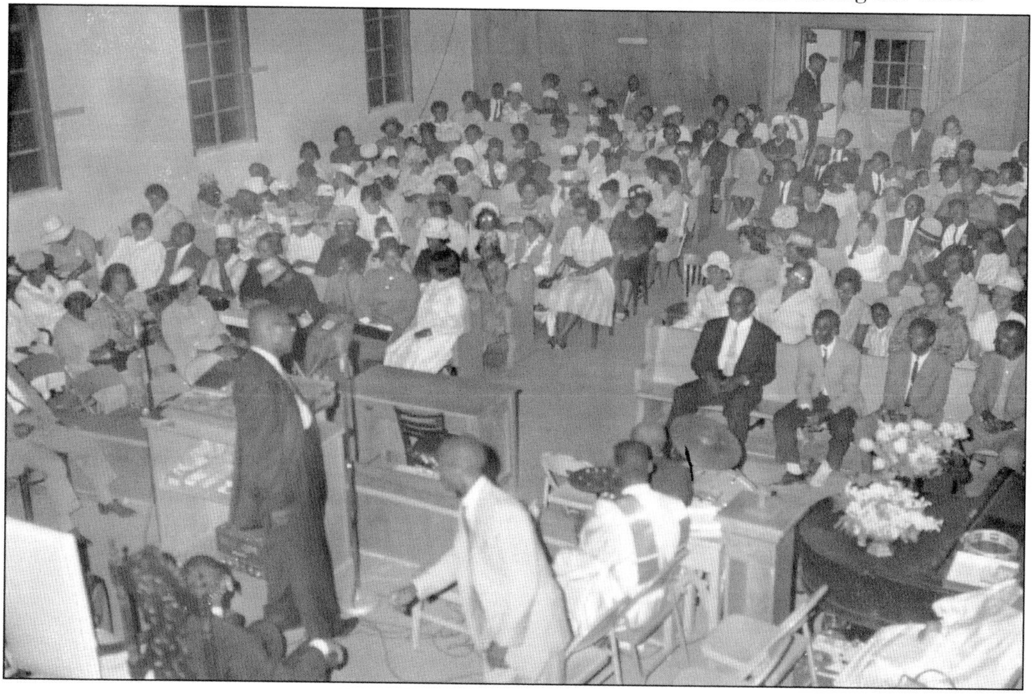

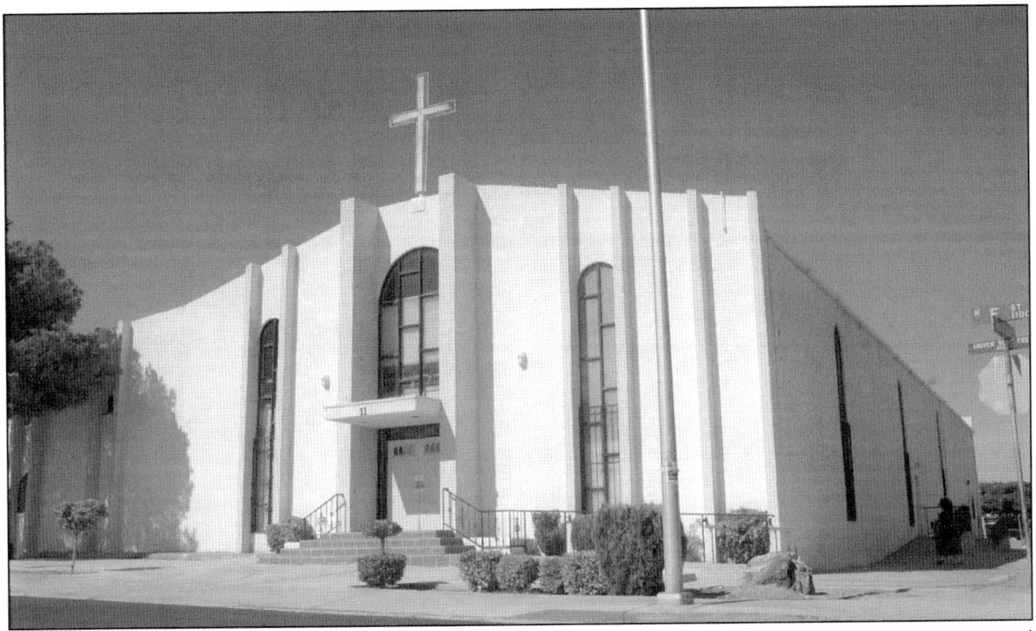

Pentecostal Temple, Church of God in Christ, 2011. Overseer Clyde Carson Cox started his ministry in 1939 and was noted for his great teaching and social advocacy. He also became the first unofficial mailman for the community residents. Arson struck down the original brick structure in 1976, but the determined congregation had a new, 750-seat church a year later. (Courtesy Steve Eagle.)

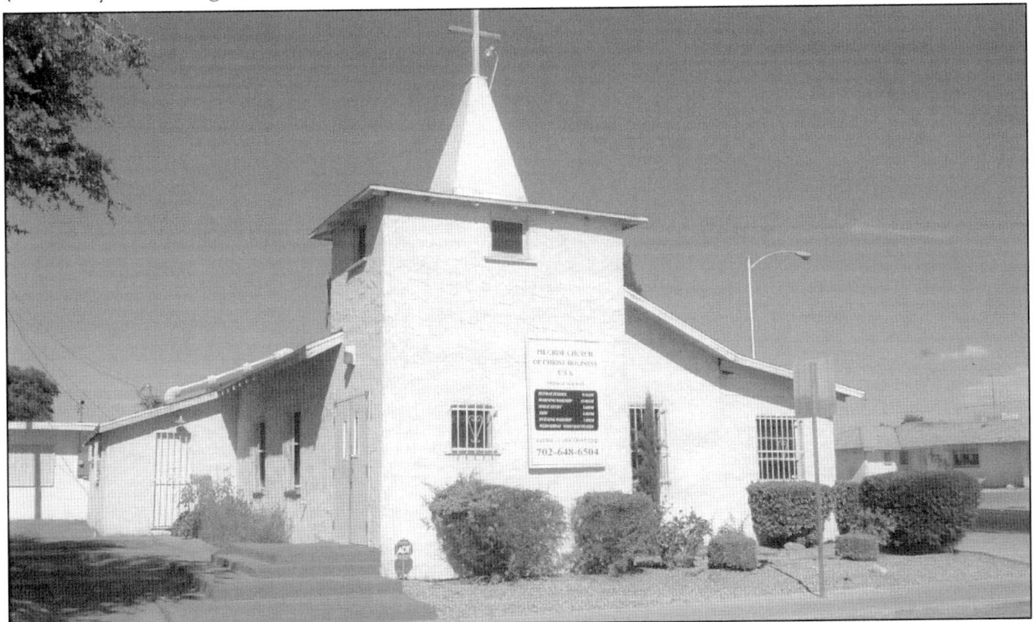

Pilgrim Church of Christ. This humble building and annex on D Street was the first church on the Westside, established in the late 1920s. Despite a few modern renovations, the basic structure remains as it was many decades ago. Seating about 50 parishioners, it has remained the heart of churches in West Las Vegas for its simplicity and perseverance. Note the simple wooden cross atop the steeple. (Courtesy Steve Eagle.)

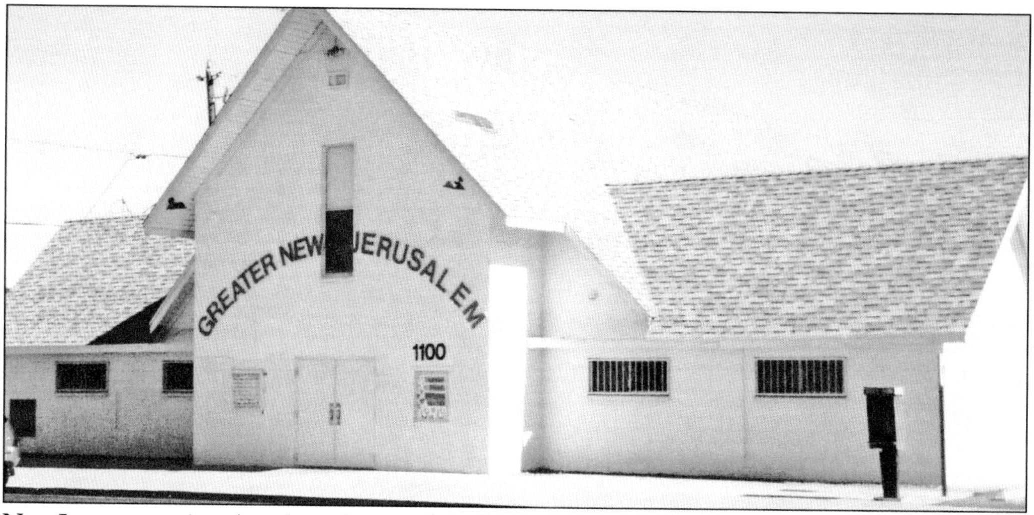

New Jerusalem. Another classic house of worship is New Jerusalem. In a more updated photograph, one easily recognizes the iconic presence. The only public image of New Jerusalem's presence in the community is a image of a shack near its back entrance taken during the mid-20th century.

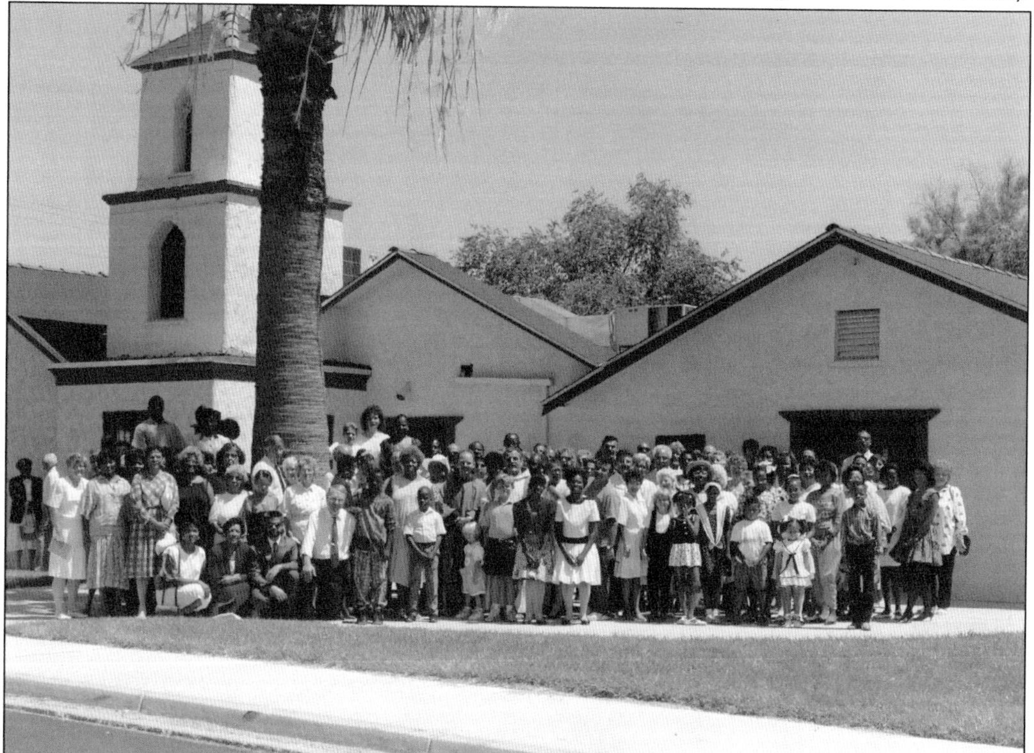

St. James the Apostle Church. The second Roman Catholic Church in Las Vegas and the first in West Las Vegas was founded in the early 1940s. Before the church's construction, a priest would celebrate Mass in various area homes. The Mission-style building was later expanded to provide for its growing population, which changed from largely Latino to African American in the 1960s. Seen above, the entire congregation poses for a picture outside of the old church building complex that today houses both a Christian and a Muslim group.

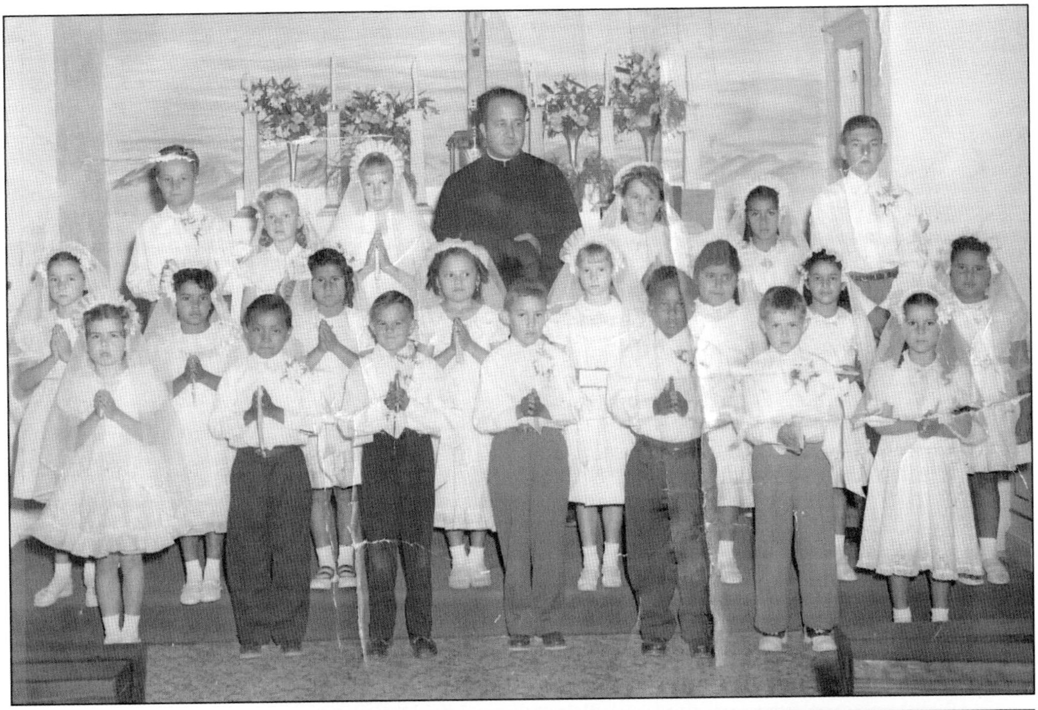

First Communion. Angelic youth await an important step in their faith journey at St. James the Apostle Roman Catholic Church. The picture was most likely taken in the 1950s, before the parish became a beacon for Catholic African Americans. At right, one of the most popular priests and pastors, Father Mike Blackburn, a Franciscan, celebrates Mass in the small interior of the old church. (Both, courtesy St. James the Apostle Church.)

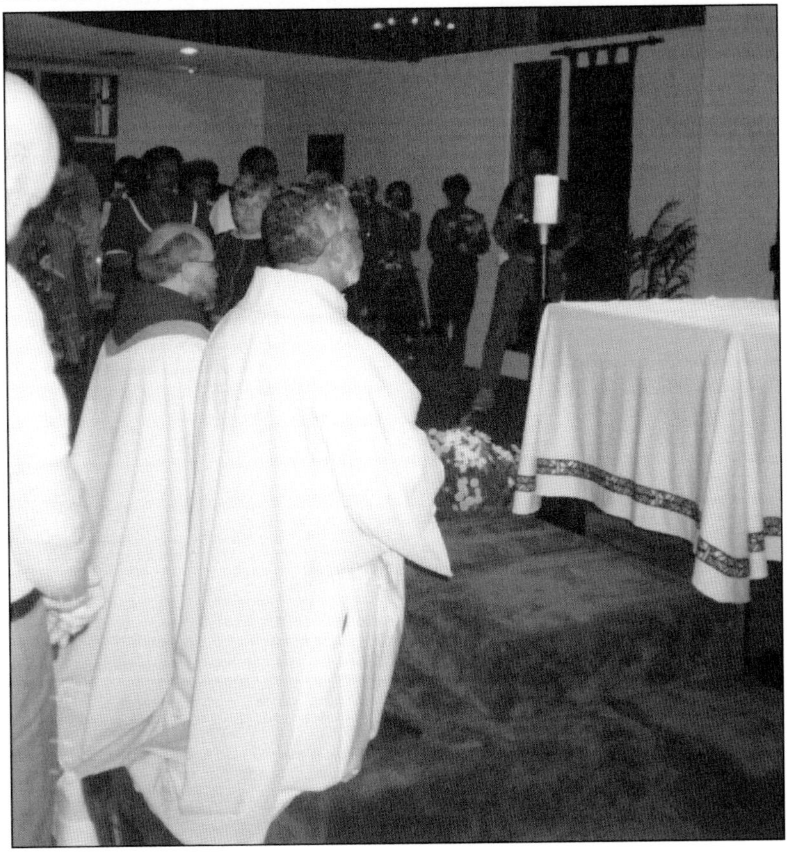

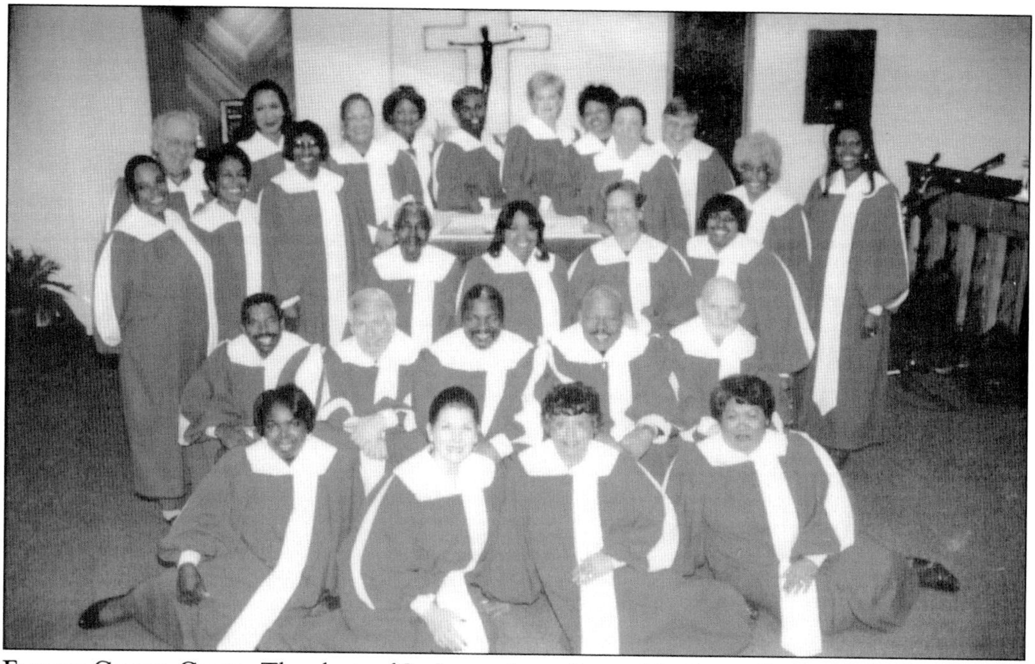

FAMOUS GOSPEL CHOIR. The choir of St. James, long directed by Susan Briare, widow of a former Las Vegas mayor, is famous throughout the state for its engaging and soulful gospel music. Many of its members have been educators, civil rights leaders, local entertainers, and elected officials. Even Calvin "Eagle Eye" Shields played percussion for the choir at one time. (Courtesy St. James the Apostle Church.)

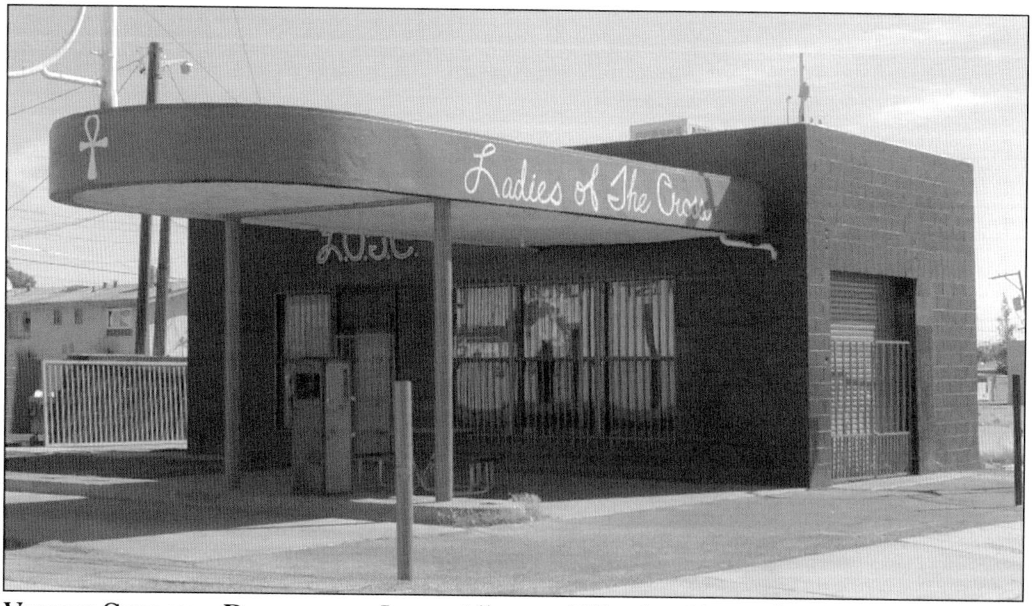

VARIOUS CHURCHES DOTTING THE LAND. All around West Las Vegas, churches of various sizes and storefront centers of prayer dot many blocks. Along Jackson Street, beyond F Street, are approximately a half-dozen churches, and rounding the corner, one runs into several more places of worship. Most are Christian, and some have unusual missions like the Red Ladies of the Cross. Sometimes one can hear the peal of church bells.

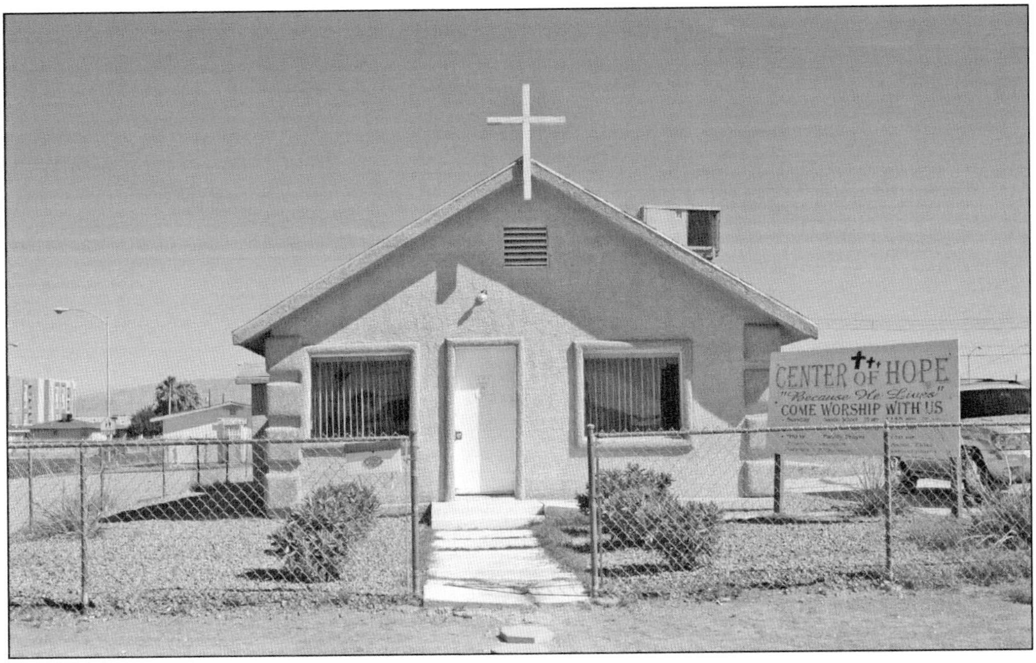

Blocks of Churches. It is nearly impossible not to run into a church on the Westside, no matter which street one is traveling or in what direction. Here are just a couple, and one with a readily recognized steeple is sandwiched between the Second Baptist Church and Hamburger Heaven. Victory Missionary Baptist Church on Monroe Avenue has been on the spiritual, social, and political front lines for decades. Under the ministerial leadership of the powerfully spoken Rev. Robert E. Fowler as of 2011, the congregation has grown to 10,000. In all, about 30,000 cars visit West Las Vegas for religious services and programs every week.

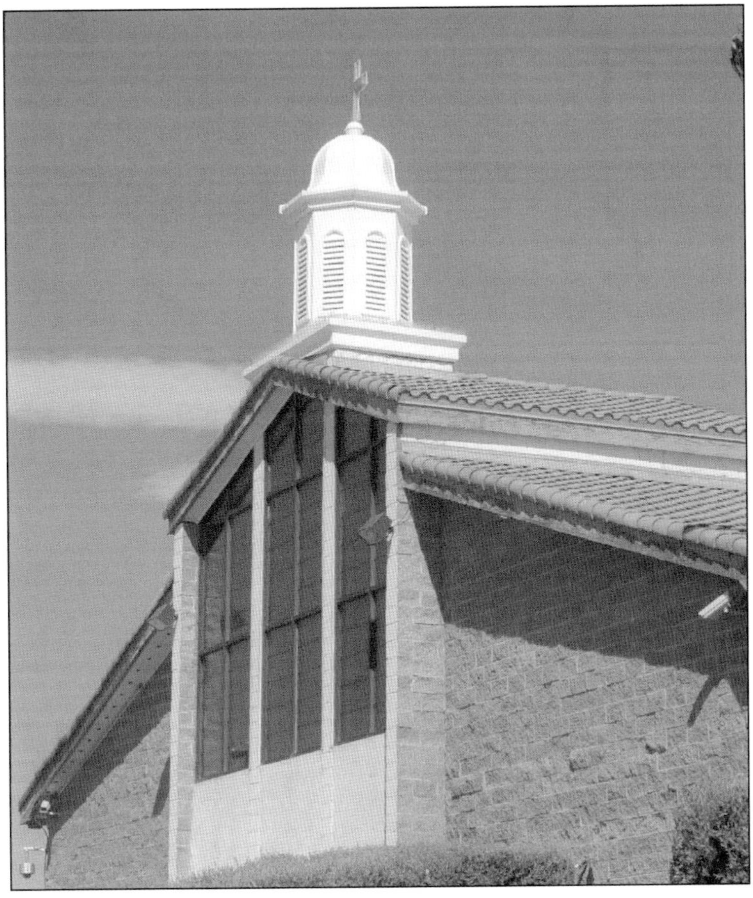

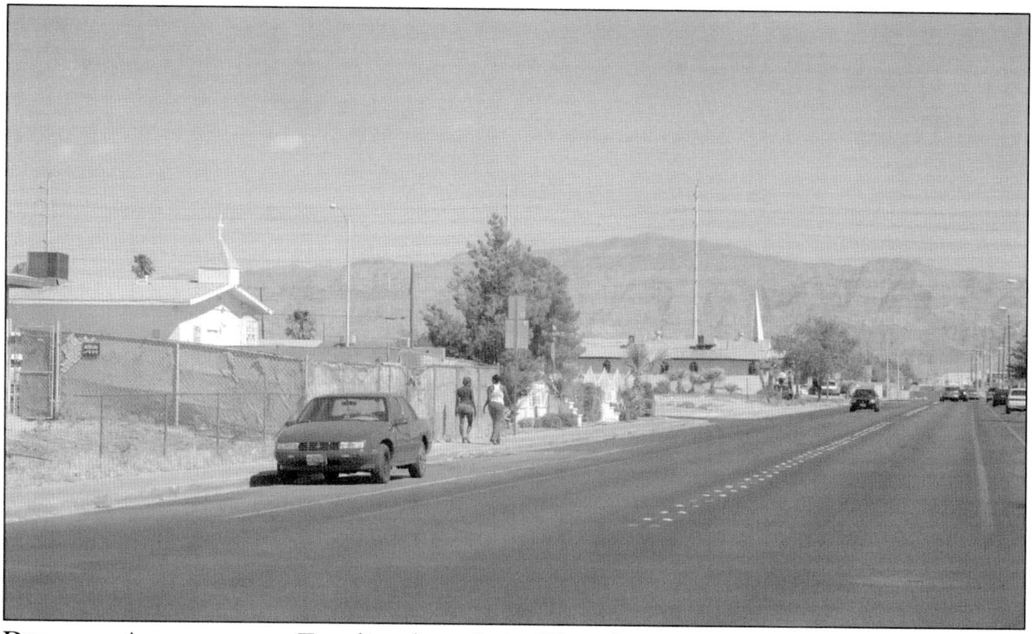

DIFFERENT ARCHITECTURE. Traveling through the Westside, one encounters all types of buildings and architecture used for churches. They range from decades-old sites to small homes. Some are laid on expansive lots; others may be bunched together, one after the other. Further northwest as one travels west on Revere Street, beyond the heartland of the Westside but still a strong appendage of that community, lays Las Vegas Heights. Dr. S.S. Rogers presides over the Greater Mount Sinai congregation at the edge of a small community park, which is currently the site of monthly Ministers Alliance meetings and other important civic gatherings. For the past 40 years, Dr. Rogers has been leading the community in various marches and vigils. Here is the annex across the street, likely built in the 1940s.

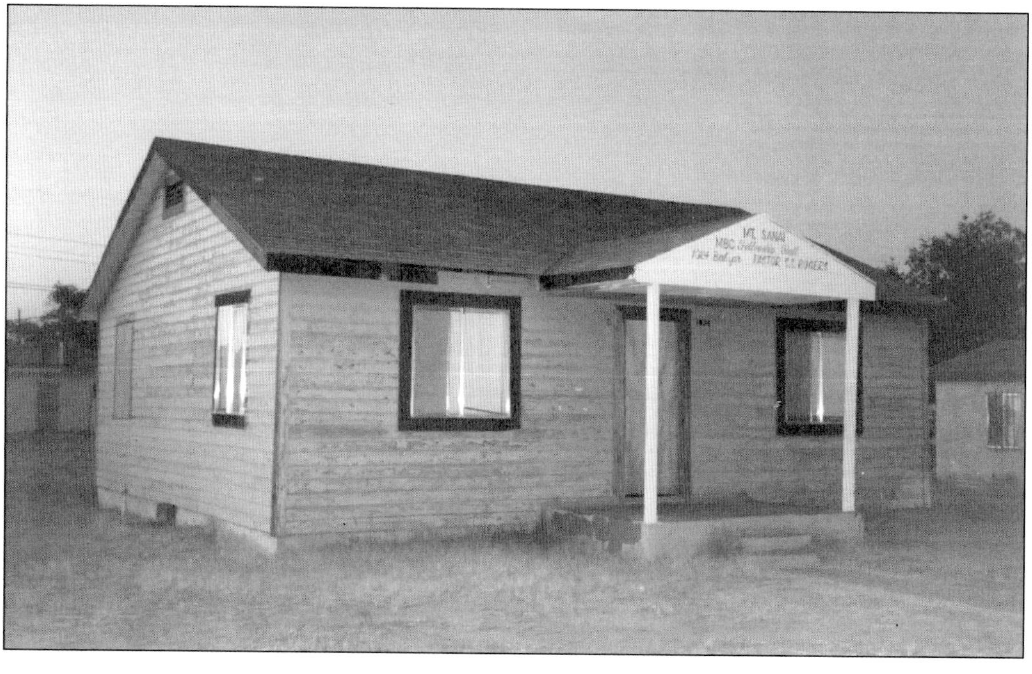

Seven

EPILOGUE
NEXT GENERATIONS REVIVING WEST LAS VEGAS

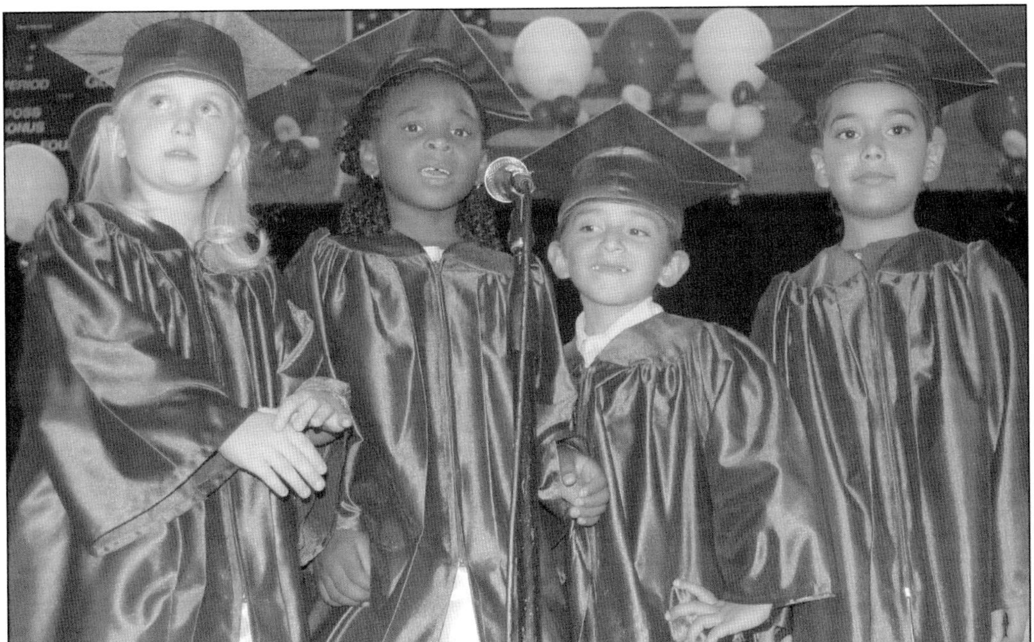

FUTURE GENERATIONS ALONG EDUCATION CORRIDOR. Four smiling West Prep Academy kindergartners, class of 2022, joined the first high school graduating class of 2010 last June. West Prep, Andre Agassi, Rainbow Academy (kindergarten through the fifth grade), and Kermit Booker Elementary Schools comprise an educational backbone on the Westside on or near Lake Mead Boulevard, dubbed the "Education Corridor." Under the umbrella of School Trustee Dr. Linda Young's "It Takes a Village to Educate a Child" approach, many area schools are collaborating to ensure that all children are provided a quality education inside and outside the classroom. (Courtesy West Prep Academy, Las Vegas.)

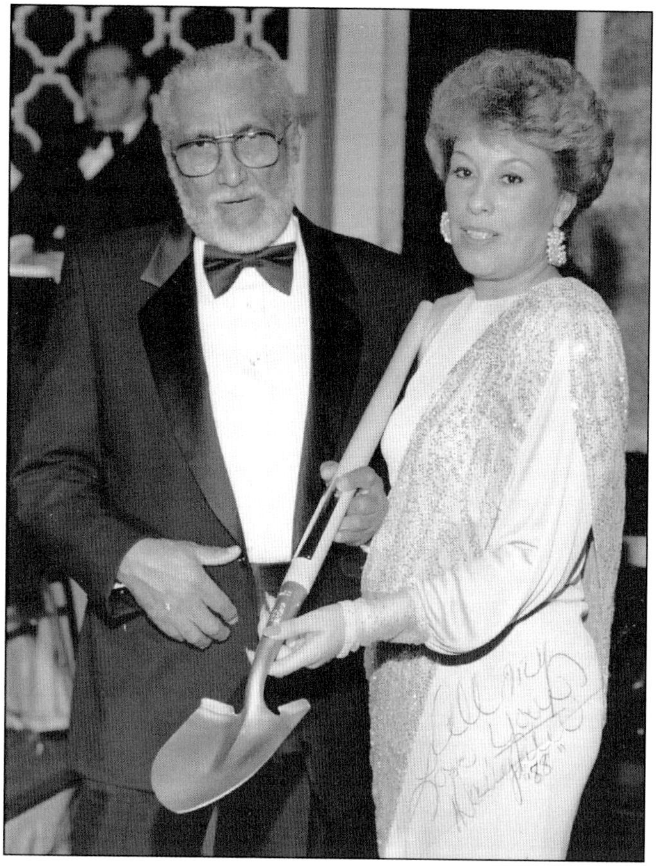

Dr. McMillan and Daughter Jarmilla Arnold. Earlier in the history of West Las Vegas, a tradition of passing the baton to the next generation was evident. Here, Jarmilla joins her late father in a special honor being bestowed upon him. Today, she is quite active in Councilman Ricki Barlow's Neighborhood Advisory Committee and numerous other causes. (Courtesy Jarmilla McMillan Arnold.)

Grandchildren Bursting Forth. Here, seven-year-old author Skylar poses with her adopted godmother, Erma Walker, chief executive officer of What About Us, an educational corporation focused on school readiness, high school dropout prevention, and job skills. This effort is one of many numerous community companions to West Las Vegas schools. (Courtesy Erma Jai Walker.)

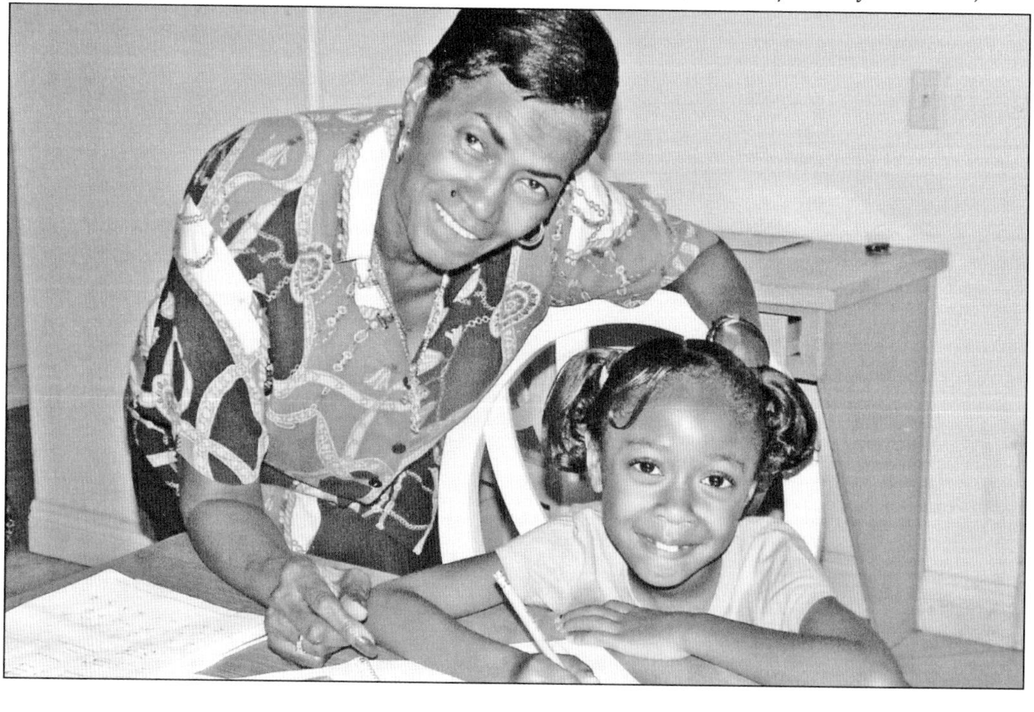

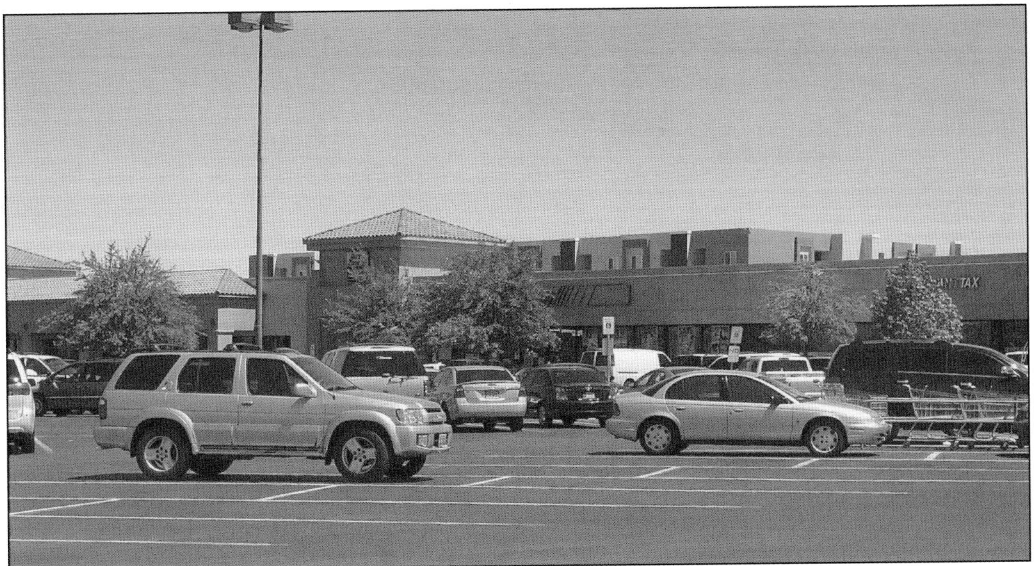

New Generations of Buildings and Businesses. There has also been a rebirth of business, restoration of buildings, and new construction. In the distance, one can see the top of the new Sarann Knight Preddy apartments behind the thriving Edmond Town Center. (Courtesy Don Walker.)

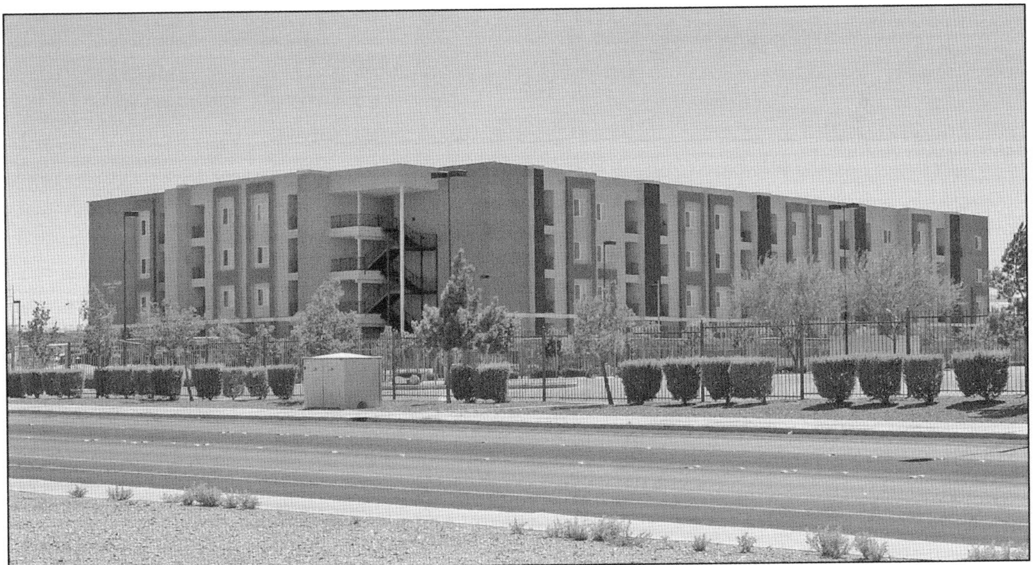

Sarann Knight Preddy Apartments. Future generations will inquire about this grand lady just based on her name being scripted across this magnificent apartment building. The several-story-high complex borders the entrance into the famous Jackson Street and can be seen for miles around. (Courtesy Don Walker.)

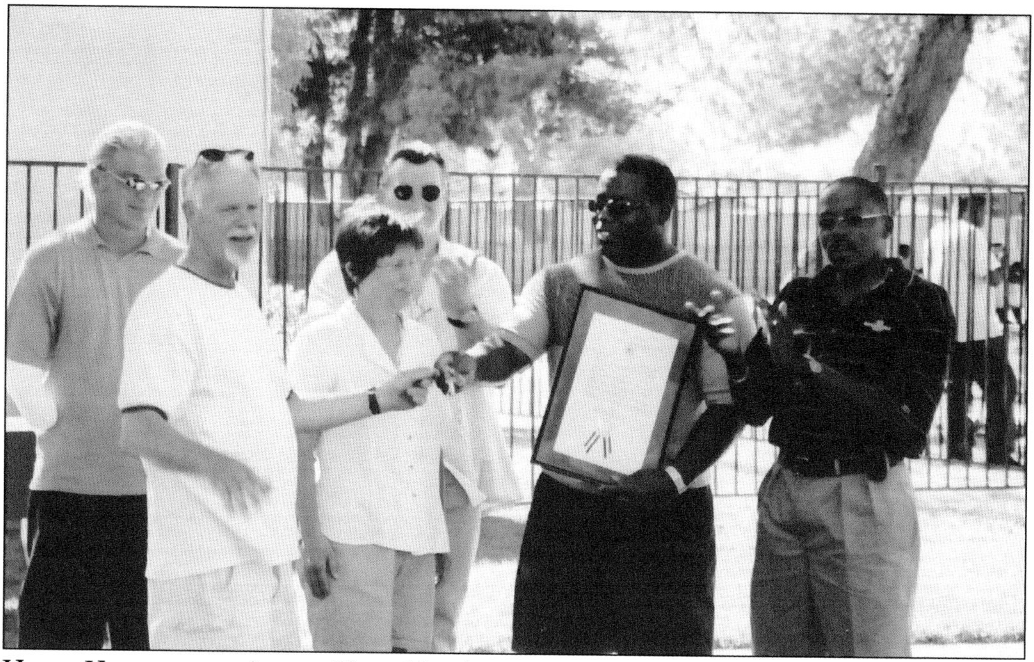

Happy Homeowners Accept Keys. New homeowners are welcomed to Whispering Timbers by Frank Hawkins and county commissioner Larry Weekly. The celebration took place in the housing complex's Senator Joe Neal Park, named after Nevada's first black state senator.

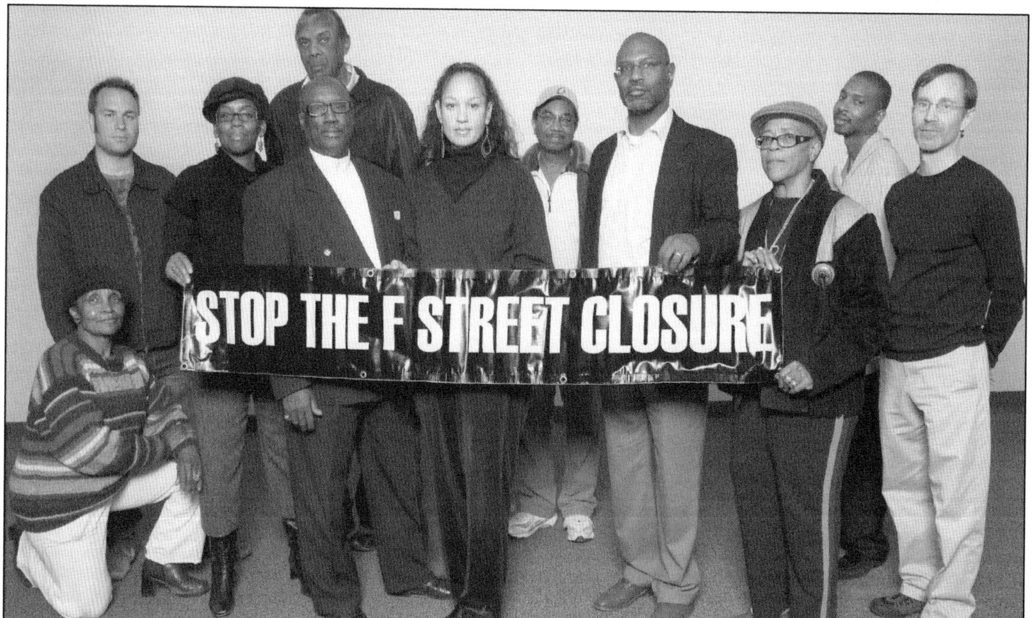

F Street Coalition. When a wall rose and blocked the popular residential throughway to Downtown from the Westside, hundreds of residents protested. Among the leaders were, from left to right, (first row) Barbara Crockett (kneeling), Dr. S.S. Rogers (forefront left), Trish Geran, Karl Armstrong, Earlene Ventura, and Dahn Shaulis; (second row) Colin Jacobs, Shondra Summers-Armstrong, Assemblyman Harvey Munford, Sam Wright, and Brandon Greene. (© 2010, Las Vegas City Life, reprinted with permission.)

Growing the Community. With a recent spurt to grow community gardens, the Westside community is literally coming alive in whole new way. The building to the right serves as a gateway to the five-acre site overseen by Roz Brooks and is open to residents, schools, churches, and businesses. It is believed to be the first community garden in Las Vegas and encourages local urbanites to plant their own vegetables and gardens. Area children visit the garden by the dozens and learn hands-on agriculture.

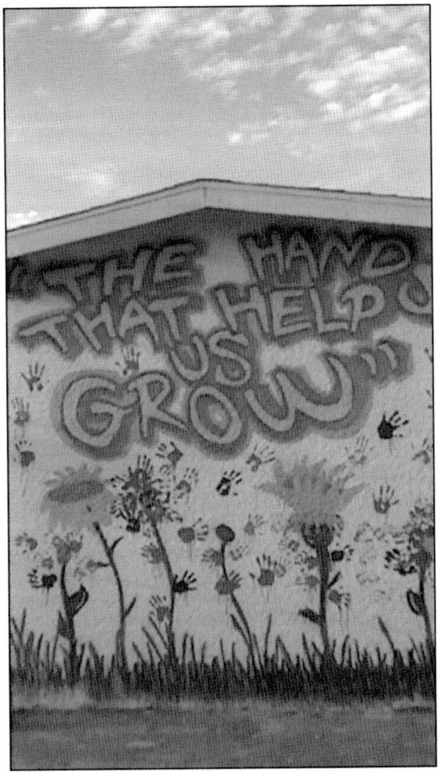

Entry into Historic West Las Vegas. A brand new marker greets visitors on the expanded Martin Luther King Boulevard in West Las Vegas. Touted as the most beautiful Martin Luther King Boulevard in the world by Councilman Ricki Barlow, the four-lane entryway leads visitors to the midline of the community.

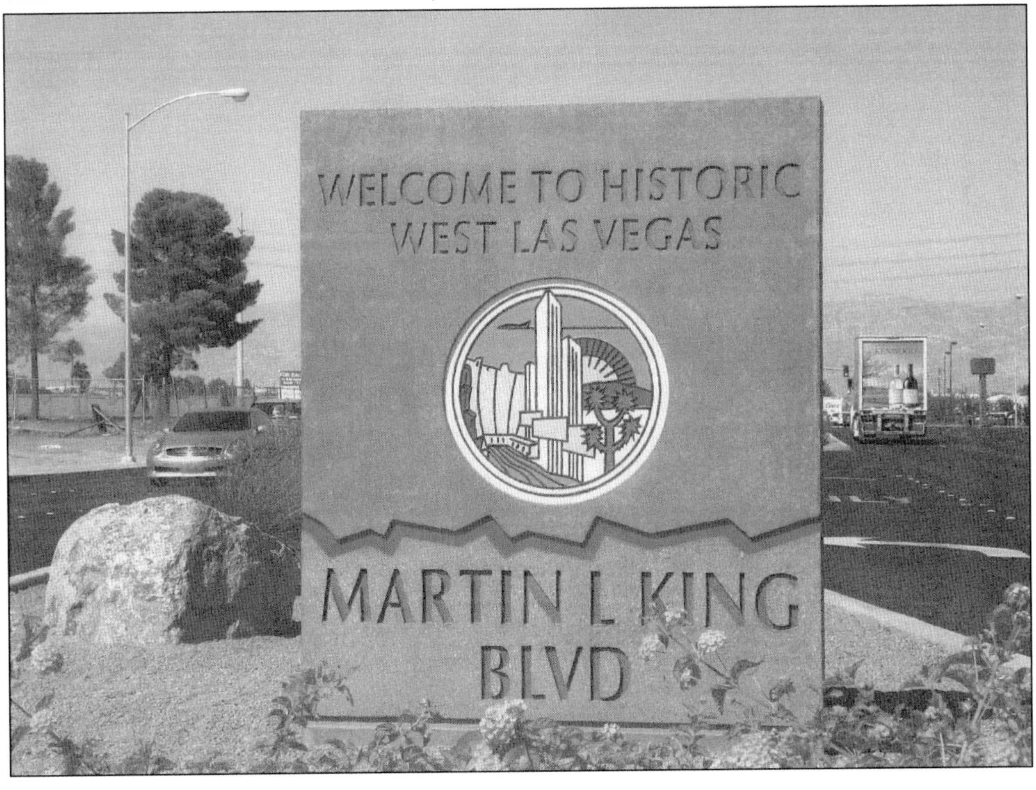